I0810876

Transfer in an Urban Writing Ecology

Reimagining Community College–University Relations in Composition Studies

Christie Toth

with Joanne Castillo, Nic Contreras, Kelly Corbray, Nathan Lacy, Westin Porter, Sandra Salazar-Hernandez, and Colleagues

Conference on College Composition and Communication

NCTE National Council of Teachers of English

National Council of Teachers of English
340 N. Neil St., Suite #104, Champaign, Illinois 61820
www.ncte.org

Staff Editor: Cynthia Gomez
Manuscript Editor: Leigh Scarcliff
Series Editor: Steve Parks
Interior Design: Mary Rohrer
Cover Design: Pat Mayer
Cover Image: Christie Toth

ISBN 978-0-8141-5518-9 (paperback); ISBN 978-0-8141-5519-6 (ebook); 978-0-8141-0084-4 (PDF)

Library of Congress Control Number: 2022950589

CCCC STUDIES IN WRITING & RHETORIC
Edited by Steve Parks, University of Virginia

The aim of the CCCC Studies in Writing & Rhetoric (SWR) Series is to influence how we think about language in action and especially how writing gets taught at the college level. The methods of studies vary from the critical to historical to linguistic to ethnographic, and their authors draw on work in various fields that inform composition—including rhetoric, communication, education, discourse analysis, psychology, cultural studies, and literature. Their focuses are similarly diverse—ranging from individual writers and teachers, to work on classrooms and communities and curricula, to analyses of the social, political, and material contexts of writing and its teaching.

SWR was one of the first scholarly book series to focus on the teaching of writing. It was established in 1980 by the Conference on College Composition and Communication (CCCC) in order to promote research in the emerging field of writing studies. As our field has grown, the research sponsored by SWR has continued to articulate the commitment of CCCC to supporting the work of writing teachers as reflective practitioners and intellectuals.

We are eager to identify influential work in writing and rhetoric as it emerges. We thus ask authors to send us project proposals that clearly situate their work in the field and show how they aim to redirect our ongoing conversations about writing and its teaching. Proposals should include an overview of the project, a brief annotated table of contents, and a sample chapter. They should not exceed 10,000 words.

To submit a proposal, please register as an author at www.editorialmanager.com/nctebp. Once registered, follow the steps to submit a proposal (be sure to choose SWR Book Proposal from the drop-down list of article submission types).

SWR Editorial Advisory Board

For the Salt Lake Community College transfer students who built the Writing Studies Scholars program, and for those who will create its future. You're making composition studies a discipline worth being.

CONTENTS

ACKNOWLEDGMENTS

THIS BOOK AND THE PROJECTS IT documents have been profoundly collaborative. Our work has relied on the contributions of dozens of faculty, staff, administrators, undergraduate and graduate students, and community supporters. We have sought to acknowledge those contributors by name throughout the text, always in relation to their specific involvement. Here, I would like to thank some of the otherwise unacknowledged people who have shaped my thinking over the years and made my contributions to these collaborations possible.

Thank you to my undergraduate institution, Bowdoin College, for providing support I have tried to pay forward in some very different educational spaces. I'm particularly grateful to Anne Henshaw and the Rusack Coastal Studies Fellowship, which provided a transformative undergraduate research experience that informed my collaborations with undergraduates at the University of Utah. Likewise, I'm grateful to professors Scott MacEachern, Liz Muther, Krista Van Vleet, Dan Levine, and Matt Klingle, all of whom were wonderful teachers and made me feel as if my writing mattered. Bowdoin College also provided me with several graduate scholarships that made it possible to attend conferences and conduct research that I would otherwise have been unable to afford.

Thank you to the mentors I found in my master's program and subsequent staff position at Portland State University. Professors Hildy Miller and the late Duncan Carter and Hugo du Coudray introduced me to the field of composition studies, gave me my first graduate research experiences, and encouraged my interest in community college writing instruction. Dan DeWeese and Jonathan Walker also provided essential mentorship along the way. PSU faculty Carol Morgaine, Barbara Brower, Candace Reynolds,

Hank Renfro, and Justin Fallon Dollard all mentored me as an apprentice teacher. Office of Institutional Research and Planning colleagues Rowanna Carpenter and Juliette Stoering offered both friendship and opportunities to research urban transfer networks.

Many thanks to my transdisciplinary community at the University of Michigan. I wasn't an especially easy doctoral student to work with, which makes me all the more grateful to Anne Gere, Scott Lyons, David Gold, Vilma Mesa, Peter Bahr, Larry Rowley, Dick Alfred, and Ruth Behar, each of whom pushed me to do my best possible work and provided pieces of the puzzle that became this book. Anne Curzan and Jeanie Laubenthal also offered encouragement at key junctures during my time in the Joint Program in English and Education (JPEE). The School of Education, the Rackham Graduate School, and the Sweetland Center for Writing all provided me with financial support and professional development opportunities while I was at Michigan—special thanks to Sweetland colleagues Naomi Silver, Louis Cicciarelli, and Anna Knutson for working with me on transfer student writing initiatives. Thank you to the University of Michigan Graduate Employees' Organization for fighting for the compensation and benefits that made my graduate experience possible.

I am grateful for the many brilliant and committed graduate student teacher-scholars who were such a profound part of my doctoral education. My JPEE Chalk and Cheese seniors were all essential mentors—special thanks to Mike Bunn, Anne Porter, Tim Green, Zac Lancaster, Moises Escudero, Randall Pinder, and of course Laura Aull. Thank you to my extended cohort, from whom I learned so much: Melody Pugh, Joanna Want, Crystal VanKooten, Danielle Lillge, Sarah Swofford, Justine Post, Liz Homan, Rebecca Manery, Will Hutchinson, Chinyere Uzogara, Lizzie Hutton, Gail Gibson, Ben Keating, Aubrey Schiavonne, and James Hammond. Special love to Merideth Garcia, who has been my teaching and writing bestie for the last decade.

Deepest thanks to my University of Michigan Community College Interdisciplinary Research Forum colleagues Brett Griffiths, Kate Thirolf, Chris Nellum, Johanna Massé, Rebecca Christensen,

Inger Bergom, and Malisa Lee. This book is so indebted to the work we did together. Thanks also to the American Indian Studies Interdisciplinary Group, especially Frank Kelderman, Sophie Hunt, Michelle Cassidy, and Becky Hill—their influence might not be so obvious, but I promise it's there. Finally, I am grateful to Ellen Cushman, Malea Powell, Andrea Riley-Mukavetz, Bump Halbritter, and Julie Lindquist, who generously extended their mentorship from East Lansing to Ann Arbor.

Over the years, dozens of community college faculty have been my mentors and collaborators. Portland Community College professor Maria Caruso and Clackamas Community College faculty Trista Cornelius and Kate Gray all facilitated my first opportunities to work with community college students. TYCA luminaries Mark Reynolds, Sylvia Holladay, Carolyn Calhoon-Dillahunt, Patrick Sullivan, and "the Jeffs"—Sommers, Andelora, and Klausman—were all wonderful mentors to me when I was a graduate student, and they continued to support me in myriad ways as a junior faculty member. While Diné College is no longer a community college, the faculty and students there who participated in my dissertation study taught me innumerable lessons about locally responsive composition pedagogy. As an assistant professor, I was fortunate to work with Holly Hassel, Joanne Baird Giordano, Howard Tinberg, Sarah Z. Johnson, Leslie Roberts, Margaret O'Rourke, Wendy Swyt, Anthony Warnke, Kirsten Higgins, Cheri Lemieux-Spiegel, Mark Blaauw-Hara, Jessica Nastal, Holly Gilman, Nicole Hancock, Leslie Henson, and Katie Hern on publications that have been essential to my understanding of two-year college literacy studies. Darin Jensen and Brett Griffiths have been my academic soulmates and my role models for fierce intellectual commitment to community college composition. And although they are not two-year college faculty, Emily Suh, Liz Tinoco, and Mya Poe keep showing me how to do this work from university positions.

I am grateful for the material support I've received from the University of Utah over the last eight years. Elsewhere in the book, I acknowledge the foundations that have supported Writing Studies Scholars since 2017. Here, I would like to thank the Office of Undergraduate Research, the Council of Dee Fellows, and the University Teaching Grant for providing compensation for my student co-researchers at several stages of this project. Likewise, many thanks to the University Research Fellowship program, the College of Humanities, and the Office of Undergraduate Studies for funding pretenure course releases that enabled me to complete this manuscript.

A huge thanks to CCCC's Studies in Writing and Rhetoric, especially Steve Parks, whose faith, feedback, and advocacy for this unconventional book has been more human than I ever expected of the academy. Thank you to the anonymous reviewers whose input shaped the manuscript, to Kurt Austin and Cynthia Gomez of the NCTE books program, and to the copyeditors who have helped me and my coauthors shine.

Thank you to my Salt Lake family—my colleagues at the University of Utah and Salt Lake Community College, my students, all of whom are also my neighbors—and our friends Chris Baczek, Frank and Thane Baczek, Dave Hyams, Jen Milner, Brian Ledbetter, Chevy Milner, Talmadge Anderson, and the whole DND crew. Thanks for the moral support over the last eight years, and for *so much food* and all the masked errands when we had a baby in a pandemic. Thank you to Kya Mangrum, Cynthia Benally, and Charissa Che for writing dates that were also always great conversations.

Thank you to my farflung Shipwreckageatology family: Drew Pizzolato and Tom Myer; Yana Domuschieva and Anton and Max Gobournov; Ashby, Robin, and Grace Cleland-Crowder; Yoon-Lin Chiew, Willie Klemm, and Henry Chiew Klemm. Our two decades of transdisciplinary nonsense have been the best possible foundation for an academic career.

Thank you to our Washington family, who took us in for nine months during the worst of the pandemic. They did most of the cooking and a whole lot of babysitting so I could finish this book. That family includes my parents, Mathew "Stuart" Toth and Cindy Williams, who gave me my most important tools: joy in learning and the knowledge that I was loved. It also includes my sister, Erika Toth, and her partner Miguel Macias; my aunt, Becky Williams; and the family I had the great luck to marry into: Faith Hagenhofer, Off White, John Daniell, Nora Carman-White, and Connor Carman. Faith and Off, thanks for letting us stay at the farm and for catching most of the rodents.

Ben, we promised that wherever we were together would be home. Thank you for your unwavering support, your pride in me even at my most graceless, and your many sacrifices, big and small, that have made Salt Lake home.

Maris, every day you become the coolest person I've ever met. Thank you.

FOREWORD

FIVE YEARS AGO, DR. CHRISTIE TOTH arrived in Salt Lake City. I met her first at a dinner during her on-campus visit, and then, a few months later, at a local brewery where she had asked a group of Salt Lake Community College (SLCC) faculty to meet with her. I didn't quite know what to make of Christie: a *scholar of two-year college writing studies*; and I didn't quite know how I felt about my profession being the subject of her research. Christie was kind, certainly, and respectful, as she moved and spoke with enthusiasm and possibility, but I was leery, nonetheless. I didn't trust the University of Utah ("U of U") to do right by SLCC.

As this book sweepingly documents, my initial response to Christie's entrance into SLCC's institutional ecology was not surprising. Relations between two-year colleges and their four-year or university "partners" are often tenuous and can break down into suspicion and disregard if not tended with care. Readers will know that this dysfunction is not isolated to the local; it has long shaped the fields of composition and writing studies, despite its being called to account from time to time (see all entries by Andelora in Works Cited).

So, I kept to the side, while Christie built relationships with my colleagues in the English, Linguistics, and Writing Studies (ELWS) department. They sought to take on the two-year-to-university transfer problem—also revealingly documented in this book's chapters—that deepens inequities in higher education. This was the heart of the institutional web, a space my years in community writing had taught me to avoid so as not to be "subsumed by it" (Dobrin and Weisser). My work, former and current, has long resided in the "'gaps' and 'fissures' of the social terrain in order to support 'alternative' alliances and collective possibilities" (Parks, *Gravyland* 32). Christie, and the others in this book, were headed to the center of the web, to its "connective spaces" where the strands meet: "the intersections and 'crossroads' that require change . . . [and call] forth possibilities" (Rousculp, *Rhetoric* xvii). They sought to change how students moved through, and too often got stuck in, the connective spaces of institutional transfer.

In the pages that follow, you'll read how they did it. Not only did the students and faculty from the SLCC ELWS and U of U Writing and Rhetoric Studies departments change their relationships and pathways, they did so in a way that, I believe, is replicable for other institutions. Certainly, local moments of fortune and good timing have played and continue to play a part in their success, as they must in all efforts to reshape structures, but the SLCC–U Partnerships in Writing Studies is more than a newly formed strand in the institutional web. Rather than being subsumed by that web, the principles that emerged from their work now serve as the foundation for other SLCC–U transfer projects that are currently underway. This authentic partnership has transformed the web itself.

A few months ago, I met with Christie at a hole-in-the-strip-mall to eat and talk about her manuscript. I now know what to make of her. She's not only a university-based scholar of two-year-college writing studies; she is the embodiment of interinstitutional functionality and potential. I invite all of you, regardless of which web you navigate (two-year, four-year, or university), to enter this book with trust, and to learn from Christie, the students, and the SLCC and U of U faculty colleagues here in Salt Lake City.

Tiffany Rousculp
Professor, Salt Lake Community College
Summer 2022

START HERE: REIMAGINING RELATIONS

THIS BOOK IS ABOUT COMMUNITY college transfer. I was not a transfer student, nor am I currently employed at a community college: I'm a tenure-track faculty member at a research university, which means I'll have to work to earn some readers' trust. Taking up a long intellectual tradition among two-year college[1] writing faculty, I'm seeking to challenge the university-centrism of composition studies. This goal is born of my broad ambivalence about the academy and my specific frustrations with this would-be discipline. I'm frustrated by the persistent underrepresentation of two-year colleges in its knowledge making and their near-invisibility in most of its graduate programs. I'm frustrated by the frequent marginalization of two-year college faculty in its professional spaces. And I'm beyond frustrated—I'm angry—about how it often fails to meet its responsibilities to two-year college students, both before and after they transfer. This book amounts to a case study of my attempts to address these inequities from my position as a professor in a department of writing and rhetoric studies.

When I first began studying composition at Portland State University in 2006, my goal was to teach at a local community college, and all my subsequent academic labor has been shaped by that aspiration. I interned at Portland Community College, researched the writing experiences of community college transfer students for my master's thesis, and went on to adjunct at Clackamas Community College and later Diné College, the associate's- and bachelor's-degree-granting tribal college founded as Navajo Community College where I did dissertation research. In 2009, I entered a doctoral program at the University of Michigan (UM) still planning to teach at a community college. At UM, I worked on research teams investigating the post-transfer experiences of community college students and developed a study of two-year college faculty professional engagement that connected me with mentors in the Two-Year College English Association (TYCA). When I went on the job market in fall 2013, however, I followed the path laid out by my graduate program and applied for positions at four-year institutions. That choice involved complex emotions and competing values, but it was grounded in a sincere belief that challenging the disciplinary marginalization of two-year colleges required committed university-based colleagues. The focus of this book—the writing experiences of community college transfer students—is thus the nexus of the career I thought I was pursuing over a decade ago and where I find myself working today.

Transfer in an Urban Writing Ecology: Reimagining Community College–University Relations in Composition Studies emerges from teaching and research I undertook with many collaborators between 2015 and 2021, my junior faculty years in the University of Utah's Department of Writing and Rhetoric Studies (WRS). I've experienced these years as a fraught experiment, an uncertain attempt to enact disciplinarity in ways that account to and for two-year colleges. At the national level, I've worked with TYCA colleagues on white papers and position statements, research projects, and professional development resources. I've sought to produce scholarship useful for making change at both local and disciplinary levels and tried to amplify two-year college voices in professional spaces where they might otherwise be ignored. Over these years, I've also become committed to researching, teaching, developing programs, and writing with community college transfer students.

As a scholar, I am primarily in conversation with *two-year college writing studies*—or, as Darin Jensen, Emily Suh, and Joanne Baird Giordano are teaching me to call it, two-year college *literacy* studies (Suh and Jensen; Jensen and Giordano)—a transdisciplinary field to which I am intellectually responsible and in which I am always a guest. Sometimes I've been a lousy guest, most often when I have failed to maintain awareness of how my interactions are being shaped by my privileges as a middle-class white woman in a tenure-track university position. In their introduction to *Working toward*

Racial Equity in First-Year Composition (DeLong et al. 4–6), Taiyon Coleman and colleagues discuss my failed 2016 attempt to coedit a collection on race in two-year college writing instruction. They refrain from naming me directly, but I owe them the accountability of a public apology. I am sorry, which does not undo the harm. At the time, I thought I was using my position to advance the conversation they initiated in their article "The Risky Business of Engaging Racial Equity in Writing Instruction." However, through a series of whitely missteps exacerbated by my position at a university, I perpetrated academic colonization. I failed to navigate the racialized power dynamics of cross-sector scholarly publication ethically, and my failure reinscribed harmful community college–university relations in composition studies.

Six years later, I hope I'm wiser. I'm certainly slower, more cautious about publication, more circumspect about what and how I might contribute to conversations in two-year college literacy studies. I am aware that my scholarly collaborations with TYCA leaders do not automatically confer trust, nor do they make me an insider. I have counterhegemonic commitments to community college writing instruction that sometimes feel unwelcome in university spaces, but two-year college colleagues might understandably suspect that my interest is academic careerism. Because of who I am and who currently employs me, I must have a more compelling reason to write than "There's a gap in the literature." One way I have acted from this awareness is by focusing on inequities that can only be addressed through collaboration between community college and university colleagues. Transfer is one such issue, as is the status of two-year colleges in disciplinary knowledge making and graduate education.

This book chronicles—and, I hope, enacts—what I think I've learned so far about community college-university relations in composition studies, and what those relations mean for the students who move between our institutions. Along the way, my collaborations with community college faculty and students have shaped my reasons for staying at my university, as well as my understanding of the responsibilities stemming from that choice.

While I'm not always comfortable with where my path has brought me, my journey-so-far leads me to believe that valuable work can be done from this position, and there is much work yet to do.

A CHRONICLE OF "HIGHER" EDUCATION

Here is the story we tell in this book. In 2014, I joined the faculty of the new WRS department at the University of Utah ("the U"). Shortly thereafter I began working with several faculty colleagues and a team of students from Salt Lake Community College (SLCC) to expand writing-related opportunities for transfer students. In 2015, the team conducted a mixed-method study of transfer student writing experiences at the U. This research helped us develop a local portrait of the unique capacities SLCC transfer students bring to writing and institutional barriers hindering their ability to achieve their goals.

Through this research, we identified two groups of SLCC transfer student writers to whom our interinstitutional disciplinary community had distinct responsibilities: those transferring into any U major and those pursuing a WRS degree. To address these responsibilities, we developed two new writing courses. The first is WRTG 3020: Write4U, a "writing-in-and-against-the-disciplines" course for transfer students in all majors that fulfills the U's upper-division writing requirement. The second course, WRTG 3030: Writing across Locations, is a co-taught summer bridge course for SLCC students considering the WRS major, minor, or certificate in professional and technical writing. Launched in 2016–17, both courses take an antideficit approach informed by the framework for *transfer receptive culture* developed by critical higher education scholars Dimpal Jain, Alfred Herrera, Santiago Bernal Melendez, Daniel Solorzano, and Iris Lucero. The courses value transfer students' identities, languages, literacies, and rhetorical capacities while encouraging critical transformation of disciplinary discourses dominated by white, colonial ways of knowing and languaging. Both courses are offered for free to prospective transfer students at SLCC.

Courses alone, however, cannot dismantle the barriers many transfer students face. Countering the inequities of community college transfer requires a combination of academic, social, and material support. Since 2017, we have developed a support program for SLCC students transferring into the WRS major, minor, and certificate called Writing Studies Scholars (WSS). With input from dozens of transfer students and funding from local foundations, WSS now provides the following:

- Pre- and post-transfer advising and mentorship
- A $2,000 transition scholarship
- Additional completion scholarships as needed
- A free one-credit study group each semester
- Monthly get-togethers, workshops, and online events
- Paid opportunities to work as co-researchers, co-teachers, and program co-developers
- Career coaching
- A network of WSS alumni

WSS has fostered a more diverse student community in WRS, become part of the department's institutional profile, and influenced transfer initiatives in other departments. Some Writing Studies Scholars have become forceful advocates for transfer students, influencing U policies and practices.

Supporting transfer students required reimagining how we related to one another across institutions; reimagining those relations has changed our local disciplinary ecology in ways I could not have anticipated at the outset. In 2018, for example, SLCC colleagues launched a stand-alone AS degree in writing studies. This program fosters community and enables WRS to connect with prospective students much earlier in their educational journeys. In 2019, SLCC changed the name of the "English" department to "English, Linguistics, and Writing Studies" (ELWS). Our collaborations have created new research and teaching opportunities for U graduate students, facilitating multiple dissertation projects and leading to the development of our Community College Professional Apprenticeship program in 2019–20. We have also developed a range of collaborative faculty professional development activities, including interinstitutional reading groups and an online symposium on interinstitutional transfer and writing centers.

In 2022, the story is still being written. The COVID pandemic intensified the material and emotional strain on already overextended transfer students, particularly immigrants, students of color, LGBTQIA+ students, students with disabilities, and students with family caretaking responsibilities. The Salt Lake Valley's rapid population growth has fueled a crisis-level housing shortage and skyrocketing cost of living; enrollments at SLCC are down while the U scrambles to serve a record number of admits. The outcome of the 2020 elections created an opening to improve funding structures for postsecondary education, but economic uncertainty and the looming midterms make much-needed reforms unlikely. We face massive turnover among staff and administrators at both SLCC and the U who were key supporters of our disciplinary transfer collaborations. Perhaps the publication of this book marks the end of the beginning of our attempt to reimagine community college–university relations in the Salt Lake Valley. Understanding that beginning requires examining specificities of our local institutional and disciplinary contexts.

COMPOSITION AT THE U

The U is the state's "flagship" research institution, and, as administrators often remind us, now a member of the PAC-12 and the Association of American Universities. It attracts a growing number of students from out of state and is pushing to increase undergraduate enrollment from twenty-five thousand to forty thousand by the end of the decade. With its new Utah Asia Campus (UAC) in South Korea and microcampuses elsewhere in Asia, the U is seeking to establish itself as a global research university. My first day on the faculty was WRS's first day as an independent department. Our story has been shaped by the resources and constraints of an R-1 institution striving to elevate its status in the academic "marketplace," as well as the possibilities of a new department figuring out what it might become.

WRS evolved from the University Writing Program (UWP), which was established in 1984 to oversee first-year writing and came to offer upper-division courses supporting student writers across the disciplines. UWP was an independent unit led by faculty appointed to the departments of English and Communication. Over the years, several prominent composition scholars were associated with UWP, including Susan Miller, Tom Huckin, Maureen Mathison, Raúl Sánchez, Jay Jordan, and Casey Boyle. In 1993, UWP began offering interdisciplinary master's and PhD programs in rhetoric and composition admitted through English, Communication, or Education. During the 2002–03 academic year, the UWP established the University Writing Center and a minor in literacy studies. It launched the WRS major and a revamped minor in 2013. The U has a long history of composition studies, but new disciplinary possibilities emerged through the 2010s.

The independent WRS department was approved by the University in 2014. That fall, we had twenty-five undergraduates in the major, four tenure-track faculty, and seven career-line colleagues. By 2021, we had grown to nearly one hundred majors, more than half of whom were transfer students, with ten tenure-line faculty and eight career-line colleagues. This larger faculty is more diverse—racially, culturally, linguistically, and in interdisciplinary expertise. We offer the WRS minor at the UAC, the major at the U's Sandy campus, and the new certificate in professional and technical writing on the main campus. Our graduate programs are now fully under our department's auspices, and we are working toward offering our major online and at the new joint SLCC-U facility at SLCC's Herriman campus. The department is "always in the process of becoming" (Syverson 6); what we are becoming is being shaped, in part, by our relations with SLCC.

When WRS launched, there were already longstanding relations between the English departments at SLCC and the U, and those histories came with baggage. Most notorious was "The Great Credit Grab of 1997," which took place when the Utah System of Higher Education (USHE) shifted from quarters to semesters. During that process, the U English department renumbered several 2000-level courses to 3000-level, which meant those courses could no longer be offered at SLCC. This move, a "grab" for student credit hours, signaled skepticism about the rigor of SLCC courses and took away literature courses SLCC faculty enjoyed teaching. Memory of the Great Credit Grab, compounded by other slights and insults, animated SLCC faculty members' resentment of university elitism for decades (Ruffus and Toth).

Until 2016, when USHE began pushing for transfer systemwide "pathways," there was little incentive at either institution to bridge these rifts. By state mandate, the required first-year writing courses—ENGL 1010 and 2010—articulate across all public institutions, but each college or university has freedom to design curriculum relevant to its mission, students, and degree offerings. While Eli Goldblatt might suggest that such conditions work against "deep alignment" of regional writing curricula (84), this autonomy enabled composition studies to flourish at SLCC in distinct ways.

COMPOSITION AT SLCC

SLCC enrolls more than thirty-four thousand students across ten campuses and high school programs, and its faculty have long engaged critically and creatively with knowledge making in composition. Its longstanding Writing Certificate of Completion—now the Writing Certificate of Proficiency—focuses on professional writing. Since 2014, Tiffany Rousculp has headed the Writing across the College initiative to support the writing practices of SLCC faculty and staff as well as students ("Everyone"). Beginning in 2015, full- and part-time SLCC writing faculty and students have worked to create OpenEnglish@SLCC, a locally responsive Open Educational Resource organized around department threshold concepts in writing used by composition faculty across the country (Blankenship et al.; Jory)—we use selections from OpenEnglish@SLCC in several courses at the U.

SLCC faculty have also made Salt Lake a national hub for writing center studies. They established one of the first community college writing centers, now called the Student Writing and Reading Center (SWRC), which has been directed by Clint Gardner since 1990 (Gardner, "Centering"; "Our"; Gardner and Rousculp). In 2001, Rousculp cofounded the Community Writing Center (CWC), subsequently directed by Andrea Malouf, Melissa Helquist, and Kati

Lewis, which provides writing coaching for community members, facilitates workshops with community partners, and publishes community writing (Rousculp, "Connecting" and "When"; *Rhetoric*). Both writing centers are staffed by SLCC and U students who develop programming and present at conferences. In 2008, Lisa Bickmore and Charlotte Howe launched SLCC's Publication Center, where students can gain experience with a range of print and digital publishing technologies. The Pub Center supports an annual cycle of student-authored publications and in 2018 hosted a National Endowment for the Humanities Summer Institute on the history and future of the book. Through these programs, SLCC students have more hands-on writing-related opportunities than most lower-division undergraduates at the U.

SLCC faculty are also highly engaged in the regional and national composition community. They fill key leadership roles in TYCA-West and regularly host its annual conference. SLCC faculty have been officers in National TYCA, the Conference on College Composition and Communication (CCCC), and the National Council of Teachers of English (NCTE), and they also participate in the International Writing Center Association (IWCA), the Coalition for Community Writing (CCW), the Council of Writing Program Administrators, the National Conference on Peer Tutoring in Writing, the Rocky Mountain Writing Center Association, and the Rhetoric Society of America. They have published in composition collections and journals, and Rousculp's 2014 monograph, *Rhetoric of Respect: Recognizing Change at a Community Writing Center* was published by SWR and won the IWCA Outstanding Book Award. SLCC has received four TYCA Outstanding Programs in English awards and two CCCC Writing Program Certificates of Excellence. In sum, there has been a lot of composition studies happening at SLCC for a long time, much of which would not have been possible in the academic culture and reward structures of a research university.

IT TAKES AN ECOLOGY

Despite striving for global status, the U is still a commuter campus dependent on transfer students—the majority of whom come from

SLCC—to constitute a third of its undergraduates. As I discuss in Chapter 3, SLCC transfer students account for a disproportionate share of Latinx, Black, Native American, and Pacific Islander undergraduates at the U. However, transfer from SLCC to the U declined through the 2010s, even as the region's population grew, the Salt Lake Valley became less predominantly white, and SLCC's student body became more racially, ethnically, and linguistically diverse.

The reasons for this decline are complex. A robust local economy attracted some students into the workforce. Transfer rates to the U have also been impacted by the growth of Utah Valley University (UVU), a community college-turned-university in neighboring Utah County. I have deep respect for UVU's access mission, but it receives less per-pupil funding from the state than does the U, it has lower degree-completion rates, and its alumni network does not offer the same connections to local, national, and transnational power structures. Declining transfer from SLCC to the U means students in the Salt Lake Valley, a growing percentage of whom are students of color, might be diverted away from the best-resourced transfer destination in the region. Supporting transfer students has been a priority of the U's Center for Equity and Student Belonging (CESB), TRiO Program, Dream Center, and School for Cultural and Social Transformation (TRANSFORM). However, these efforts have not always received the recognition or resources they deserve. Some academic units on campus have looked down on transfer students; many have taken them for granted.

My collaborators and I have sought to hold the U accountable to its oft-stated goal of being "the University *for* Utah." While I don't think global and local commitments are inherently at odds, I want to ensure that the U's aspirations don't foreclose access to the state's best-resourced public institution for the diverse residents of the Salt Lake Valley. Many local students enter postsecondary education via SLCC, and many more would come to the U if they could afford it and felt welcome. I want WRS to play a meaningful role in *broadening* local access to the U, particularly for low-income and working-class students, immigrants and their children, and communities of color long structured out. My own commitments matter little, however, in an elitist academic culture that calculates value based on how many students an institution recruits from afar or turns away. Fortunately, several converging factors helped create favorable conditions for reimagining our interinstitutional disciplinary relations around a shared commitment to expanding educational opportunities for community college transfer students.

The first was the fresh start we got WRS. Credit articulation for first-year writing courses is the usual exigence for interactions across two- and four-year English departments. Those interactions often devolve into turf battles over curriculum and enrollment. Becoming a new department created a different basis for interinstitutional collaboration. While WRS is responsible for first-year writing, it was no longer existentially concerned about maintaining enrollment in 1010 and 2010. To survive as a department, it needed to grow the major, and SLCC was fostering interest in writing among many prospective students. The benefits of major-based partnerships were reciprocal. A clear "pathway" to WRS provided exigence for SLCC colleagues to create a new AS degree in writing studies. That degree became an opportunity to develop new 2000-level writing courses at SLCC that articulated into the WRS major: a gratifying reversal of the Great Credit Grab.

The second factor was supportive leadership and faculty colleagues at the U. Essential to reimagining our disciplinary relationships were three consecutive WRS department chairs who "got it": Maureen Mathison, Jay Jordan, and LuMing Mao. Also essential were WRS faculty who contributed directly to teaching and mentoring WSS students: Jenny Andrus, Nona Brown, José Cortez, Samah Elbelazi, Kendall Gerdes, David Hawkins-Jacinto, Tracey Daniels-Lerberg, Joy Pierce, Natalie Stillman-Webb, Jon Stone, Hua Zhu, and especially Romeo García. Leaders in the College of Humanities Dean's Office like Taunya Dressler, Diane Harris, and Stuart Culver, as well as Office of Undergraduate Studies (UGS) leaders Marti Bradley, Anne Darling, and Jim Agutter, provided funding and visibility for our transfer programs. By the time Ruth Watkins assumed the U presidency in 2018, with "transfer student success" as part of her institutional "roadmap," our interinstitutional disciplinary partnerships were already well underway.

The third factor was the vision and grace of my SLCC faculty colleagues. Particularly key were Brandon Alva, Lisa Bickmore, Chris Blankenship, Anne Canavan, Nathan Cole, Jennifer Courtney, Clint Gardner, Jerri Harwell, Charlotte Howe, Justin Jory, Kati Lewis, Alice Lopez, Stephanie Maenhardt, Andrea Malouf, Bernice Olivas, Tiffany Rousculp, and Stephen Ruffus. They mentored me through my many mistakes, advocated for our partnerships with their administrators, helped me navigate unfamiliar college bureaucracies, introduced me to their students, and invited me to campus events. They taught, presented at conferences, and wrote with me. Much of this labor was beyond their job descriptions and institutional reward structures; they redefined their professional roles to encompass these partnerships.

The fourth essential factor was the labor of staff at SLCC and the U who helped us connect with and support students. At SLCC, academic advisors Sidney Brown, Philip Asosike, and especially Luz Gamarra helped many students find our transfer programs. The staff and student organizations in SLCC's Office for Diversity and Multicultural Affairs (ODMA) allowed us to table at events and shared information about our programs. At the U, we relied on WRS academic advisor Lisa Shaw, Transfer Center advisor Terese Pratt, and CESB advisors Paul Fisk and Martha Hernandez. Paul and Martha helped many, many transfer students in WSS navigate oppressive bureaucracies. Alonso Reyna Rivarola and Xris Macias at the U's Dream Center and Brenda Santoyo at SLCC's Dream Center provided essential mentorship and advising for DACA and unDACAmented students in our programs. Over the years, staff in the U's Women's Resource Center, LGBT Resource Center, Center for Disability and Access, Student Success Coaches, TRiO, Office of Undergraduate Research, MUSE Scholars Program, and Office of Equity, Diversity, and Inclusion also supported WSS students. College of Humanities Internship Coordinator Ned Khatrichettri and Career Coach Megan Randall became the WSS career team, and Donna Ziegenfuss and Dale Larson created dedicated library resources for transfer student writers. Mark St. Andre and Beth Howard in UGS were important institutional advocates, and College of Humanities Development officers Lindsay and Lexie Kite were fierce and ambitious fundraisers. WRS Administrative Manager Polly Light managed program finances, and WRS executive secretaries Andrea Pischnotte, Kris Hirschbeck, and Kelli Borrowman provided logistical support. These colleagues were essential collaborators in the intellectual and programmatic work this book documents.

Finally, students were key agents in reimagining our local disciplinary ecology. Every transfer student who participated in these programs contributed to shaping them. Many played formal roles on the transfer team: reading and discussing scholarship; helping design studies; collecting and analyzing data; presenting to campus leadership and at conferences; creating recruitment materials; connecting with prospective transfer students; building web content; designing curricula; co-teaching courses; working with peers in the summer writing studio; advocating for transfer students on the U campus; communicating with donors and community partners; supporting one another; telling me when I was messing up; pushing our departments to do and be better. They also wrote with me, both as coauthors and by offering feedback on parts of this book that tenure criteria required I write "alone."

Some of these student collaborators appear elsewhere in the book, and some are only named here, but burying them in the acknowledgments feels wrong: Katherine Allred, Tanya Alvarado, Natalia Anderson, Rita Anderson, Jem Ashton, Jarrod Barben, Sabita Bastakoti, Emily Beck, Jake Becker, Joanne Castillo, Nic Contreras, Kelly Corbray, Lisa Donaldson, Illise Ellsworth, Margarita Lafarga, Russ Fugal, Angie Gamarra, Kimberly Gamarra, Cassie Goff, Michael Goodman, Heather Graham, Kayden Groves, Cristina Guerrero Perez, Keyon Hejazi-Far, Kate Henderson, Victoria Hunter, Winnie Jenkins, Nathan Lacy, Oti Langi, Jose Loeri, Anthony Magro III, Rachel Mills, Joseph Moss, Matt Nepute, Lupita Porras, Wes Porter, Sam Rivera Aguilar, Sandra Salazar-Hernandez, Claudia Sauz Mendoza, Davor Simunovic, Jacque

Thetsombandith, Adi Tolentino, Rebecca Trusty, Andrea Valverde, Stephanie Weidauer, and Yazmín Zarate Sandoval. Several graduate students also made essential contributions to our transfer programs: Charissa Che, Shauna Edson, Nina Feng, Nkenna Onwuzuruoha, and Justin Whitney. This ecology of collaborators shaped the possibilities for reimagining disciplinary relations. Without them, there would be no book, and, really, no reason to write one.

PATHS THROUGH (AND BEYOND) THE BOOK

Transfer in an Urban Writing Ecology is an experimental text that combines student writing, personal reflection, and academic analysis to make meaning ecologically. It includes a polyvocal chapter coauthored with students; three chapters single-authored by me; textual artifacts and images; and reflections, responses, and mini-essays written by me, students, and faculty at both SLCC and the U. The book is arranged as three parts, with individual chapters separated by interstitials that open with a student-authored text, followed by my commentary on how that student's intellectual work contributed to our collective projects and the (now-graduated) student's 2021 response. "Part I: Polygraph" theorizes the ecological framework that has emerged through our collaborations. "Interstitial I: Nic's Theory of Mentorship" presents Nic Contreras's 2016 essay "Down the Rabbit Hole," a foundational influence on my approach to collaborative research with transfer students. It is followed by Chapter 1, "Composing Salt Lake's Writing Ecology," coauthored by me and six student co-researchers: Nic, Sandra Salazar-Hernandez, Westin Porter, Kelly Corbray, Claudia Sauz Mendoza, and Nathan Lacy. Taking up Rousculp's conceptualization of Salt Lake as a writing ecology, we tack between our individual, emplaced literacy experiences and scholarship in composition studies. The chapter cycles through six themes emerging from our consideration of Salt Lake's writing ecology: *relations*, *identities*, *valuing*, *motion*, *difference*, and *change*. We suggest decentering academic institutions in conversations about transfer to consider how our ecology is being continuously co-constituted through the mobility of students, their writing across and beyond schools, and the lands on which we live and learn. In this ecological frame, writers at SLCC and the U are already interrelated. The question becomes how we cultivate our relations with intent to counter inequities and make positive change.

"Part II: Transfer-Conducive Disciplinary Ecologies" alternates between interstitials featuring texts by transfer student coauthors and single-authored chapters written by me. Each chapter takes a different methodological approach to the question of community college–university relations in composition studies and how we might reimagine those relations to expand opportunities for transfer students. "Interstitial II: Nate's College Calculus," opens with an artifact from Nathan Lacy's college decision making that frames a discussion of the systemic inequities of transfer as an impetus for reimagining community college–university relations. It is followed by Chapter 2, "A Discipline Worth Being," which situates this project within composition's disciplinary turn. Observing that traditional notions of disciplinarity have marginalized two-year college faculty, I argue that composition studies must discipline differently. I historicize this argument through an examination of a century of fraught relations between two- and four-year composition faculty. I discuss recent efforts among two-year college faculty to assert a more inclusive disciplinary vision, culminating in the recent teacher-scholar-activist (re)turn, which calls on university-based composition scholars to enact solidarity with two-year college colleagues. I identify implications of these histories for reimagined relations in Salt Lake.

"Interstitial III: Claudia's Theory of Writing" presents Claudia Sauz Mendoza's essay "Reflexión" and describes how she shaped the pedagogical and political orientation of our transfer programs. It is followed by Chapter 3, "Toward Transfer-Conducive Writing Ecologies," which puts critical higher education studies in conversation with scholarship in composition. I take up the concept of *transfer-receptive culture* and suggest a discipline-specific contribution: *transfer-conducive writing ecologies.* Such ecologies cultivate collaborative disciplinary relations across institutions that facilitate the physical, intellectual, and discursive mobility of community college students. Transfer-conducive writing ecologies honor the diverse rhetorical capacities students bring from their personal and community experiences, embracing an antideficit orientation with a commitment to expanding educational opportunities for transfer students on something closer to their own terms. This chapter presents findings from our mixed-method study of transfer student writing experiences at the U that shaped the collaborative programs we developed.

"Interstitial IV: Joanne's TYCA-West Keynote" presents Joanne Castillo's speech "The Work beyond Access" and discusses what she taught me about reimagining local disciplinary relations to enact broader institutional change. It is followed by Chapter 4, "Pathways and Ecologies," which describes the interinstitutional initiatives we developed to create a more transfer-conducive Salt Lake writing ecology. I discuss how we built on the findings of our local study and made strategic use of statewide policies pushing for transfer "pathways." I narrate the emergence of our two transfer writing courses and the WSS program. The first four years of these collaborations produced unanticipated ecological change at the U, at SLCC, and within the discipline. Based on our experiences, I suggest that a university writing department operating from reimagined relations with community college faculty and students can use the affordances of disciplinarity to make meaningful change.

Part II concludes with "The End of the World as We Know It." Reflecting from the vantage point of summer 2021, I take stock of our collective work. In 2020, the network of relations and material resources we cultivated helped WSS students weather the academic disruptions, economic challenges, and emotional difficulties of the COVID pandemic. However, it also made clear that persistent inequities in community college transfer cannot be countered by small, privately funded programs like WSS. We must consider how we can use our interinstitutional disciplinary relations—our writing ecology—to advance policies that enable all transfer student writers to thrive.

"Part III: Emergent Principles for Partnership" resists textual closure by presenting a collection of short essays by SLCC and U faculty, graduate students, and transfer students. In 2018, we developed an interinstitutional vision statement: *Articulating SLCC-U Partnerships in Writing Studies: Reimaging Relations, Making Change*. This document identifies seven "Principles for Partnership" to guide our collaborations: *recognize inequities*, *be colleagues*, *value difference*, *center students*, *address material conditions*, *educate for social justice*, and *engage with communities*. Part III contributors respond to these principles—extending, complicating, and challenging them, and exploring implications for our local writing ecology and the futures we might imagine for composition studies. In ecological fashion, Part III grows beyond the print book in a living webtext. We are continuously expanding our collective thinking through new essays by faculty, staff, and student collaborators at https://transferwritingecology.lib.utah.edu.

NOT THE DESTINATION

This book is not the end of the path. It exists because I had to produce a tenure monograph, although we ended up calling it a "polygraph" because it seemed neither honest nor advisable to write such a book alone. I wouldn't have produced a book if that weren't the price of staying in my uncomfortable position. In 2017, as we were drafting Chapter 1, Nate offered what still seems to me like the best articulation of our project. "This book," he wrote, is

> but a byproduct of the real work that was done to make tangible differences, however large or small, in the lives of those we've interacted with during our research. I'm certainly proud of the work that went into it and hope it will be useful in some way to those who take the time to read it, but this book is not the goal, not the solution, not the thing that made change. However, like a long-term deposit, maybe it will be doing the work for us when we're busy spinning plates elsewhere.

By the time you're reading this, we'll all be spinning other plates. This book is one push in a collective effort to reimagine community college–university relations in composition studies, our small contribution to the ongoing process of co-constituting a discipline worth being.

PART I:
POLYGRAPH

Interstitial I: Nic's Theory of Mentorship

Down the Rabbit Hole

IT'S THE FIRST DAY OF SCHOOL IN THE new country. I'm sitting on the frame of my dad's bike and trying to memorize how to say "Hola, mi nombre es Nicolas" in English. As I look at the road ahead I feel the wind whipping my face. I keep expecting to see the school around the next corner, or the next street. I don't know what it looks like. I don't know how far away we are from it, or from home. I'm trying my hardest to mouth out the words my dad taught me a few minutes earlier, words I heard only the night before, and keep the same rhythm throughout the sentence—I don't want people to know that I don't know a sixth word in English. That means no mumbling. No stuttering. No long spaces in between any of the words. Nothing that might indicate that I have to think about saying my own name. I figure, if I say this one sentence just right, they'll have no basis upon which to doubt me.

That was sixteen years ago.

Since then, I've moved five more times. I've learned how to relearn. I've learned how to move through new spaces. I've learned that if you ask the right questions, you'll get the right answers. I've learned that the right words can do a lot of that work for you. You just have to find them.

Early on in my life, perhaps even that same day on the bike, I realized that words have a great impact on our world (both internal and external). It's the reason we had such a hard time with the word "mentor" while writing this. It's the reason we have a problem with this rhetoric of deficit that surrounds community colleges and transfer students. It's the whole reason I'm in this ~~business~~ field to begin with. You see, some people think transfer students might not be as good as other students. That we stand still, unsure of where we are or where we should go, in a state of paralysis, or crisis, or something. I think it might be quite the opposite. I'm not a big fan of absolutes, but I think we all *know* where we're going, or, at least, where we *aren't* going. My life's made it obvious that, if anything, you're not anywhere for very long. Things do make a lot more sense once you realize where you've been, however.

For example, a few days ago I was in the Salt Lake County Jail facilitating a creative writing workshop. Flash fiction, I think. Now, I don't know if what I do is mentorship—I wouldn't even really call myself a teacher—but I think explaining what I do there will help illustrate my point.

Every week I go to the jail and do my best to help our students understand and learn the day's material. The challenge is that no two classes are ever the same. Every week I go in there are different students. There's a different guard on duty (some nicer than others), and a different workshop to teach. The participants' lives are just as convoluted and strange as mine. And yes, there's transfer happening even here, in these holding units. Our students are moved around, they switch cells, pods, roommates, even facilities sometimes. Nevertheless, my job is more or less the same every week.

I go in, with my tote bag full of golf pencils, paper, and our curriculum, and I do my best to teach the workshop and explain materials as best I can to that day's class. I ask questions (as I've been taught to do by the Community Writing Center) and facilitate conversation. I use everything in the room to gauge what and how things need to be said to create the learning environment I'm looking for. Essentially, I try to meet them in the middle—wherever that is. This means I have to understand my position in relation to theirs. I don't always find their "bicycle story," but I know that some version of it is there, and that's good enough for me. I walk into these workshops with a simple idea in mind: that I can do something good for these students, as long as I work in conjunction with them, and not from a position of power. Not that I always have that position either—I've learned that too. Whether it's a good day at the jail, or a bad one, my time with these men and women always gives me something to take home.

It's amazing what happens when we leave our egos behind and approach each other as two travelers should—with understanding. We live better. I'm humbled by the knowledge my students bring, and they by mine. It's reflexive. It creates dialogue and mutual respect. It also means I am constantly revising my analogies, my linguistic choices, my curriculum—my entire approach, really—to better fit the students of the day. I do the same thing in my other classrooms—the ones at the college and university. I mean, it's the nature of the place, right? Or of the job? The beast, maybe.

Truth is, I often struggle to find the right metaphor for transfer. Are transfer students pinballs ricocheting across the educational board? Or are we more like commuters with great knowledge of the public transit system? Does that make literacy sponsors pinball wizards or bus drivers? Our research team has a joke about us all being rabbits in lab coats—you know, transfer students studying transfer students. That might be the most appropriate metaphor. I think that effectively makes me both the joker and the punchline, too. And while it can be hard explaining our study to people I meet, I never get angry. Just as I never get angry when people ask me where I'm from. I just find it funny. People I meet know I'm not from here, whether I be at the university or on the street by my house. I can tell by the way they ask. "Where are you *from?*" they say. The joke is: I don't know anymore. I've moved around so much that I can only identify with transfer really. Ironically, it's been the only constant in my life: living in between places, between the lines. It can get confusing, but I think it's probably because I haven't found the right words yet. As I mentioned, that's part of the game.

The important thing to remember here is the goal. It's simple: help someone learn something new in a way that is engaging—and, if possible, fun. I find that this works best when I use my knowledge in conjunction with theirs, and I've learned that from my own mentors. It's in those rare moments where two people stop and share with each other that knowledge is made, that a connection sparks—whether it be in a jail or in an office. I find that you learn more about yourself through your other (I have Jacques to thank for that). No two paths are alike, as my coauthors have shown, which is why my favorite mentors, the ones who have helped me the most, have been the ones who stop to listen, assess, and adapt—it strikes me that they must be transfer students too, in a way. It inspires me to do the same with the people I meet.

As I journey through the academy, and the world at large, mentors find ways to bridge people and situations together. Sometimes they help you make sense of an assignment; sometimes they help you make sense of your life. Sometimes they put you back on that bike. All I can hope for is to do the same with my work. Essentially, I become that bridge, and I think that's really what our study and work is all about. We're working hard to connect two schools and their students who have been wading the waters of transfer alone.

I think that's what makes this study so important. It provides sponsorship to us, transfer students, and also serves to bridge the socioeconomic barriers between these two schools—effectively creating more opportunities for future transfer students. Building this bridge is huge because it is a step in a direction that, although some would say is obviously beneficial, has rarely been taken. I never quite understood why; I saw both of these schools as part of the same group. A group dedicated to providing students with the best education possible—if you're reading this, that group probably includes you. So, why shouldn't we work together?

I hope our words will make clear that transfer can be positive. And also, that it can be negative. But that's not really the point. The point is understanding—understanding that you just might find yourself back on that bike tomorrow and that there're rabbits walking around in lab coats today. Get it?

◈◈◈◈

Christie Toth, Emily Beck, Shauna Edson, Nic Contreras, Wes Porter, and Nate Lacy at TYCA-West 2016 in Las Vegas. Photo credit: Charissa Che.

Nic Contreras wrote "Down the Rabbit Hole" in fall 2016 as part of a collaboratively authored essay titled "Traveling Together: Rewriting Transfer Student Literacy Sponsorship." His coauthors included four members of our transfer research team—me, Nate Lacy, Wes Porter, and Shauna Edson. The team spent the 2015–16 academic year researching transfer student writing experiences at the U, but this essay, written by invitation for the inaugural issue of the e-journal *Mentoring across Disciplines and Cultures*, was our first effort at composing together.

We developed our initial ideas as a presentation for TYCA-West in Las Vegas and spent the remainder of the semester writing and revising together. Even as we wrote ourselves into new and deeper relationships, the 2016 presidential election heightened longstanding dangers faced by Nic and other students who were denied access to US citizenship. Composing together amid that cataclysm deepened my awareness of my many privileges and subsequent responsibilities to these fellow travelers.

I am, in varying ways, different from my student coauthors, and many of those differences have conferred unearned, compounding advantages over the course of my life. I was born a citizen of the United States, the white cis daughter of two career military officers. I grew up in late-twentieth-century military communities with well-funded schools. I scored high on assessments that privileged my family's white, middle-class languaging and literacy practices, and I attended a private liberal arts college right after high school. While I no longer identify as straight, I've been married to a white cis man since 2009. I have a terminal degree and a job with health insurance. While those advantages have put me in the institutional position to "mentor" transfer students, my coauthors are the experts on the phenomena we have researched and written about.

Our academic collaborations are fraught with the risk of white saviorism, so let me say this as clearly as I can: *Being white and middle-class makes me bad at this work.* There is much I don't know, and there are many reasons for students—particularly working-class students, BIPOC students, undocumented students—not to trust someone who looks and talks like me. The purpose of our transfer projects is not to magnanimously grant community college students access to an elite university education, but rather to try to change the structures of that education in deep collaboration with students who are marginalized by academic "business as usual." As Dimpal Jain and colleagues write in *Power to the Transfer*, "In terms of policy and practice as related to transfer, students of color should not merely be consulted; rather their voices should be an integral part of the decision-making process" (24). My student coauthors have been integral collaborators researching and voicing transfer student writing experiences, developing supports that counter the inequities they face, and making institutional change. This book could not, would not, and should not have been written without them.

As Nic observes, the phrase "rabbits in lab coats" became a running joke on the team. To me, the joke signaled my coauthors' awareness of the power differentials between researcher and researched as well as between professor and student, heightened and complicated by our other differences. It foregrounded the sometimes uncomfortable in-betweenness of the roles we were negotiating from our different positions. I worked hard to be vulnerable: to acknowledge my power and privilege in this situation as well as the limits of my perspective and the fact that I screw up. During our research team meetings, I did the best I could to create spaces for everyone to speak, and to listen with intent, often functioning as the whiteboard note-taker so everyone could see—and, if necessary, correct—what was emerging through our conversations. While I didn't delude myself that it was possible to set aside the power asymmetries inherent in our positions, I strove to stay open to being changed by what these students knew, said, and wrote. And Nic's theorization of mentorship in "Down the Rabbit Hole" did change my understanding of what we were doing together: I felt, and feel, a keen responsibility to live up to his ideals. In our best moments, I hope our research team approached his vision of "dialogue" and "mutual respect," that we used our knowledges "in conjunction" with one another.

In some ways, that vision bumped up against the university's model of "undergraduate research," a competitive "opportunity" in which students learn to think, act, and write like professional academics. Nic's essay nudged me to self-consciously reject the replication model and prioritize the relationship-building aspect of our work together. As we grew and adapted, we found ways to involve everyone who said they wanted to be on the team, no application required, and valued their contributions in whatever form they took. These students' coursework, alongside-school responsibilities, and personal well-being were more important than "research," and our collective priority was supporting their efforts to achieve their goals. Roles on the team were flexible and open to ongoing negotiation: the important thing was sustaining our connections.[2]

One of my greatest trepidations throughout this project has been the risk of exploiting my co-researchers—all first-generation college students, many of them students of color—for my own professional gain. I could not disentangle this book from my tenure requirements and the fact that my future as a university professor hinged on its publication. From the outset, I was open with my student coauthors about how our work together fit into the reward structures of the academy, how the neoliberal university commodifies intellectual labor and operates on a self-serving star system, and how I stood to benefit from our projects. I shared my discomfort and anger regarding that reality. I have tried to ensure that, whether the book ever made it to print, the work that went into it benefited SLCC transfer students: those who co-researched and coauthored the book, and those who came after.

Academically, the benefits for students included much of what is typically associated with undergraduate research: the learning that comes with reading and discussing published scholarship, collaboratively designing and conducting research, presenting at conferences, writing and revising together, and engaging in many critical and metarhetorical conversations along the way. Involvement in the project also contributed to students' efforts to complete their degrees. Student co-researchers had the option of enrolling for undergraduate research credits, which moved them closer to graduation and, in some cases, enabled them to carry enough credits to qualify for financial aid. We used university funds to travel to conferences in Houston, Las Vegas, Portland, Boulder, Louisville, Pittsburgh, and Reno. The conferences weren't always welcoming (or, frankly, interesting) to undergraduates, but they were an opportunity to raise the visibility of community college transfer in disciplinary spaces. More importantly, traveling and presenting together strengthened the students' relationships with one another.

The relationships students formed with one another were in many ways more crucial than their relationships with me. They created a loose but mutually sustaining community, supporting one another in and beyond classrooms in which they might otherwise feel isolated or minoritized. This community of co-researchers was the kernel for the Writing Studies Scholars program discussed in the preface and Chapter 4, which aims to cultivate and extend such relationships across SLCC and the U. As Nic writes, students became the bridge. They showed me that my job was to help create the conditions under which they could forge and sustain connections with one another, and to engage my faculty colleagues in the never-complete work of becoming a department in which all students can feel as though they belong.

In feedback on a draft of this interstitial, Nic told me to hit this point hard: I always sought to ensure that student co-researchers benefitted *materially* from their contributions to these projects. Most were paid hourly wages for their labor, first through the U's Undergraduate Research Opportunity Program (UROP), MUSE Internship Program, and a University Teaching Grant, and then through foundation grants, at which point I was able to raise their pay from twelve to fifteen dollars an hour. When the first external grant arrived in 2017, we awarded all still-enrolled transfer students on the team two-thousand-dollar scholarships. With the help of colleagues across campus, I found ways to secure additional scholarship funding for those who needed it to complete their degrees. I've tried to use what social and cultural capital I possess to support these co-researchers' academic and professional goals. I've written letters of recommendation and served as a reference for scholarships, employment, and graduate school. I still send them position announcements. They have reciprocated by sending me opportunities from their workplaces to share with current WSS students.

I've also tried to ensure that proceeds from this research benefit transfer students long-term. I promised the team I would donate all income associated with our work—speaker fees, honoraria, awards—to a department scholarship fund for SLCC transfer students. That promise holds for any royalties from this book. I allocate a percentage of my salary to that scholarship fund, an amount that increases with merit raises, tenure, and promotion. Those funds support transfer students in our department who do not qualify for federal financial aid, including undocumented students and those who have exceeded their lifetime aid eligibility.

I've made mistakes in our co-researcher relationships. Those mistakes were often born of the limitations of my experiences and perspectives as a middle-class white woman. Some were exacerbated by the stresses and chronic overextension of junior faculty working conditions, by my complacency when things seemed to be going well, and by misplaced trust in a few colleagues. When I've recognized these mistakes or when students were willing to say something, I've apologized, sought to make amends without burdening them with my emotional processing, and done my best to change. I'm sure I've made other mistakes that my student collaborators chose not to call out. This reality of our power dynamics—that because of my positionality I won't always be told when I've hurt someone—haunts me. I hope that uncertainty has made me more vigilant.

I never wanted anyone involved in this project to feel like a rabbit. My best indication that we've approached Nic's vision of "making knowledge in conjunction with one another" is where we are today. According to a 2015 Transfer Process Working Group, 65 percent of transfer students at the U graduate within six years, a figure that aligns with national statistics for community college transfer students at public universities (Jenkins and Fink). Nationwide, Black and Latinx[3] students who transfer from community colleges complete bachelor's degrees at about half the rate of white students (Shapiro et al., *Completing College: A National View of Student Attainment Rates by Race and Ethnicity*). Between spring 2017 and spring 2021, all student coauthors of this book graduated with bachelor's degrees, and all have stayed in touch with one another and with me. Well into their post-graduation lives, they have come back to the table to revise and edit this book. Some continue to write in support of program grants, some regularly connect me with prospective students. Most still live in the Salt Lake Valley, and all have gone on to endeavors—teaching, youth mentorship, student or social services, graduate school—that resonate with the work of this book.

FROM NIC IN 2021

Truth be told, I was hesitant to touch any of this old writing anymore. Even rereading it can be disorienting, almost nauseating. I feel embarrassed at my optimism when I read what I wrote and my attempt at imitating the tone of the Vonnegut novel I'd just finished reading. The fact is, I can't change what I wrote all those years ago (and I'd rather not anyway), but when Christie offered me this spot as an addendum of sorts, I figured the least I can do is contextualize and clarify some things that have changed since then.

Right off the bat, one glaring error in this piece is that I thought I'd read enough deconstructionist theory that I was free from all these structures and systems at play. I say in the original piece how I could meet people with this knowledge (inside a jail of all places) and not be influenced by my position of power, as if those things weren't already present in the room when I walked in. This was something I learned later on, that even though you might not believe in hierarchies or systems of oppression or race or what-have-you—that doesn't mean they aren't still there, affecting everything you see before you even see it. It's something I expressed to Christie this past year. I made sure to tell Christie and I'll tell you too, reader, that simply because you place value on your students' words, their ideas, or their wholeness as people and listen to them doesn't mean others will. I know there were and still are many people who will look at the work our team attempted to do and scoff at it. That's fine; it's to be expected.

The second thing I'd like to address is how optimistic I was back then—or at least, how optimistic *this version of me* reads. To be fair, I think I was young and simply excited about writing anything at that point. I remember looking around at what other folks were doing and feeling inspired. I wanted to show what I could do and how I might theorize my viewpoint of the world I'd seen so far in a fun and creative way and not as some identity (Latin American, immigrant, etc.) that was placed upon me. I resisted, and I often still resist, the task that so many times feels like an obligation to me as a member of a minoritized group, to write one-dimensionally about my woes and share "my story," explaining again and again what it might mean to folks who so many times won't remember or won't understand it even after I've gone to such lengths. Instead I opted to write something that made sense and felt validating for me. I won't apologize for that.

However, in the years since the writing of the piece, I have admittedly felt less like a traveler and more like a fugitive. Looking back, my life as an undocumented immigrant in this country has always felt this way, no matter who was president—but I thought that idea might be harder for the reader to relate to. Nowadays, though, I've become more comfortable with the idea of using my voice to speak in ways that might make *others* less comfortable. This is in part because the United States' flirtations with fascism and its unapologetically inhumane and self-serving actions as a world power have made it very clear to me that the work that follows must actively disrupt the status quo for things to change. If this work is to lift the voices and the peoples that have been ignored, then those who would hold our backs to the wall can no longer be suffered merely for comfort's sake. They must be disarmed and made to see that they are victims of this oppressive system, too. I think that for the changes we'd like to see take place in academia and in the world—are they not the same?—we must hold one another accountable in uncomfortable, yet loving ways, if at all possible. I hope to still meet travelers where they may be, but I think I'll carry the colloquial "big stick" with me just in case.

And that's it, really. That's all I want to say for now. Being tied to any piece of writing for too long starts to feel like wearing a ball and chain, or in my case like carrying around a time capsule that maybe you'd just rather keep buried. I feel sort of like a relay runner who's been holding onto this baton for too long, running and running, waiting for the person I'm supposed to hand this off to. I'm ready to pass this on.

There is this comment at the beginning of "The Art Spirit" where Robert Henri refers to art as "Signposts towards the future . . . towards greater knowledge." That feels like what we were trying to do with all this writing. I'm hoping that once this book is published, we can nail this post down and keep walking forward. This was never about me, I feel, so I try not to be too attached to it anymore. And I mean that in the best way possible! Our work and ethos always appealed to me because it felt so contrary to the normal hierarchies of the institutions we belonged to. We always talk about "not pulling up the ladder behind you" on our team. I am thankful to have found a place and a group of people who were concerned with undoing the very nature of academic work, and instead promoting something different and new, some way forward for the people in the back who were still making their way.

I think my team would agree that we were always and still are dedicated to the idea that if we could somehow help pave a way forward from where we are now, or at least leave some breadcrumbs behind to show how we'd come to be here, someone else might follow behind and continue where we left off. As with all art, I can only hope this book and the writings I was able to help co-create might propel you forward into some action, further down the rabbit hole you might be peering into, contemplating whether you should jump in. Just as a bike ride or maybe some book you read in college might have led you here, so I hope that what I've written will lead you to write whatever story and (in this way) whatever future you see when you close your eyes at night. After all, *this* only ever was a dream we dreamed up one afternoon and now it's a book. Maybe you're on some college campus reading this, or in some room without any windows, but I want you to know we were there once, too.

And so, I want to finish my addendum to this time capsule with the hope that it may help the reader forward, and that way—at least for the near future—I won't have to read it or talk about it any longer. I'm someone else now, somewhere else now, further down the road from this signpost, and I'd rather not have to come back every year to check whether it's still here. You, my friend, can feel free to do whatever you like with this after you're done. Maybe you can see to it that the wind doesn't knock it down. Or maybe you'll want to put it all out of your mind and forget about it.

Either way, here you go—I think I'm done with this now. It's your turn to carry it on.

1

Composing Salt Lake's Writing Ecology

TRANSFER ORIENTATION

AS WE WROTE THIS CHAPTER, it became clear that our references to various parts of the Salt Lake metro area held meanings, values, and ironies for us that would be lost on readers unfamiliar with our region. Phrases like "up on the hill" and "down in the valley" appear throughout, and they represent more than just topography. They describe the social geography of the Salt Lake Valley, a geography that is what Nedra Reynolds calls "the where *of writing" (176) for transfer students moving between SLCC and the U. Such phrases signal location, but also decenter the U, which is perched on the edge of the valley "bowl." Inside that bowl are swaths of wealth and poverty, privilege and marginalization, laid out along five hundred square miles of gridded streets whose numbers locate you relative to another imagined center: downtown's Temple Square, four miles west of "Emigration Canyon." This northeast corner of the valley the Eastern Shoshone call co'kar-ni is where, in 1847, thousands of white Latter-day Saint settlers and at least three enslaved Black men first arrived on Shoshone, Goshute, and Ute lands that were, at the time, still claimed by Mexico (Q. Taylor). We can only sketch an impression of the physical environment of the Salt Lake Valley and the social and material relations it co-constitutes (see Ríos, discussed below). However, we hope this sketch will orient you, help you glimpse the complexity of our local writing ecology.[4]*

Salt Lake City lies southeast of the Great Salt Lake, between two mountain ranges mapped with settler names: the Wasatch to the east (given much attention by hikers and skiers), and the Oquirrh to the west (whose attention comes primarily from the Kennecott Utah Copper Corporation). Those mountains nearly converge at the southern end of the valley. At the northern end, the Wasatch jut west, cornering downtown, with neighborhoods spreading north and east into the foothills that contain the state capitol and tiers of wealthy households. On one foothill, the university's large white "U" is visible from vantage points across the valley. On the other side of that spur of mountain are the refineries and rail yards of North Salt Lake.

By and large, the further east you live along "the Bench"—the stretch of foothills along the base of the Wasatch that includes, at its northern end, the U campus—the higher the elevation and the wealthier you and your neighbors are likely to be. If you live further west, past I-15 and the railroad tracks, you are in communities like Rose Park, Glendale, West Valley City, Taylorsville, and Kearns, where you and your neighbors are more likely to be working-class, immigrants, and/or people of color. Go far enough west, past the airport, and you hit the refinery town of Magna, which sits at the base of the Oquirrh Mountains, just south of the tailing ponds and landfill. Up on the hill, the U offers a breathtaking view of this bowl. On good days, it's breathtaking because you can see the entire valley, the Kennecott Garfield Smelter Stack beaconing like a lighthouse where the Oquirrhs meet the rapidly receding Great Salt Lake. On bad days it's because the valley's natural inversion effect traps particulate matter from vehicle emissions and refineries, resulting in air quality so poor you can't see downtown.

The ten campuses of Salt Lake Community College (SLCC) are spread across the valley, all close to or west of I-15. The main Taylorsville-Redwood campus is located ten miles southwest of downtown, the geographical center of the bowl. These locations facilitate access, particularly for communities on the west side. They also mean that, for the 54 percent of SLCC transfer students who head to the U each year ("SLCC"), their physical trajectory is from "down" in the valley to "up" on the hill. Although the U is the state's flagship, it is also an urban commuter campus. Most students live off-campus, and about a third of U undergraduates are transfer students of some kind.

The U's location sends mixed messages about access, particularly for those in the western part of the valley. University Neighborhood Partners offers community-based programming on the close-in west side, and a small satellite campus in Sandy, a prosperous bedroom community at the south end of the valley, offers general education and high-demand major courses. However, on the main campus, where most students complete their coursework, parking is expensive and in short supply. U students have free access to the Utah Transit Authority (UTA), and those who can live or park near the light-rail system ("TRAX") have a direct line to campus, but UTA service is often inadequate and potentially unsafe for students who live or work beyond the more expensive close-in neighborhoods. The U's relative inaccessibility maps onto the inequitable social geographies of the Salt Lake Valley, and for some transfer students, navigating those geographies can be an uphill climb. Despite the challenges, their physical and rhetorical movements between home, work, campus, and community enact the metro area (see Edbauer). These students are agents in the Salt Lake writing ecology: before, during, and after transfer.

Now that we've oriented you to where *we are, we will orient you to* who *and* how *we are, and* why *we've chosen to write this chapter the way we did. "We" are Nic Contreras, Sandra Salazar-Hernandez, Westin Porter, Kelly Corbray, Claudia Sauz Mendoza, Nathan Lacy, and me (Christie Toth). I am a junior faculty member in the U's Department of Writing and Rhetoric Studies (WRS), and the rest of the team are SLCC transfer students who majored in WRS and dedicated time and energy to this project over the last seven years. Nic, Sandra, Wes, and Nate have been part of the project from the beginning, working on our 2015–16 study of transfer student writing experiences at the U. Claudia and Kelly joined the project the following year, when we were piloting the writing courses we developed based on that study.*

When we started drafting this chapter in 2017, the student members of our research team ranged in age from twenty-two to thirty-eight; I was thirty-four. We came back together to revise in summer 2019 and again in summer 2021. All six student coauthors are in the first generation of their families to attend college. Wes and Nate graduated from the U in spring 2017, Nic in spring 2018, and Claudia in spring 2019. Sandra graduated in fall 2019, and Kelly in spring 2021. Nic identifies as Hispanic/Latino, Claudia as American-Latina, and Sandra as Mexican American. Kelly is Black, and Wes, Nate, and I are white. Nic and Claudia immigrated as children from Argentina and

Mexico, respectively, and Sandra, Wes, Nate, Kelly, and I were born in the United States. Nic, Claudia, and Sandra are bilingual in English and Spanish. All seven of us are cisgender—four women, three men. Three of us identify as bisexual or queer.[5] *Two of us are neurodivergent, and some of us have histories with trauma and other struggles with physical and mental health. We note these intersecting identities here, but in our individual sections we each made our own choices about how to represent ourselves.*

This chapter begins theorizing interinstitutional writing transfer by putting our individual experiences and perspectives in conversation with disciplinary scholarship. It establishes context for the findings and programmatic developments presented in the chapters that follow. This structure is an enactment of the kind of ecological orientation we're seeking to advance. As Kristie S. Fleckenstein and coauthors assert, "All knowledge is always situated. This realization is a prelude to diversification: a commitment to increasing the range of perspectives, the ranges of voices, speaking in any one study" (401). Our writing experiments with such diversification in form as well as content. It is nonlinear and thematically recursive. Influenced by cultural rhetorics methodologies (Powell; Powell et al.), we seek to constellate our perspectives on writing, transferring, and co-researching here in Salt Lake. We lay these perspectives alongside each other to see how they "ping," as we took to calling it, and what they contribute to our understanding of community college–university relations. In the process, we encourage readers to reimagine those relations ecologically.

Our methods for composing this chapter were iterative. We began by reflecting on our study findings, our personal experiences, and ecological theories in writing, rhetoric, and literacy studies. For our collaborative presentation at the 2017 CCCC convention in Portland, Oregon—the homelands of the Multnomah, Clackamas, and Cowlitz and the Confederated Tribes of Grand Ronde—each team member composed a reflection on the writing ecology of Salt Lake from their vantage point. After the conference, we systematically reviewed our pieces for recurring themes that seemed central to our emerging ecological understanding of transfer student writing experiences. The themes that surfaced were relations, identities, valuing, motion, difference, *and* change.

Justin Whitney, Kelly Corbray, Sandra Salazar-Hernandez, Shauna Edson, Nate Lacy, Wes Porter, Claudia Sauz Mendoza, Nic Contreras, and Christie Toth at CCCC 2017 in Portland. Photo credit: Jay Jordan.

I drafted passages discussing each theme in relation to scholarly literature on writing, rhetoric, and literacy ecologies, then brought those drafts back to the group for feedback and revision. These passages thus "sound" more like me (specifically, the "me" produced through my academic interactions). I took on much of the labor of scholarly reading and synthesis because I had the immediate professional pressures and the privileges of training and time. However, every use of the term "we" in these sections has been reviewed by the entire team—most recently, during the copyedit stage of the publication process in summer 2022—and, when necessary, reworked until every coauthor was satisfied. Each coauthor revised their individual section in response to team conversations throughout 2017, reviewer and editor feedback in 2019 and 2021, and during copyediting in 2022. Although these revisions extended over more than five years, we drafted this chapter before the rest of the book. In some ways, it now feels like an artifact, but the intellectual and interpersonal connections it enacts became the heart of the project.[6]

Charissa Che, Wes Porter, Darin Jensen, Nic Contreras, Sandra Salazar-Hernandez, Claudia Sauz Mendoza, and Nate Lacy in Portland's Chinatown during CCCC 2017. Photo credit: Christie Toth.

This chapter's representations of Salt Lake's writing ecology are inevitably partial, reflecting our embodied experiences and perspectives. However, we hope our approach counters what Fleckenstein and colleagues call "the distortions of a singular account" (389). Like the Salt Lake Valley itself, our stories are not neatly reconcilable, but they are interconnected. They demonstrate the diverse and co-constitutive nature of the writing ecology we inhabit. They are emplaced, but also suggest negotiations transfer students might be undertaking in other settings. Ultimately, we believe our work demonstrates why inquiring into transfer students' experiences matters. We hope it encourages others to consider how they might collaborate across institutional, professional, and disciplinary differences to center transfer students' experiences and interests.

Nic

Let me be clear: I do not trust you. I don't mean this to be offensive, nor should you take this statement personally. Simply put, my life has taught me that mistrust, or doubt, is possibly the best way to generate knowledge and remain safe. My distrust of institutions and authority figures stems from my childhood, and, for reasons I'll explain later, I am wary.

This is all sort of uncomfortable for me. See, I can't see your face right now, reader. I am not sure where you live. I don't know where you grew up or where you went to school. I don't know whom you voted for in the last election or even what your favorite album of all time is (my own way of getting to know someone). I can't look you in the eyes nor feel you out in any way, so I don't really know how to play my cards. I don't know where to begin. Though it is not my first time addressing academics, professors, or strangers, this all feels so much more permanent, so I choose my words carefully:

You, reader, most likely belong to the academy, a place that prides itself on its ability to be critical, even of itself. However, you and I both know there is a bubble there; it exists around the university and protects everything inside. I feel it when I walk on your campus. It keeps everything Steady Eddie and safe. A friend of mine once told me, "If there's ever a time where you start to feel comfortable, that's when you're fucking up." What she meant was that the moment you think you've got it figured out—you don't. That's when accidents happen. And for me that's where a lot of the blame lies. It is in the hope that I can unsettle you, then, that I write this—if only so that you, too, will see my dilemma.

Now, my story begins at the CWC. If you don't know the CWC (the Community Writing Center), it's situated on the plaza of downtown Salt Lake's City Library. Begun in '01 by SLCC English professor Tiffany Rousculp, it's a center that focuses on promoting literacy in the community. It's also where I worked all through college. It's the place where I learned about community work and, really, where I was introduced to academia. It was there that I met many of the people who now compose this research team. It was there where we first met Christie. If you'd told me when I met her that I'd be helping to write a part of her book later, I'd have laughed my ass off.

I recall receiving an email about this "research opportunity" back in the late spring of 2015. Apparently, some professor at the

University of Utah was looking for writing students to help with some project. I figured I'd at least listen to what they had to say—even if things didn't pan out, it'd be good to know someone up on the hill before I transferred there in the fall. I only hoped my short time at SLCC and the few months I'd spent at the CWC had prepared me to answer her questions—or whatever it was she wanted from us.

When the day finally came I was still nervous about what I'd have to say on the subject of "writing." This was back when I thought you had to have infallible truths to present to the world if you were going to be an academic. I was surprised, however, when Dr. Toth walked into the center. She didn't look stuffy, or old. She wasn't wearing a tweed coat as I knew all professors did. She insisted we call her Christie before she got right to business.

The lady spoke at what felt like a hundred mph. She dropped academic verbiage I was still trying to learn to pronounce. I wish I could tell you exactly what we talked about that day; it had something to do with transfer students, I'm sure. All I remember is feeling my brain strain as we worked at connecting the dots between the ideas Christie threw on the whiteboard and the ones we had in our minds about the university and "research." There was lots of head scratching on our parts and enthusiastic outbursts from Christie when we presented our half-baked notions of what we thought we were dealing with. I'm thankful that our meetings nowadays are at least somewhat more coherent.

I bring all this up because, as I look back, something crucial happened in that moment. Up until then, academia, in my eyes at least, was a world removed from the rest of reality. But here was this university representative, a person, who was taking time to come listen to *us*. I can't stress enough how valuable that is. I'd seen little of academia, and as a first-gen student I had (and still have) a very limited understanding of this world. In high school, we'd been assured that college professors wouldn't care about us. When I arrived at college I learned that advisors and student services were also very much on the same boat. The message I received was "We help those that help themselves," which isn't much help at all; it feels more productive to bang your head against your desk.

During my first few years of college, I asked few questions and figured out what I could on my own. I was used to it. I grew up undocumented, and, early in life, I developed a deep mistrust of institutions and anything that was associated with the state. When I was a kid, places labeled *secure* by most to me spelled out *warning*. I knew it only took one ICE agent at your door for the whole jig to be up—everything we'd worked for gone, all of us cuffed and deported. So, I got good at playing my cards close to my chest, and I got even better at reading the signs and figuring things out for myself. Mostly, I was scared.

I flew under the radar, which kept me safe. It wasn't until recently that I realized it also kept me silent. This "game" kept me in the shadows where I wouldn't be found out, but it also did nothing to move me out of that place, to improve or change my situation. I mistrusted everyone. Who would turn me in? Who would help me? I waited for someone to make themselves available, to present themselves as trustworthy, but nobody did. I got by like that for a long time. I got really good at my bluff. In retrospect, I see now that it's all a gamble. Being undocumented is a lot like going to college or being a writer; you're building something and you're not sure that it's going to last or lead to anything, but you take the risk anyway.

It was no different that day at the CWC, but we all came back the week after, so we must've felt something. I think we saw that Christie seemed genuinely interested in what we had to say and bring to the table. I know I saw the project as a way to make a place for us at the university, to begin inquiry on this issue and begin to provide access for other students like ourselves. If anybody could speak to transfer experiences we could, and if we wanted to change things, we needed to be involved in the work.

This is similar to one of the first lessons I learned at the CWC. Our manual states that the CWC cannot "know what a community needs or wants without entering into full and mutually beneficial partnership with that community." The idea being that for a community resource to serve its community well, it must not presuppose or diagnose what a community needs without consulting the people it plans to work with. This Freirean approach is inherently collaborative and dependent on dialogue.

We took a similar approach with our project. In our meetings, our team would discuss what we thought needed to be done. We talked about transfer issues and the writing ecology of Salt Lake and what affordances and constraints it produced for students who were transferring to the U from SLCC. Together, we used our diverse experiences to shed light on different areas of the ecology and the transfer experience. One of the first things the research team did was interview students who, just like us, had transferred to the U.

We listened to how these students talked about their experiences navigating between schools. To this day, I see those trajectories as I would routes on a map—the interviews, classroom field notes, and student writing we've collected as a sort of traveler's log, with us performing a road worker's role, examining the structural integrity of the transfer bridge, looking for any confusing signs, potholes, or blocked entrance ramps we could fix or reopen. While we mapped the movement of student writers around town and across campuses, we also recognized the way our movements were already affecting the ecology by creating opportunities for transfer students to engage with professors and research, offering a form of representation for future transfer students, and helping to bridge a longstanding rift between two major educational institutions in our valley.

Working on this project has made it clear to me that it *is* possible for institutions of higher ed to work with their community members—if they want to. I think the project itself proves how working *with* transfer students can provide them with opportunities and access that help them succeed. I won't pretend our work didn't affect our own transfer experiences. I also won't pretend our project is perfect. I still don't trust institutions; I know better than to trust those who hold the power to hand it over willingly. I realize that just because it's possible for institutions to do this kind of work doesn't mean they will. I'm even skeptical of our team's ability to do anything truly radical for the disenfranchised if we are under the umbrella of an institution that has been complicit in their marginalization.

I don't think there's anything wrong with being skeptical, though. It can be productive. It can be generative. It's kept me on my toes, and probably saved my life more than once. If you let go of the doubt for too long you find yourself doing "amazing" self-congratulatory work—too much blowing smoke, not enough looking in mirrors. I will mistrust you all in the academy to keep us from falling into that very same trap of comfort, and *that* is not a bluff. However, I also know you have to take a chance on something if you want to make it, so that's what I'm doing. I'm writing to you all in a leap of faith—I'm trusting Christie, because she says you're good for it. And I hope that she's not wrong.

RELATIONS

Our thinking about relations is informed by the literature on writing ecologies and Indigenous rhetorics of relationality, scholarly conversations that have sometimes come into conflict. We first encountered the concept of Salt Lake as a writing ecology through the ecology itself—specifically, SLCC professor Tiffany Rousculp's book Rhetoric of Respect: Recognizing Change at a Community Writing Center. *Rousculp draws on ecological theories of writing to locate the CWC within the larger "ecosystem" of Salt Lake (16). In her analysis, the CWC functioned like an "organism" that "developed distinctively within the particulars of Salt Lake" (22), its "discursive ecology" shaped by and shaping the ecology of the city (128).* Rhetoric of Respect *offered theory grounded in the intellectual work of SLCC faculty and the community writing framework Nic, Sandra, and Wes brought from the CWC. We adapted Rousculp's ecological vision as we began tracing writing-mediated relationships connecting SLCC and the U to one another, to communities across the valley, and to places and people(s) beyond Salt Lake. Once we began looking for ecological connections, they were everywhere.*

The concept of writing ecologies has a complex genealogy. Rousculp draws the notion of discursive ecologies from ecocomposition, first articulated by Christian Weisser and Sidney Dobrin in the early 2000s. Ecocomposition puts insights from ecocriticism and environmental rhetoric into conversation with scholarship in writing studies, particularly the work of Richard M. Coe and Marilyn Cooper. Coe suggested that composition is an ecological phenomenon, calling for a scholarly focus on "systemic interrelations instead of analytic separations" (237). Cooper went on to define writing as "an activity through which a person is continually engaged with a variety of socially constituted systems" (367). Weisser and Dobrin extended Cooper's use of the term "ecology," arguing for, in Weisser's words, "place and location as a critical category (alongside race, class, gender, and culture) in understanding how texts are created and distributed" (69). As we investigated how transfer students negotiate and adapt literacies across the Salt Lake Valley, place *emerged as a critical category indeed.*

Although we encountered writing ecologies through Rousculp and ecocomposition, we have also been influenced by what Dobrin calls the "second ecological turn" (16), a "post-ecocomposition" (3) development using ecological frameworks to conceptualize writing as "dynamic," "fluctuating," "spatial, relational, and complex" (2). This turn brings together ecocomposition's focus on sociality, discursive systems, and place with insights from complexity and network theory. Scholars in this "new materialist" vein have drawn attention to the material, transitory, and emergent nature of writing and rhetorics as they are produced, distributed, and circulated over time (Dobrin). In this theoretical turn, "[t]he term ecology becomes a vehicle to unpack the complexity, interconnectedness, fluidity, and motion of discursive networks" (Weisser 70). Chris Mays sums up these complexities as "the ways writing works in, through, and on a diversity of environments, objects, discourses, materials, ideologies, cultures, technologies, genres, and so on" (568). We came to appreciate how the concept of ecology sensitized us to the complexities and dynamism of transfer students' writing experiences, and the ways those experiences are shaped by emplaced relationships.

The term also helps us account for the embodied, material nature of our relationships as co-researchers and coauthors. In "The Importance of Harmony: An Ecological Metaphor for Writing Research," Fleckenstein and colleagues present an ethical argument for researching writing with an ecological orientation:

> *An ecological way of researching directs the researcher's gaze to relationships, including the researcher's own active involvement*

> *in and contribution to the researcher ecosystem. . . . An ecological orientation to research fuses the knower, the known, and the context of knowing. . . . Thus, the interdependence of an ecological orientation includes active participation in the multiple linkages of the research web. Interdependence hauls back into the research process—or acknowledges what has always been there—the disorder and complexity of what Thomas Newkirk calls the wet, messy, rowdy elements like feelings, intuitions, and bodies: heart, mind, and guts. (395–96)*

This orientation has been useful as we work to understand writing transfer between and beyond SLCC and the U. It encouraged us to embrace the messy, rowdy disorder of bringing our own hearts, minds, and guts to bear on a complex experience in which most of us were personally immersed. Fusing the knower, the known, and the context of knowing has helped us consider how enacting this project together is reshaping our interinstitutional relations.

However, we are also aware that the writing ecologies in question are shaped by social inequities bound up in coloniality, and that such structures have shaped the literature on writing ecologies, as well. In "Writing Wakan*: The Lakota Pipe as Rhetorical Object," David M. Grant points to new materialist scholars' failure to acknowledge longstanding Indigenous traditions of relationality. Grant counters by examining the chanupa as a material artifact of Indigenous rhetorical practice that operates within the Lakota ontology of mitakuye oyasin. This term is often translated as "everything is related" (68), i.e., part of an "interrelated network" in which "relations are reciprocal" (72). This network is "in dynamic flux" and "continual motion" (69), affirms the "tensions and attractions" of "difference" (72), and is subject to "changes through the disturbance and reordering of its relations into a new, emergent order" (74). This Lakota ontology long predated parallel insights in the writing ecologies literature, and, as Grant asserts, "Given legacies of cultural appropriation, genocide, and outright theft, indigenous scholars have reason to be suspicious of work that comes so close to their own" (62). For us, the appeal of an "ecological" orientation lies in its foregrounding of emplaced relations in the adaptation of writing knowledges across contexts, institutional and otherwise. My* *own greatest misgivings spring from concerns that the term occludes Indigenous knowledge of the nature and implications of these relations.*

I have agonized over whether this baggage means we ought to abandon the term "ecology." As a research team, we have also wrestled with its connotations of scientism and the risk it might activate discourses of social Darwinism that naturalize rather than take responsibility for patterns of exclusion, marginalization, and exploitation. And, indeed, some Indigenous rhetorics scholars have opted to eschew the term. For example, to recognize the land-based literacies of Indigenous migrant farm workers from Central America, Gabriela Ríos works to "shift the ontological presuppositions inherent in the term 'ecology'" in favor of

> *an Indigenous concept of relationality that is similar to the notion of ecologies—of networked relationships existing among various human and non-human objects—however, this indigenous concept relies on a relational ontology at the level of* kinship *quite literally. . . . Indigenous relationality recognizes that humans and the environment are in a relationship that is co-constituted and not just interdependent. Additionally, Indigenous relationality recognizes the environment's capacity to* produce *relations. (64)*

We take Ríos's ontological critique of the term "ecology" seriously. We also heed Grant's observation that one key "difference between new materialist projects of descriptive power and indigenous materialisms of being" is "responsibility to sovereign constellations" (83). Ecological theories of writing do not presuppose an ethic of responsibility rooted in peoplehood and place that extends to human and more-than-human communities.

Grant helps articulate conditions under which we might employ the term "ecology" while attending to these shortcomings. He concludes new materialist and Indigenous scholarship can "work together or even in harmony," provided one is willing to "carefully articulate one's projects, be clear about relations, and take note of ontological assumptions" (83–84). Our project is to understand and strengthen relations between SLCC, the U, and the valley in which we live to better and more equitably support transfer student writers. Through careful and critical consideration, we have embraced the project-specific affordances of the term "ecology" for foregrounding our indebtedness to the place-based work of SLCC faculty like Rousculp and for affirming difference within complex and dynamic local systems that include but also extend beyond conventional academic spaces. We are operating from the ontological assumptions that our relations within this ecology are produced by place and entail responsibilities. We have sought to attend to Indigenous histories, continued presence, and futures on this land, but recognize we are not engaging with the land and our respective responsibilities to it in ways Shoshone, Goshute, Ute, and other Indigenous scholars might.

We arrived at these premises by constellating our own emplaced, embodied experiences and knowledges with scholarship in composition and Indigenous rhetorics. In "Careful with the Stories We Tell," Lisa King, Rose Gubele, and Joyce Rain Anderson write, "Indigenous rhetorics are the memories, the memoria, so to speak, of this land. . . . Recognizing and engaging Indigenous rhetorics is in part how we begin to reason together" (15–16). I am striving to make the terms of our engagement explicit. Although they acknowledge the importance of tribally specific knowledges, Andrea Riley-Mukavetz and Malea Powell suggest that co-constitutive relations with land are broadly Indigenous ontologies. As they explain:

> *Imagine a kind of four-part layered web that situates the body in a particular place across historical time, rooted in cultural practices that arise from—and are responsible to—a land base. This orientation to that set of relations, and the responsibilities that arise from maintaining "right" relations, then forms the ambiguous boundaries of something we call* Indigenous rhetorical practices. *(148)*

Without making claims on or to specific tribal knowledge and practices, I acknowledge that my engagements with Indigenous rhetorics as they have been articulated within the academy have prompted our team to look to our emplaced relations and take responsibility for cultivating them in a more "right" way.

I don't think we're enacting what Shawn Wilson calls Indigenous research methods, although I have learned much from his discussions of relationality. Rather, I follow Scott Lyons's urging to learn from the "cultural logic" of Indigenous intellectual work (211). In "Rethinking Responsibility," Lyons writes, "[R]ather than sneaking into someone else's ceremony, it would be better to consider the gifts that have already been given: for instance, the long and venerable history of Native writing, which has consistently depicted responsible living, and advocated for its importance to the world" (213). In my limited white settler understanding, I believe making visible how those gifts have influenced our team's work is among my responsibilities.

Christie

When I arrived in Salt Lake as a professor, I already had connections to the region dating back to my undergraduate years. Both my parents were career military, and, growing up, I lived a lot of places: South Carolina, Hawai'i, Maryland, Iceland, Chile, England, Germany. In the early 2000s, while I was earning my bachelor's degree on Arosaguntacook, Wabanaki, and Abenaki lands in Maine, my family was stationed at Hill Air Force Base, thirty miles north of Salt Lake City on Eastern Shoshone lands. One upside of moving frequently is that you end up with friends in many ports. As it turned out, Chris Baczek, a buddy from the international school I'd attended in Chile, was an art student at the U. Whenever I was home from college, I would hang out with her in Salt Lake.

My ties to this place are already political. My father was the grandchild of Hungarian immigrants to Munsee Lenape lands in New Jersey, and he grew up bilingual in English and Spanish because his parents worked at Universidad de Puerto Rico, which is on Taíno lands. Thanks to his language abilities, we lived in Santiago—Mapuche lands—from 1995 to 1997 while he served as an exchange student at Chile's Academia de Guerra Aérea. He called it "war college." Baczek grew up in Salt Lake, but she spent those years in Chile because her father's Utah-based mining company had business in the Andes. From the beginning, then, my Salt Lake literacies have been sponsored by American colonialism and militarism, complicit educational institutions and martial multilingualism, extractive industry and global capitalism. They were mediated through the social and material privileges of my parents' ranks, their income, and our whiteness. Those literacies were entangled in my efforts to read, think, and write my way out of the military culture in which I'd been raised, efforts that became frantic in 2002, when my father left my mother and sister in Utah to help stage the invasion of Iraq I marched against in Maine.

In *Because We Live Here*, Eli Goldblatt writes, "I had grown up in the US Army, moving every couple of years with my family when my father was transferred somewhere new, and the idea that staying put was radical—and thus heroically productive . . . seemed appealing and true" (3). I'm wary of the discourse of heroism, but, like Goldblatt, my peripatetic military childhood fueled a personal interest and (vexed) political commitment to place. I entered the professional ecology of composition with a self-conscious resistance to the academy's dislocating pressures. I earned my master's degree in rhetoric and composition at Portland State University, an access-oriented urban institution with the motto "Let Knowledge Serve the City" emblazoned across its skybridge. I only decided to get a PhD when I realized I was unlikely to land a full-time job at a local community college. On Odawa, Ojibwe, Boodewadomi, and Wyandot lands at the University of Michigan, I followed my interest in open-admissions institutions that enable students to pursue their educational goals while staying in their communities. My dissertation was a study of locally responsive writing pedagogies at Diné College, a tribally controlled institution in Navajo Nation founded in 1968 as Navajo Community College.

I completed these projects under an apprentice's constraints. By necessity, the primary audience for most of my writing was faculty at four-year institutions, and I chafed under the university-centric paradigm. Like Ellen Cushman (and my father, whose childhood bred an abiding suspicion of academics), I felt a visceral aversion to "ivory tower isolation" ("Rhetorician" 11). I was galvanized by Cushman's call for rhetoricians to consider "the civic purpose of our positions in the academy, of what we do with our knowledge, for whom, and by what means" ("Rhetorician" 23). Like her, I wanted to be among the "agents of social change outside the university" ("Rhetorician" 7). I felt I wouldn't be doing real-to-me work until I could collaborate with two-year college colleagues on projects that made concrete local change as well as contributions to composition studies.

My doctoral education deepened my misgivings about the academy's relationships with place. My community college research heightened my awareness that inequities surrounding institution type are built on an inverse relationship between local access and prestige that is not class-, race-, gender-, culture-, or disability-neutral. My time at the tribal college and my engagements with scholarship in Indigenous rhetorics taught me those inequities are embedded in structures of US settler colonialism (Riley-Mukavetz and Powell; Jackson). As Vine Deloria Jr. wrote, "Non-Indian Americans, not the Indians, are the real nomads. White Americans are rarely buried in the places they were born, and most of them migrate freely during their lifetimes, living in as many as a dozen places and having roots in and accepting responsibility for none of these locations" (254). This critique seems as true of the academy as it is of the military in which I grew up. Like Rebecca C. Jackson, I came to suspect that the neoliberal indifference university-based academia fosters toward *where* we work perpetuates a settler colonial disregard for local knowledges and relations. That disregard includes our relationships with and responsibilities to nearby community colleges.

I went on the academic job market in 2013 with no particular desire to work at a research university. What I cared about was location. I wanted to be close enough to Navajo Nation that I could maintain my relationships there, and I wanted possibilities for collaboration with community college colleagues on local projects. When the position at the U hit the job list, the importance of place outweighed my ambivalence about R-1. I already knew several SLCC faculty through TYCA and CCCC, and the U had a large transfer student population. Furthermore, there was an opportunity to help build a new department of writing and rhetoric studies that attended to community colleges from its inception. There was also a promise of life beyond academia: my old friend Chris Baczek still lives and makes art in Salt Lake. Of course, it was only through many accumulated and largely unearned priveleges that I had such a choice, and my body is an agent of colonization wherever I go on this continent, including the Salt Lake Valley. All the more reason to always be thinking carefully about what I am (and am not) doing here: why, and how, and with whom.

As I reengaged the Salt Lake ecology in 2014, I knew I needed to learn more about transfer students' experiences as they moved between the community college and the university. I wanted to undertake those investigations differently from the work at Michigan. I wanted to research *with* SLCC transfer students. I believed the project would benefit from their local knowledges, institutional experiences, and perspectives on everything from interview protocols to curriculum development. I hoped the project would also benefit my student co-researchers—that it would be a paid learning opportunity connecting them to resources, mentorship, and, perhaps, a stronger sense of community at the U.

I could not have anticipated how this work would force me to rethink my still-emerging scholarly identity, to de- and reconstruct notions of value I didn't know I held. I didn't predict how we would each, in our different ways, come to new understandings of our own mobilities, or how the political context in which we were laboring would unfold. Together, we have been co-constituting our relations with this place I have now lived far longer than anywhere else. What makes staying put "radical," at least for *this* white nomad of the settler state, is deciding to accept responsibility for this place. Speaking of reflective knowledges made with the land, Deloria writes, "Our task is to live in such a way that the information we receive through analysis becomes—over the passage of time and through grace and good fortune—our experiences also" (251). With grace I rarely deserve, my Salt Lake co-researchers have allowed me to experience this place and the complex relations it co-constitutes.

IDENTITIES

Thinking ecologically means considering the interactive, emplaced identity negotiations transfer students undertake. Stephanie Kerschbaum suggests that identities are emergent and relational. They are "always in flux, always 'yet-to-be,'" she writes, "so they are never fully known or knowable entities, and knowledge about self only comes through encounters with others" ("Avoiding" 627). This conception of identity resonates with Grant, who suggests "the philosophical question to start with might not be 'Who are you?' so much as 'How are you?' In what way is your being?" (83). "How we are" in our relational, identity-producing encounters—including the myriad encounters involved in interinstitutional transfer—is always co-constituted with place.

*In their argument for an ecological approach to composition, Dobrin and Weisser assert that "identity—and how it is manifested by discourse—is shaped . . . by our relationships with particular locations and environments" (567). Relational identities are produced in and by places that enact forms of inclusion and exclusion. Asao Inoue writes, "places may have important associations with particular groups of people who typically inhabit those places, identified by class, social standing, language use, religion, race, or other social dimensions. Work done in such places can be affected by these associations" (*Antiracist *78). Not all writing-related identities engender the same kinds of social recognition or rewards, and these place associations mean privileged writing-related identities are not all equally accessible or attractive to everyone.*

Place, identity, and writing are thus profoundly intertwined with social inequities. Salt Lake's writing ecology offers wide-ranging but uneven possibilities for identity-(re)shaping encounters. The U's location in the affluent and predominantly white foothills east of downtown, for example, does not produce the same identities as SLCC's locations in the more racially and linguistically diverse working-class neighborhoods to the west and south. Likewise, the CWC sponsors different identity encounters than either SLCC or the U, declaring through its motto and interior design that "everyone can write," although the identities produced in its spaces are also inevitably differential and constrained. And there are countless other sites throughout the valley, in and out of schools, where encounters are shaping writing identities in complex, often inequitable ways.

For us, an ecological orientation foregrounds the complex, emplaced identity negotiations transfer students encounter as they move between *and beyond postsecondary institutions. Some of these negotiations are related to demographic categories Kerschbaum calls "visible and measurable"—and thus easily commodifiable (*Toward *43). Community college students are more likely than those at most four-year institutions to be BIPOC, immigrants, older/returning students, students with disabilities, and/or veterans—all groups historically underrepresented in postsecondary education. They are also more likely to be first-generation college students, to come from low-income or working-class families, to have children, to be working full-time and attending school part-time. As they move through these various spaces and social situations, transfer students negotiate a range of in-flux and interrelated identities that have claims on their time, attention, energies, and money.*

*While university-centric research might characterize such claims as "interference" (Brittenham 527) or "environmental pull" (Bahr et al., "A Review" 488) that diverts transfer students from their studies, an ecological perspective recognizes that alongside-school identities are often embedded in relationships, forms of cultural participation, sources of motivation, and access to financial and other resources that sustain students as they pursue their degrees. For students from "nontraditional" backgrounds, coming into the identity of "college student" can be challenging. Popular media continue to project normative representations of a residential four-year college experience. As Wes and Nate suggest, transfer students may also have encounters that reproduce stigma associated with attending community college, even as they are grappling with identity and values conflicts produced by encounters in differently diverse and more self-consciously elite university spaces (Alexander et al.; Bahr et al., "A Review"; Toth et al., "Traveling"). Inoue argues that academic settings privilege what he, building on Pierre Bourdieu, calls a "local white racial habitus" in spoken and written discourse (*Antiracist *92). This hegemonic, Inoue asserts, places unjust burdens on students of color, multilingual students, and first-generation college students as they negotiate identities as college writers.*

Those who transfer must reconstruct their student identities first at the community college and then at the university, and they face additional negotiations as they enter specific disciplinary discourses (Mathison; Gere et al.; Toth et al., "Traveling"). These encounters can challenge students' conceptions of their own identities. Even when those challenges are ultimately beneficial (and not all are), students must still undertake the intellectual and emotional labor of this renegotiation. Depending on their circumstances, the time, energy, and support required to work through the conflicts that sometimes emerge can be a greater cost than some are willing or able to bear. All these experiences can shape transfer students' sense of belonging, their self-concepts as learners and writers, and their motivation to persist in postsecondary education. However, such experiences can also foster rhetorical awareness and knowledges students draw on as they face new academic, social, professional, and political challenges.

Sandra

In 2005, I was in fifth grade, attending Ford Boulevard Elementary. Mrs. Simpson gave my mom and me a small booklet during one of our parent-teacher conferences, and I remember it being a lot less attractive than the Goosebumps books I *did* read. I was not about to open up a book with the title "How to Get the Main Idea." That book was *not* made for me or to take home to my Spanish-speaking parents. This booklet remained unopened, but my mom has held onto it for many years. I think she has kept it as a keepsake from when we lived in East Los Angeles. Mrs. Simpson shared with me that she once visited the Great Salt Lake and how she went in the lake and walked around in it. I believe this was our only nonacademic conversation.

In the fifth grade, and probably a few times in primary school, I recall being moved temporarily and tested for my reading retention. The types of writing found in comprehension tests or those immersion programs in the early 2000s left me confused and downcast for some time. The composition tests in East Los Angeles and in Utah were not meant to aid but to fail me instead. They shared examples of situations I couldn't make connections with, that had nothing to do with my own reality and culture, which led me to believe that I was not good at English and therefore not good enough for school. Not once did I think that there was valid writing outside of academic spaces. In school, that's where I was told what writing should look like. This writing remained inside the walls of my school. I did learn at an early age that I was not a writer.

My mother and I in unison, " . . . ocho por una . . . ocho, ocho por dos . . . diez y seis. Ocho por diez? Ochenta!" This chanting and memorizing was done on school nights over in our East Los Angeles living room. I learned to love math in third grade. Those moments are very important to me because here we were communicating with each other that the math language transcends spaces. Until that time I hadn't realized that something from school stretched over to my home and was accessible to both of us. I would walk home, underneath a freeway and past a McDonald's, two auto mechanics, and a bus station to get to my house. I walked this path every day and ignored what was obvious writing, like the graffiti on the side of the freeway, a seventy-nine-cent special for a large drink at McDonald's, the destinations the buses displayed or the name of the street I lived in. I didn't recognize that as writing, and so I ignored most of the writing around me for a long time.

When I was ten, my mom found a paper ad about free English Tutoring and signed me up immediately. Here is what I remember. My mentor was tall, white, and drove a white Chevy Impala. He would talk about the boring workbook on reading comprehension and point to it, and I sat there confused, trying to figure out how this related to me—at this time, it didn't. My writing tutor would drive from downtown LA, down to East LA and into the comfort of my home—with this knowledge that only made sense to him. My only memories of this part of my life are of my mom mopping furiously before the tutor arrived, a comment from him on how our bathroom was tiny, and me showing off my guitar skills by playing a piece of Cielito Lindo on an acoustic guitar during our very last session. I can't exactly remember how many sessions or weeks this lasted, but it didn't really help me any new skills to use in school or help with my understanding of writing.

During the first two years I worked at SLCC's Community Writing Center, I wanted to get a social work degree. But then I realized that the writing and rhetoric department at the University of Utah actually talked about community, connection, local disparities, and gendered writing. The way our professors talked about systems and rhetorics sparked my interests. They kept me engaged and enraged at the same time because I was reading on how America became "America." And it wasn't and still isn't good. I did not speak up a ton in class, but through our writing assignments we were given opportunities to talk about what mattered to us students.

With the WRS courses, I was given opportunities to problem solve, read writing from philosophers and writing from current professors who let us into why they teach what they teach. During my time with the CWC, we facilitated writing workshops in and around Salt Lake City where in one of my favorite writing groups I became known as the "writing lady." Every week I had a one-hour slot reserved to talk about creative writing inside high schools, inside a refugee housing complex, a hospital, a youth shelter, and in jail. I'd be rushing over to one workshop after another. Most of the curriculum planning came from what I learned in my writing classes at the U and hanging out inside my car jotting an agenda for my workshop that started in five minutes. My 1996 green Toyota Corolla was my office.

I had many moments at the beginning of my employment at the CWC thinking, "What am I doing here? . . . I am not a writer." There would be many times people would assume I had an English degree (which I did not have) or wrote for a living (never once had I written a poem). I was exposed to all kinds of community writing—people's writing process, ideas, and writing related questions—or could just be there, present, to offer an extra pair of eyes on their writing. And so there I was—the unwriter talking about writing, seeing people struggle with writing, telling people that they shouldn't worry so much about grammar.

So what now?

I encourage you to keep advocating and continue to support your students in composition. Choose a book that just got released and listed as the #1 *New York Times* bestseller. Talk to your students about social injustice issues that they care about and actively participate in. Pick a book, pick a song, one of your favorites, or a show that's streaming that the kids are talking about now. Share career advice, too. Get creative. Make book copies for your students (if you can). Encourage your students to see that there is valid writing outside of academic walls. Here is my mantra. WRITING IS A SOCIAL PRACTICE. WRITING IS NOT AN ACADEMIC PRACTICE JUST FOR ACADEMICS. WRITING IS FOR EVERYONE. AND ANYONE CAN BE A WRITER.

VALUING

An ecological framework has the capacity to decenter the U—and, for that matter, SLCC, and the entire academic enterprise—to situate transfer students' writing experiences within a more varied and complex ecology. In Literacy: An Introduction to the Ecology of Written Language, *David Barton writes that "an ecological approach aims to understand how literacy is embedded in other human activity, its embeddedness in social life and in thought, and its position in history, in language and in learning"* (32). *Barton's emphasis on the social and historical situatedness of literacy reflects decades of research that questions the supremacy of academic ways with words. We might understand that trajectory as a disciplinary process of learning to* value *writing differently: to challenge received notions of what is good, desirable, and worthwhile, and to interrogate whose interests assessments of value serve.*

*Inoue calls for antiracist writing assessment that "struggles through the ways language comes to mean and be valued and how our bodies and environments affect that meaning and valuing" (*Antiracist *81). For Inoue, an ecological orientation offers a way to understand writing assessment as embodied and co-constitutive of place and power:*

> *[A]ll ecologies are associated with political activities, with the ways that people and environments affect each other and the interests that particular groups have to change or maintain a given environment or place. And so, ecology is always a reference to the political (or power) relations between people and their environments, between people in environments.* (Antiracist *81*)

Institutional assessment ecologies shape—and are shaped by—the ways languages, discourses, and writing are valued in local contexts. Such evaluations usually reflect the interests of dominant groups. Left uninterrogated and unchallenged, they reproduce the inequities that give rise to them. Transfer students—who are already more likely to come from groups disadvantaged by the ways languaging and literacies are valued at the university—enter these particular assessment ecologies midway through their college education.

Invoking the Freirean praxis of problem posing, Inoue argues for placing critical conversation about how writing is valued at the center of writing instruction, asserting "healthy writing assessment ecologies have at their core dialogue about what students and teachers know, how students and teachers judge language differently, so that students are also agents in the ecology, not simply objects to be measured" (Antiracist *84*). *Inoue's ecological approach encourages teachers and students to see the power relations informing what we value and to recognize how privileging conventional academic literacies can devalue language practices in other parts of the ecology, thereby marginalizing the communities that practice them. He suggests teachers and students work together to understand "the complexity and holistic nature of assessment systems, the interconnectedness of all people and things . . . without denying or eliding linguistic, cultural, or racial diversity, and the politics inherent in all uneven social formation"* (Antiracist *77*). *While Inoue is focused on first-year writing, we can extend his logic to the inequities transfer students experience in university writing-assessment ecologies.*

Our collaborative research could be seen as a version of the kind of problem posing Inoue calls for, and, in our conversations together, we have often returned to the issue of valuing as it relates to community college transfer students. How do we develop resources and produce scholarship that challenge deficit discourses surrounding transfer students' writing experiences—particularly reductive notions of "preparedness" that assume the primacy of conventional academic literacies—and instead value the knowledges, experiences, perspectives, and languages transfer students transform as they move across Salt Lake's writing ecology? In considering these questions, we have found ourselves grappling with the material conditions that influence those transformations.

As an alternative to evaluating students' written performances based on a local white racial habitus, Inoue argues for classroom assessments based on labor, *which "can be measured by duration, quantity, or intensity"* (Antiracist *80*). *In his view, "to favor labor over the gifts of racial habitus sets up assessment ecologies that are by their nature more ethical and fair"* (Antiracist *80*). *He asserts, "Labor is a more equitable and fair measure. Everyone has 24 hours in every day"* (Antiracist *84*). *We find the notion of valuing labor over an inequitable notion of "writing quality" compelling, particularly when we consider that most transfer students are also workers. It does seem fair to "compensate" students in predictable ways for the labor they put into their schooling. However, based on our research and experiences, we question whether* time *is an equitably distributed resource.*

As Kelly and Nate describe, many transfer students juggle demands like work, family caretaking, and community engagement and leadership. They might also be managing debt, physical and mental health issues, transportation or housing concerns, and/or mandatory engagement with government agencies (e.g., social services, immigration offices, community corrections). They don't have as many hours in a day to devote to school as traditional-age university students whose expenses are subsidized by family. We might seek to make visible and reward the intellectual and emotional labor (and often-hidden sacrifices and tradeoffs) transfer students undertake as they navigate interinstitutional writing ecologies. We might choose to value the labor of transferring and transforming prior writing knowledge, which researchers agree is a time-intensive and intellectually demanding task (Wardle; Driscoll and Wells), rather than ignoring the reality that transfer students might need to labor differently—often, harder—than their nontransfer peers in these transitional moments. Recognizing this labor might enable teachers to help cultivate the adaptability and rhetorical awareness interinstitutional transfer can foster.

We believe valuing such transfer labor helps achieve Inoue's goal of creating "a more equitable ecology, particularly for those who may come to it with discourses or habitus different from the dominant ones" (Antiracist *80*). *It furthers Cushman's call to recognize that "what counts as knowledge and evidence of this knowledge—what is valid—is to be found in all peoples' understandings and rhetorical struggles"*

("Decolonizing"). Transfer students might be uniquely equipped to question, critique, and challenge ways of valuing writing that have been naturalized in university settings. Such critical labor is something to be recognized, encouraged, and rewarded.

Westin

On May 10, 1869, thousands gathered at Promontory Point in northern Utah for the driving of the Gold Spike—the ceremonial merger of the Central Pacific and Union Pacific railways to complete the first transcontinental railway system in the United States, constructed across Indigenous lands, largely through the labor of Chinese and Irish railroad workers. The site was not a destination, but a point in time and place that marked the rapid industrialization, mobilization, and ongoing colonization of North America. Local legend has it that the ceremony was delayed because the track carrying the Central Pacific engine with president Leland Stanford, who drove the final spike (and later founded the elite private university), was washed out by high springtime river in Weber Canyon, just outside of Ogden, Utah. The story goes that Stanford and his men began celebrating early, passing the time drinking, and, by the time they finally arrived at the event, Stanford was too drunk to drive the spike and missed several times.

A white Salt Laker by way of English American Latter-day Saint settlers and Italian American railroad workers, I grew up in that rural county of Morgan, Utah, Shoshone lands appropriated and settled by my Mormon ancestors generations before. A blip on the map of Northern Utah, Morgan County is now a valley of cattle ranches, dairy farms, wardhouse steeples, and mink sheds all woven together by a single interstate and railroad track.

Years later I would bounce around the Wasatch Front from Dad's to Mom's house, a stone's throw from the refineries and railyards of North Salt Lake where my parents labored, sustained their unions, and organized other workers. At night I would pry my window open and pray for breeze in the dry heat, while the too-close sounds of train whistles blew me awake, sometimes till dawn.

Like a lot of students, I began college a few years after high school, and took classes when I could afford them and work around them. Friends and I pinged around different parts of the city: downtown to Sugar House, Riverton to Rose Park, working where there were jobs, and living where there were rooms. I was one of the lucky ones for whom college was a realistic possibility. There is a joke around town about attending JSLCC—Just Salt Lake Community College. The "just" acts as a strategic hedger to both define and apologize for your status as one who can just afford to attend the community college, while simultaneously not alienating those who can't afford any college. For nearly three years I attended SLCC, shuttling between satellite campuses in the valley, under the shadow of the maybe-someday University of Utah.

I found work at the SLCC Community Writing Center in those years, a nonprofit extension of SLCC that serves to "support, motivate, and educate people of all abilities and educational backgrounds who want to use writing for practical needs, civic engagement, and personal expression." It was here that I met Nic, Sandra, and Christie, and, by extension, Nate, Kelly, and Claudia, as well as the other folks who have been part of this research team over the years.

The CWC became the Grand Central Station of our urban writing ecology, for me at least. It was the hub through which all tracks of the ecology I was traveling on at that time passed. Quite literally, the CWC is located at the heart of downtown Salt Lake City, and it is the most central point between several SLCC campuses and the U. TRAX, the light-rail train that networks the city, has one of its most popular stops across the street. Unable or unwilling to pay the outrageous price for parking at the U, I would continue parking at the CWC downtown and ride the train up the hill to class long after I finished at SLCC.

Having a hub like the CWC afforded me the opportunity to intersect with others. Other students, other writers, other residents of the valley—all key players. Those intersections revealed and provided access to other parts of the writing ecology. On a daily basis, I got to work with all kinds of writing and writers. I also got to work with all kinds of students, all of us coming from different places, going in different directions, but crossing paths, sharing a station temporarily. For nearly three years I worked at the CWC, simultaneously completing my coursework at SLCC, transferring to the U, and moving through the city in different capacities. The CWC taught me that Salt Lake's writing ecology is constituted by the routes through which we are constantly moving. It is dynamic, situated in and shaped by time as much as by place. I'm privileged, lucky, to have been able to go to college, but was even more lucky to be able to work at the CWC while I did, and find faculty who were willing to embrace "nontraditionality" as resource rather than restriction. As you think about your own urban writing ecology—where the tracks lead to and from and what the whistles sound like—I encourage you to recognize students as agents of that ecology, regardless of the routes they took to reach your institutional hub.

Postscript from 2019: When I wrote and rewrote my section as I approached graduation in 2017, I was mostly scratching for a way to situate myself as a first-generation transfer student who might be able to offer a unique perspective to academics. Demographically speaking, though, I am in some ways the student you might be most familiar with: I am a young, white, able-bodied cis man. While those identities may not have determined my success, they did create safe spaces wherein I could fail. I could come to college mostly because my parents picketed, struck, and negotiated fairer wages and working conditions for blue-collar jobs. Their entrance to the middle class and the means by which they were able to build houses and raise a family came from the security of a unionized workforce—my mom in the Communication Workers of America, and my dad first in the Oil, Chemical and Atomic Workers, then the United Steelworkers. Coming from that labor milieu gave me an understanding that the world spins askew on an axis of power and that the only thing anyone gets from the power brokers is what they're willing to fight for; understanding, too, that my parents fought from a place of considerably more privilege and safety than many nonwhite workers do.

Leverage. Both my parents, I believe, would have been humanities students had they gone to school. My mother gardens and my father reads. They instilled in me a love for language and art as well as curiosity. College was the place for people with a love for language and art as well as curiosity. Not the refinery. Not the phone company. But leverage, real-world bargaining power, is what college was supposed to afford me. College, we thought, was the path by which one could circumvent the minefield of the American workforce. It's ironic that we never saw how the institution that granted me a diploma did so not entirely differently than did the industries that cut my parents' checks: by taking more than it gave.

I operate from an incredibly privileged position. And I wouldn't give up my education for anything. Already it has afforded me opportunities that I never would've had without it. My point is this: Universities are threshers. They take exorbitant amounts of money, labor, and intellectual contributions from students. And what is too often thought of as the "ability" to successfully navigate those threshers—to come out as the wheat, not the chaff—maps directly onto the kinds of capital that privileged identities like mine have to spend. If you are employed by a university, whether you like it or not, you work on behalf of the machinery that determines and separates wheat from chaff. Unless you don't. The work this book documents is a testament to the real power and responsibility you have to change those systems to more equitably serve and reward students—to give more than you take.

MOTION

Just as an ecological orientation enables us to decenter academic ways of valuing, it also encourages us to decenter the U in our study of interinstitutional writing transfer. As Fleckenstein et al. argue, an ecological approach requires recognizing "that scholars [must always] draw a circle around the pertinent feedback pathways to delineate the span of the research ecosystem and that the circle is always mutable and permeable" (396). Given the interconnectivity of writing and the movement of feedback across ecological systems, we must make intentional choices about how we bound the scope of a study and be willing to rethink received boundaries that have limited our understanding of writing phenomena.

For example, Fleckenstein et al. argue, "the line circumscribing a research ecosystem can include the cultural and personal lives of the students outside the classroom" (397). By redrawing the lines circumscribing the study of transfer student writers—by respecting what Rousculp calls the "'wholeness' of a person or collection of people" (Rhetoric *xiv)—faculty can decenter the institutions that are the focus of their professional lives to recenter students and their movements within a broader ecology. This methodological choice has ethical dimensions. Deloria writes, "[T]he goal should be to allow the life-worlds to intrude into the world of systems and to make certain that institutions serve human beings, thereby eliminating the real possibility that institutions will completely dehumanize us" (186). Being willing to recognize transfer students' movements beyond institutional systems keeps them—and faculty researchers—human.*

Motion is key to the permeability of writing ecologies. Margaret Syverson suggests writing ecologies have "physical, social, psychological, spatial, and temporal dimensions. . . . [T]he social dimensions of composition are distributed, embodied, emergent, and enactive" (23). Jenny Edbauer builds on Syverson to assert that rhetorical ecologies are co-constituted through action and motion. As she writes, "We do city, rather than exist in the city" (11). Syverson and Edbauer help us see that Salt Lake's writing ecology is always in process and being (re)made through our movements.

This orientation enables us to view SLCC and the U as what Wes calls hubs *in the valley's writing ecology. These hubs play important roles in the regional economy and function as key sites of literacy sponsorship (Brandt), but they are by no means the only places where transfer students are writing, either before, during, or after they move between SLCC and the U. Instead of the conventional conception of "vertical" interinstitutional transfer, which imagines students moving "up" from the community college to the university in one idealized, linear ascendance, an ecological model recognizes lateral, multidirectional mobility across and beyond these institutional hubs.*

Students' movements through our writing ecology are rarely linear. Many students "reverse" transfer from the U or other universities to SLCC, sometimes but not always with plans to return to a four-year institution. They "swirl" between SLCC and the U and/or other regional universities. They stop out or drop out for a host of intersecting reasons: financial pressures or work schedules, family obligations, health issues, religious missions, boredom, burnout, uncertainty about their goals, and other personal needs or interests that take at least temporary precedence over school. They might complete a certificate or associate's degree at SLCC and not decide until years later that they want to pursue a bachelor's. When they are enrolled and not—and whether they ever complete their degrees—students compose for many nonacademic contexts and purposes.

Stuart Blythe calls for research on writing knowledge transfer proceeding from "an ecological mindset" (65). Such a mindset foregrounds the various forms of knowledge transfer students undertake as they travel their idiosyncratic literacy paths. They encounter writing knowledge through their formal postsecondary experiences, as well as in their families, workplaces, and other community contexts. They navigate these complex, ever-shifting writing ecologies in ways that make sense, meet needs, and are possible for them at a given moment in their lives. In the process, they acquire and adapt many different kinds of writing knowledge, with varying consequences, across and beyond institutions.

The Salt Lake writing ecology is co-constituted in no small part by the movements of transfer students—their bodies, their money, their ideas, their languages and literacies, and the materiality of their writing—across our institutions and the wider community. While that flow is never the same students or the same writing, their continuous movements connect SLCC and the U to one another and to the rest of the valley in complex, dynamic ways. Likewise, where faculty and staff at both institutions choose to put their own bodies, dollars, ideas, languages, and writing is also co-constituting the ecology. Their movements create—or fail to create—what Norbert Elliot calls "opportunity structures" for SLCC students, particularly those who are "least advantaged" due to race, class, age, gender, sexuality, language background, immigration status, disability, and other identities and experiences. The social justice implications of such mobility suggest that university faculty have a responsibility to get down off the hill and do city—or in our case, do valley*—differently.*

Kelly

As Michelle Cleary states, "Overwhelming research on writing transfer assumes students move from grammar to high school to college to work in one uninterrupted progression" (661). When most people think of college students, what comes to mind is a bunch of late-teens and early twenty-somethings. I will admit, this is how I thought of students in higher education, right up to the day I finally returned to school to chase down my own degree at thirty-two. I now know people recognize their drive for education and choose to attend school at different stages in life, from those fresh out of high school to the empty nester pursuing an incomplete bachelor's or graduate degree.

My first attempt at a degree was at the age of seventeen, during my time in the Job Corps. My second was when I was nineteen, back in my hometown of Yakima, Washington. During my formative years, most of my interactions and associations were outside of my racial "category" of African American. As of the 2000 US census, the white population of Yakima was 68.8 percent and the Hispanic population was 33.7 percent, far outnumbering the 2.0 percent in the city of African American heritage ("Yakima"). What this meant to me, in terms of race relations and identity, was shaped by my reception and interactions in the places I frequented the most: home, school, and church. At home, racial inequalities were discussed as a factor of the past, whereas at school and church my race was rarely, if ever, mentioned. I spent my childhood in a training ground of "neutrality" and, though I was aware of my difference, I learned not to focus on it.

I moved to Portland, Oregon, at twenty-one, where I boomeranged from Mt. Hood Community College to Portland Community College and back again twice before settling into a job-to-job existence. What precipitated my movement between careers and schools was a number of things: boredom; the dissolution of a position; harmless irresponsibility (in my estimation at the time, anyway) which led to my termination from a couple of jobs; curiosity; impulsiveness; and feelings of failure when it came to my haphazard attempts at school. I have often wondered why I never heard from the schools during the times I became truant, which always happened before I decided to quit. Is all the focus in these schools on admission and little or none on retention? Did it have something to do with assumptions teachers or advisors made about me? I am aware that my own tendency toward a neutral view of race does not change the fact that I am Black. I cannot change the truth that when people see me, they see first: Black, female, and obese. I know that all of these things about me are seen, and that I am judged often based upon the stigmas that are inextricably linked to all of the surface identities to which I am bound.

I know too that whether or not I choose to view the world and myself through a "color-blind" lens, I am being affected by these aspects of my embodiment, which I consider just parts of a whole and which society at large often prefers to separate and demonize. Or to champion, depending on the perspective from which they are viewed. Minorities attend two-year schools in disproportionately higher numbers than white students. Whether this is simply a matter of affordability or easy access to these types of schools, I cannot say. But completion rates among Brown minorities in two-year schools are eye-opening. The six-year associate's degree completion rate of Hispanic students who began at a community college in 2012 was 35.7 percent, and for Black students was 27.5 percent. Bachelor's-degree completion was even more rare, at 13.2 percent and 19.5 percent, respectively. These numbers are in comparison to the 48.1 percent community college and 26.2 percent bachelor's degree completion rates of white students during the same period ("Community"). Are schools aware of the fact that a number of the students who enroll will not complete a degree and therefore turn a blind eye to students—particularly Brown students—who may only require a bit of encouragement to stay?

I bounced through a number of careers during my twenties and early thirties, from crowd management to residential aide to nanny to Certified Nurse Assistant to culinary school and some years working in kitchens. When I was attending culinary school, I continually heard the question, "So you want to be a chef?" and assertions like: "I bet you'd love to be on *Hell's Kitchen!*" My answer to these questions was always an emphatic "No!" The boredom I mentioned earlier was typified by my impulsive decision (facilitated by misleading recruitment and predatory lending tactics) to attend a career school out of a desire for knowledge of the craft, coupled with some small aspirations that one day I would possess the picturesque family I have always hoped to enjoy and the ability to wow them with the gourmet fare I had learned to create. In hindsight, I realize that I could have obtained similar knowledge through a much more financially feasible route: via a community college or hands-on in the workforce. The sad truth is that for-profit schools are just that: for the banknote, not the students who fill the seats. And I now know that for-profit schools aggressively recruit students of color—and particularly Black students—like me.

While completing my culinary education, and thus proving to myself that I *could* focus on school long enough to finish, I moved to Utah for a six-month externship. However, the Great Recession of 2008 had tanked the job market, which made my search for a position at the end of my externship daunting, and in the end unfruitful. This led me to return to my home state for what I assumed would be a few months, until I found a permanent position elsewhere. A few months became a few years, and after bouncing between culinary positions in and around Yakima, I eventually returned to the state of Utah, which I had fallen in love with, planning to return to school. I enrolled in SLCC in the fall of 2013, electing the pursuit of a Paralegal A.O.S. degree. Late in the game, when I realized that paralegals do much of the same work as does a lawyer, without the benefit of a lawyer's credentials or pay rate, I decided to transfer to the U, with the goal of eventually attending law school. As I began to speak with advisors at the U, it became evident that the advising I had experienced at SLCC was insufficient for my needs. Not only would the majority of the classes I had taken in my paralegal program not apply to my degree, but I had not been informed that all of the years I spent attending schools while not completing degrees would be counted in my grade point average, bringing it well below what was necessary for admittance to the university. After some research, I was relieved to find that there was an admittance sponsorship program through the campus's Transfer Diversity Scholars program that allowed me to enroll in the spring of 2016.

In the fall of 2016, after an extremely rocky start at the U, I had a catalytic discussion during a class and came to realize that what I love the most about the law is drafting an argument or brief—essentially, the craft of the *writing* involved—and what I loved about culinary school (other than the great food) was developing amazing menus, then finding exciting ways to describe what I had created. So, I decided to focus my education on what I love best: writing.

Looking back now, I know that the path I took to higher education was a long one, unique to my life. The interconnectivity between each of my jobs, educational paths, interpersonal relationships and life choices I have made over time has carved out a distinct direction, and I now realize that self-improvement, whatever that may be, can take many forms and happens when a person is ready for it, not on society's timeframe. Because I know what it is like to look up one day and assess my life choices—everything from where I live to my career path—I realize that many adults who have pursued multiple interests make the same decision to return to school each day. According to the National Center for Education Statistics College Navigator, in the fall of 2014 27 percent of University of Utah students and 37 percent of Salt Lake Community College students were over the age of twenty-five. It is not easy to change direction in what could be considered the middle of a life, but people all over the country are doing just that.

By the age of thirty-three, I had not exercised my brain in an academic capacity for quite a long time, although I had done things like technical and medical writing, and some accounting and record keeping for work. I realized after I returned to school that what I remembered of being a student, the experience I expected to have, and the experience that I would have along this journey were very different things. Many challenges can arise when a person has been outside of traditional education for what can equal tens of years. Family, community engagement, religious and political obligations, financial struggles, etc., can all compete with studying for priority. My path, through career *and* education, has been shaped by physical and mental health issues, as well as financial difficulties and all of the baggage that can come along with interpersonal relationships. My race probably also played a part in these experiences. Yet, these seeming obstacles can also provide resources. The rich life experiences of older students, especially those from diverse ethnic, cultural, and socioeconomic backgrounds, can be a great addition to an institution's chorus of voices; and the challenges may be mitigated in part when curricula account for these rich backgrounds (see Gleason).

What diverse older students take back to their equally diverse communities when requesting assistance from friends, family, and coworkers brings the university to places where it may not normally go, like my oldest friend's living room as we discussed my studies. Or Facebook messages as I requested editorial assistance from my sister. This action of "transporting literacy" (Michaud 245)—a kind of ecological mobility—widens community awareness of the institution, but can also awaken universities to the need to create alternative methods of teaching and expand access for nontraditional and returning students through the creation of more options for communication and contact. Older and returning students are bringing with them a vast array of engagements within the local writing ecology. Writing is embedded in and shaping our communities, both in schools and outside of them. The differences in students' paths should be viewed not as a disadvantage but as a dynamic function of a changing ecology.

DIFFERENCE

A key affordance of an ecological perspective is that it foregrounds the value—indeed, the necessity—of diversity. Barton asserts, "An ecological approach emphasizes diversity, and in the original biological senses of ecology, sees it as a virtue. Diversity is a source of strength, the roots of the possibilities of the future. This is just as true when applied to the diversity of languages and literacies" (32). Fleckenstein and colleagues draw on the concept of biodiversity to develop their ecological metaphor for writing research:

> Beyond the economic and spiritual values of biodiversity, a multiplicity of life forms is essential for the resilience and productivity of ecosystems . . . because an ecosystem exists through its interactions. So, if the number of participants in an ecosystem (or the number of ecosystems) is eroded, the interactions are affected, and the intricate network of life destabilizes. (401)

In this metaphor, it is the quantity and diversity of interactions that sustain a healthy ecology, make it resilient and productive. This logic, Fleckenstein and colleagues argue, extends to "the complexity and messiness of twenty-first-century meaning making" (389). The more generative interactions we foster across a wide range of traditions and practices—the more relations we cultivate—the more robust and adaptive our writing ecology will be as we head into an unknown future.

We follow Kerschbaum in preferring the relational term "difference" over the commodified term "diversity." Informed by the work of Mikhail Bakhtin, Kerschbaum encourages us "to see differences as dynamic rather than as static entities, as relations between people rather than individual traits, and as interactionally emergent, not as properties that can be bought, transferred, or sold" (Toward 55). Kerschbaum's insistence that "difference, rather than being presentable through categories and remaining relatively inert across time and space, is dynamic, relational, and emergent" resonates with the literature on writing ecologies ("Avoiding" 623). As she argues, "Difference is not 'out there' waiting to be found and identified but is always coming-to-be through the here-and-now of interaction" ("Avoiding" 626). Thus, the differences that emerge through transfer students' interactions at the university do not have static or inherent meanings. Their meanings are, rather, a function of what everyone involved in a particular emplaced interaction chooses to display (or has no choice but to display), what their interlocutors notice and choose to act upon (and the nature of their actions), and how all parties respond to these dynamics as the interaction unfolds (Kerschbaum, "Avoiding" and Toward). Difference is thus always being co-constituted within emplaced ecological relations.

The recognition that the meanings of difference emerge through interactions—that "diversity" is valuable, but its value is instantiated, *ignored, or undercut by how we make meaning of difference—invites us to push back against abstracted, monolithic, and purportedly neutral constructs of "academic preparedness." It encourages us to embrace the plurality of languages, literacies, knowledges, and life experiences transfer students bring with them from their various educational pathways. In an ecological orientation, those experiences and social networks can be mobilized to support writing transfer and adaptation. As Syverson argues,*

> *[I]n the process of enacting ourselves and our world, we use whatever resources we can bring to bear on our situation, including our past experiences, our present resourcefulness, and our interactions with others, which inevitably reflect their past experiences, as well. Writers (and readers) are notoriously opportunistic in the kind of bricolage that seizes upon any experience or interaction that can be useful for enacting their textual worlds. (72)*

With their varying backgrounds and "nontraditional" trajectories, transfer students bring wide-ranging rhetorical "resources" that contribute to the writing "bricolage" we undertake in classrooms.

*These differences may be helpful for fostering what Fleckenstein and colleagues call "critical self-awareness" (401). Inoue, for example, urges teachers to "create sustainable places that depend on local diversity for critical examination of writing and the habitus that produces that writing and readers' expectations" (*Antiracist *80). He argues that the "local diversities" within and beyond our campuses can help us interrogate how language and writing are valued in academic spaces (68). An ecological approach that understands difference as critical capacity rather than deficit aligns with principles of culturally relevant and sustaining pedagogies articulated by education scholars (e.g., Ladson-Billings; Paris; Paris and Alim). It can further the vision of CCCC's statement on Students' Right to their Own Language and calls to mobilize the cultural and political power of rhetorical difference put forward by generations of scholars of Black, Latina/o/x, Indigenous, Asian and Asian American, and feminist rhetorics. It can incorporate insights from recent disciplinary turns toward code-meshing and* *translingualism (e.g., Horner et al.; Young and Martinez). Likewise, it can respond to decolonial critiques of epistemological universalism put forward by Indigenous and Latinx rhetorics scholars (e.g., Cushman, "Decolonizing"; Powell et al.; Riley-Mukavetz and Powell; Ruiz and Sánchez; García and Baca), encouraging us to recognize the local knowledges transfer students live, adapt, and transform. It furthers efforts in queer theory to deconstruct the normativities surrounding academic rhetorics, literacies, and educational paths (Alexander), and it advances calls in disability studies to broaden conceptualizations of "access" and "accommodation," to question the assumptions about neurological and sensory processing, bodily abilities, and time from which literacy technologies, pedagogies, and institutional spaces often operate (e.g. Yergeau et al.; Womack; Wood).*

A critical ecological approach can recognize that difference is cultural, linguistic, discursive, epistemic, and embodied. That is, writers write—and are read—from bodies marked in complex and intersecting ways by socially constructed categories. Our embodiments interact with our environments, (re)producing relations that are often unjust, and this affects students' experiences moving across and beyond postsecondary institutions. As Syverson asks:

> *If writing and reading . . . are embodied processes, how should teachers think about the differences between a hungry student and one who is well fed, an exhausted student and one who is rested, a battered student and one who is well loved, a disabled student and one who is "normal"—and the whole complex range of physical conditions that lie between or among these poles? (188)*

While Syverson's language is dated, her point remains: students experience differences in their embodied, material circumstances that shape their writing and can impact the time, space, attention, motivation, and money they devote to their academic pursuits.

An ecological approach enables us to see this kind of material difference and reckon with its inequitable consequences. Some people are harmed by their experiences in our writing ecology, and no amount of "grit" can counter those material injustices. However, without lapsing into bootstraps rhetorics, we might recognize that these experiences sometimes also have the potential to foster resilience, or what our co-researcher Justin Whitney calls "callouses." While painful, such experiences can motivate and inform rhetorical work. As Claudia suggests, writing offers ways to make new meaning from these experiences of difference to pursue personal and social change. Ecological orientations suggest that supporting transfer students is not just a matter of raising awareness or adapting pedagogy: it requires addressing material conditions that affect educational access and outcomes. It requires political *labor that extends far beyond the syllabus, the department website, and the university's development offices.*

Finally, we believe our work together on this project evidences the value of difference within the disciplinary ecology of composition studies. As Fleckenstein and colleagues argue,

> *An ecological orientation to research emphasizes the need for* research *diversity: multiple sites of immersion, multiple perspectives, and multiple methodologies within a particular discipline and research project. . . . Traditional approaches to research have crafted a monoculture in which the identities of the researcher and the subject of research are carefully controlled and carefully separated. An ecological orientation destabilizes that monoculture, requiring researchers to consider who is empowered to ask questions and solicit answers, who can be the object of the study, who can be authorized to analyze the data, and who can conduct and report research. (401)*

Our collaborative, constellated research—what Nic calls being "rabbits in lab coats"—complicates the monoculture with a multiplicity of voices and perspectives. Our team's multifaceted identities and experiences, varying languages and literacies, and different investments in academic knowledge making have presented challenges, but they are, ultimately, a strength: a source of generativity and resilience. The meaningful differences produced through our interactions have invited a more diverse cohort of transfer students into the project and the WRS department. We hope our work challenges the research monoculture and contributes to enacting more just disciplinary ecologies.

Claudia

It was my first semester at the University of Utah, where at a transfer student event an enthusiastic professor sold me on a class—"Write4U"—the then-pilot course for transfer students. Nic, the research assistant, emailed me to be a participant of the transfer student study being conducted for the pilot course. I thought: "I'll get a $20 gift card to the University Bookstore for being questioned by a stranger for an hour. That's hella above my pay rate." Once in the interview I realized I had met Nic once before, about two years earlier. Back then we were both at SLCC and had only exchanged small talk. I vaguely remember him saying he worked at the SLCC Community Writing Center and my "who the hell needs writing" attitude.

The interconnectivity that allows transfer students to flow between academic worlds would later prove its value because agreeing to be interviewed for the pilot course—by someone who also spoke Spanish—was the beginning of my search for evidence to provide answers to the questions of my identity, ironically through the writing I felt so inadequate to do. "How long have you been here? You barely have an accent!" is the usual follow-up from people who don't know me and are determined to single me out, after they've asked, "Where are you from?" I tend to ignore those microaggressive questions, because asking where I'm from is the wrong question if you want to understand my writing in relation to this place. And I can't tell you about Salt Lake without letting you in on a little secret: I'm an infiltrator—my foreign words immigrate over the border and into the writing ecology of Salt Lake.

I'm driving—no, racing—with excitement to get my parents' garage, where I'm sure I'll find just the right piece of writing to share with you. I want to give you physical evidence—a textual artifact of my existence.

I got to the garage and began digging up dusty boxes of my dad's old notebooks, taxes, and bills that ended up going to collections. Despite spending hours looking I came up empty-handed. Defeated, I went inside the house to try and explain to my parents this loquera thing I was doing for school, so I told them: "Esque estoy buscando papeles donde yo haya escrito de cuando vivíamos en Mexico." Mi Mama dijo, "Y para que los quieres? Si escribias en Espanol." I told her, "Esque es como evidencia de mi contribución a la escritura de aquí (SLC) fuera de la escuela y antes que llegaramos."

My dad pulled out photographs from his drawer. He saved those little windows into our world that my mom, my sister, and I would send him in the mail while he lived in Salt Lake and the three of us in Mexico. I remember sitting en la cocina with my mom, who would help me form sentences out of my longing to see my father. Now, as my parents and I sifted through these relics, I noticed my mother's eyes becoming teary, and she said, "Siento mucha nostalgia cuando me acuerdo que antes te podía enseñar a leer y escribir, algo que ya no pude hacer en Estados Unidos." My mom passed down her self-perception of inadequacy and powerlessness that comes with moving and learning a new language to me.

In 2002 my family left Guanajuato, Mexico, and resettled in Magna, Utah, a township famous for its drinking water, "rich in minerals." The open-pit Kennecott Copper Mine is our contaminated backyard, after all. I sat in the Magna library writing this very piece for you. I looked toward the Wasatch Mountains, surrounded by hiking trails and deer, where an emblematic symbol is carved. The symbol is one letter: "U" for the University of Utah, and I wondered if the U could see us from up there.

I have been struggling to connect the fibers of my experiences within the writing ecology of Salt Lake, even though I live here. The letters I sent my father in 1999 had materialized here, but in some ways I never did. The following questions loom over the rest of my paper: Why does academia need data to validate experiences? What evidence should I include to convince you my experiences are real? For even I had to find evidence to believe my own writing existed. So who am I for you to believe? I can't find answers to questions and realized I don't need to. What I do now is make sense of why I ask and what is asked of me.

Within this text I've written myself out of SLC—always the outsider looking in, for various reasons, as my skin bears the colors of mixed ancestry: Toltec, Spanish, French, Black, or as my grandma would say, "Somos lo que quedo despues de toda la cogedera." I'm used to being the outsider—an involuntary participant—but even more I let myself become a victim to my beliefs about beauty, intelligence, racism, and other self-deprecating notions that influence my idea of self as a not-writer. A person who is not and cannot fully be. The process of not being is continual, and a constant battle with myself, mitigated, in part, by how much I can actually bring into the classroom. Often I have had to leave my gender and ethnicity at the door. I come and go from all the places I inhabit, whether physically, or in dreams and desires of what could've been if I'd stayed in Mexico, where I didn't question my origins.

The initial shock of being forced to leave my home caused a part of me—call it my mind or spirit—to have stayed behind in that place where I used to belong. My body crossed over the border, and I had found artifactual evidence of myself here, but I have never consciously been a part of Salt Lake. I want to be here. I choose to stay here. No matter if my writing will always give me away. I have chosen to let go of my long-lost home so I can be *here*. The following passage comes from the in-between, another realm of existence that I inhabit in my language of nurture and in the form of verses, the way I've used to make sense of my story which at this point has had no beginning, middle, or end. I wrote a letter to my hometown "Cortazar" to unravel myself from it.

Querido Cortazar,

Hace ya más de 15 años me fui de ti, una niña solloza. Hoy regreso a platicar contigo como mujer porque despues de tanto tiempo te llevo dentro de mi, y quiero que sepas que aunque te deje, jamás me quise despedir.

Me pregunto si tu aun te acuerdas de mi. Si me
extrañas si te hago falta y me necesitas.
Y si regreso a ti me estarás esperando o te
habrás olvidado de mi?

Porque debajo de este cielo compartido, yo a ti
te extraño.

Si supieras que si pudiera volver aquel momento
cuando me tuve que ir, si pudiera volver el
tiempo jamás me hubiera separado de ti. But
there's no going back and there's no pretending
that we still speak the same tongue. If you let
me go I'll always come back to you as you return
to me in dreams.

In this parallel world
Of my spectral existence
Your borders are the labyrinth of my melancholy
And your prose peace to my rebellion.
Filling the void of your absence
With foreign warmth
I've let you go.

Ahora me pregunto quien se quedo contigo, y si eres feliz.

As I seek reconciliation between the places I've been in both physically and spiritually, I do so faced with the reality that there is no going back to my romanticized idea of "home" because that would mean a mother with two daughters living in a town where more and more dead bodies are appearing and people are disappeared. I returned about ten years ago now, at eighteen, and found myself ousted once more, faced with the sentiment of "Tu no eres Mexicana, ya eres gringa." Perhaps this was my saving grace—I realized I no longer had the privilege of living in ignorance. I knew it was time to let go, to fully embody myself again:

So I sat down to be interviewed about writing by another transfer student, who proved to be a reflection of the work I am capable of doing. At the time, I didn't understand why anyone wanted to ask questions about my connection to writing as far back to when I was a kid who didn't speak English. I didn't know someone cared. But after four months and three interviews I had collected $60 worth of gift cards and picked up pieces of my life I never had the opportunity to reflect on. I had been writing all along in the United States and actually liked it—just not in school. With the little poems I would write in my basement to pass the time, helping my dad with his résumé to apply for jobs, proofreading my sister's essays, and teaching my mother to write in English.

Providing opportunities for students to reflect on the forms of writing that they've used outside of school, in other languages, or unconventional ways is crucial for our understanding the role that writing plays in shaping identities here in Salt Lake. It enriches the writing ecology of any place—by having multiple voices involved. I went from feeling inadequate, detached, impotent, to later finding unfilled niches, i.e. through this research project. One of the last questions Nic asked me was: "Do you feel like you belong at the University?" I answered, "Yes. I belong as an outsider, there are always outsiders, and we belong by not belonging." I'll always be an infiltrator to some, but I'll never be a foreigner to myself.

CHANGE

In her book title, Rousculp pairs the ethic that emerged at the CWC, a rhetoric of respect, *with the idea of* recognizing change. *An ecological approach helps her theorize discursive change over time in relation to place. Ecological theories of writing have long emphasized the inevitability of change. Cooper writes, "An important characterization of ecological systems is that they are inherently dynamic; though their structures and contents can be specified at a given moment, in real time they are constantly changing, limited only by parameters that are themselves subject to change over longer spans of time" (386). Writing ecologies are, in Syverson's terms,* emergent*—always "in the process of becoming" (6). Sometimes change emerges gradually, through the accumulating interactions of those within the system, while in other cases it can result from what Syverson calls a* perturbation. *In these situations, "some factor outside the system can trigger a perturbation that propagates, in which a change in the state of the relative activity of the components of a system leads to further changes of state either in the same components or in other components" (129). Grant identifies a similar ontology in the Lakota narrative of Taté's lodge, in which a "perturbance of a network" and the "decisions made by network actors" results in "a subsequent realignment or equilibrium" (75). Because of the complexity of ecologies, it is often not possible to predict which perturbations will lead to state changes, or what the resulting equilibrium will be.*

*The unpredictable, dynamic nature of ecologies is co-constitutive. In Inoue's words, "the ways that environments affect people are discursively, performatively, and materially, changing us as we dwell and labor because we dwell and labor in those places" (*Antiracist *90). We are, in turn, always changing the environment through our actions, including our languaging. In this dynamic, Inoue sees possibilities for Freirean praxis, asserting that "the link between the world and the word is reflection that is action, which is labor, the engine of becoming and change, the engine of ecologies" (406). Change is inevitable, if not inevitably positive. Inoue suggests we can work together to understand our current relations and act collectively to create a writing ecology that is more just, fair, and healthy for everyone with whom we dwell.*

Changes in our local writing ecology have real implications for the lives and opportunities of the transfer students within it. However, the actions of those students are also co-constituting that ecology at any given moment. Thus, transfer students and researchers, and transfer-students-as-researchers, have agency, albeit constrained, to reimagine and remake the writing ecology through their actions. As Fleckenstein and colleagues assert:

> *Rhetorically enacted, an ecological orientation offers teacher-scholars the hope of* making *a difference in the material conditions of one's reality. . . . [R]hetorically enacted, research is something that is undertaken for reasons that go beyond the motives of satisfying one's degree requirements or providing material for promotion and tenure considerations. . . . [R]esearch is undertaken so that new knowledge can be a difference that* makes *a difference. (406)*

In this framework, research can be purposeful action that not only produces knowledge, but also changes the ecology in the process.

We have spent the last seven years working with *transfer students and* as *transfer students,* with *teachers of writing and* as *teachers of writing, to remake our writing ecology. We have done so through public acts: proposals, presentations, publications, engagements with university communications that became contentious when we suspected our differences were being commodified. We have also done so through "everyday" rhetorical practices (Powell et al.) and what Cushman calls "the daily interactions when the regular flow of events is objectified, reflected upon, and altered" ("Rhetorician" 12). We have sought to recognize and tend to local interinstitutional relationships that were invisible or neglected, to forge connections, and to show what kinds of disciplinary relations are possible and why they might be desirable. We have done what we could to bring bodies and languages and knowledges and perspectives into academic spaces where they weren't acting before. And we have seen ecological change—small from a systemic view, perhaps, but not so small in our own lives or those of students we've met along the way.*

In his Keywords in Writing Studies *entry on "ecology," Weisser states that "an ecological conception of writing emphasizes complex adaptation and the constant motion of discursive systems" (68). If adaptation is central to writing, then transfer students may be better primed than most for such discursive motion. They are, after all, defined by movement between academic institutions, and they often travel across many other borders to get there—political, socioeconomic, cultural, linguistic, and gendered. Many do so under material conditions that demand adaptation for survival. They know change, and that knowledge can yield forms of rhetorical awareness that facilitates writing transfer. In line with Dimpal Jain and her colleagues' principles for creating a transfer-receptive culture, an ecological approach helps us appreciate the intellectual and rhetorical capacities community college transfer students bring* "because *they are transfer students" (253)*: because *of their multifaceted identities and knowledges, their mobilities, and their experiences with and desires for change.*

As teachers, students, and writers, as departments and institutions, we are all always in the process of becoming. But Indigenous rhetorics—the memoria of this land—remind us such change does not undo the emplaced histories and relations that came before (Deloria; King et al.; Powell). In Lakota ontology, "[p]rior orders still continue and have a lasting effect, yet the network as a whole progresses through cyclical states of becoming" (Grant 74). As we move into the future and new spaces, remaking our ecologies through our actions and responding as best we can to perturbations beyond our control, we also encounter and carry traces of prior ecologies making the here and now in which we dwell (Edbauer). Those ecologies are not gone, not lost, nor are they truly escapable. Whether we choose to recognize them or not, our relations persist across time and space, as do our responsibilities. An ecological approach helps us see that our relations will always be (re)writing us, even as we strive to (re)write them. This awareness may be our best resource for facing the inevitability of change.

Nate

[Dénouement]

The week leading up to my graduation, I would walk out to the top floor of the parking garage at my job and consider how my life would soon be reorganized. Each day it became more apparent to me that the academic structure in which I had found some form of comfort was about to collapse around me. I would get angry when

I saw buildings on campus whose construction wouldn't be finished until after my graduation, knowing I'd never step inside them as a student. I'd think, "You aren't supposed to build things *after* I leave!" Like finishing a book and finding the world around you profoundly unchanged and indifferent to the emotional turmoil you'd just experienced, I found that the universe wasn't going to warp time and space to make the narrative of my graduation any more cinematic, and didn't seem inclined to rush in and wrap up unfinished storylines in my life.

I saw college as the only realistic means to alter the future I'd envisioned for myself based on the circumstances of my upbringing: a future of financial insecurity, no employment opportunities outside of manual or service labor, and genetic predispositions to substance abuse. As a child of teenage parents, and as a first-generation college student, I had no roadmap that led me through school, and, now having graduated, no clear path leading me to the more secure life I've been working toward. I'm not trying to paint my college experience as being uniquely harder than those of other students, because that certainly wasn't the case—as a "traditionally college-aged" (young), straight white man, I could comfortably visit campus day or night without anyone so much as batting an eye. I understand that my ability to pay for school hinged on an unusually high-paying job as a security guard where I likely benefited from being "traditionally military-aged" (young), white, and able-bodied, and the benefit of living with a roommate whom I could depend on to pay rent every month. While acknowledging my positionality and perspective is important, discounting my own experiences discounts the experiences of others with similar experiences, so I'll try to limit that here.

For a student with no economic safety net in place to soften the impact of failure, I took the safest route I could through college. Two years passed before I dared take more than two classes per semester while I worked full-time. My class schedule (and even my eventual selection of a major) was built to accommodate the job that paid for it. I quickly gave up looking for scholarships after I found that most required full-time enrollment, or hours of essay writing that would be better spent working for guaranteed compensation. Splitting my time between work, school, and other activities created the sense that I didn't quite fit into any of the communities I was participating in—not quite a worker, not quite a student, but some sort of distracted amalgamation of the two.

When I was invited to be a member of this research team, it felt as if the university itself was reaching out to formally ask me to be a part of its community. I knew I couldn't give it all of my time, but I knew that without this solid connection between me and the school, I would continue to feel as removed as I had throughout my years at the community college. While it certainly didn't help the sensation of spinning plates, it managed to instill some much-needed confidence that I was capable of earning a bachelor's degree. One of the pitfalls of being a first-generation college student is being inherently untrusting of people who say you're capable. Are they saying that I'm just as capable as someone of a more affluent and educated background, or do they mean that I'm more capable than they think someone from my background would be? Are they even credible enough to know the difference? I've always feared, and assumed, that I'd merely managed to exceed their lowered expectations.

Two weeks after my graduation, the team reconvened to begin talking about how we might approach writing this chapter. Going on our third year of doing research together, and this being the book we'd been planning all this time, it felt too daunting a task to summarize our experiences throughout every iteration of this project on a few pieces of paper. Furthermore, I struggled with the notion that *this* would be the work that is recognized on our CVs: not our interactions with students over the years, nor our building relationships with faculty at Salt Lake Community College, or any other experience that wouldn't appear on paper. How could this be the paramount achievement of our endeavors, above all else?

I find this book to be but a byproduct of the real work that was done that made tangible differences, however large or small, in the lives of those we've interacted with during our research. I'm certainly proud of the work that went into it, and hope that it will be useful in some way to those who take the time to read it, but this book is not the goal, not the solution, not the thing that made change. However, like a long-term deposit, maybe it will be doing the work for us when we're busy spinning plates elsewhere. We learned throughout countless meetings and hours spent writing that the best way to invoke change was by working directly with members of the ecology.

As the services offered to me as a transfer student weren't terribly useful, given how they seemed to only apply to the full-time, nonworking student, I want to make sure that the stuff I help create for others is actually useful to them. Receiving a gift you neither wanted nor needed is an exercise in patience; you're expected to feel grateful, yet you can't help feeling disappointed by the wasted gesture. Over the course of this project, I've read about and encountered researchers who felt they knew how to help "the community," without ever knowing its members by name. It seems to me that these disconnected researchers are doing more harm than good when speaking on the behalf of those they haven't met, whose voices are silenced through the very act of not being invited to speak for themselves. In thinking of our communities as living, breathing things, with kaleidoscopic values and resources, scholars can take accountability for our position in the ecology, and make interpersonal connections that remind us why the work is being done in the first place.

As we continue to speak to students, fellow educators, and academic peers, we are continually reconfiguring our position in the ecology and finding the areas that could best use support. Even the courses we've designed after years spent researching how to better facilitate interinstitutional transfer will need to be reworked and continually calibrated to meet the shifting needs of students and faculty. We've found that there is no "one-size-fits-all" solution to supporting students; the notion that there could possibly be one is laughable. As community members, we must be willing to adapt to our ever-changing landscape, and be willing to engage in new situations.

PART II:
TRANSFER-CONDUCIVE DISCIPLINARY ECOLOGIES

Interstitial II:

Nate's College Calculus

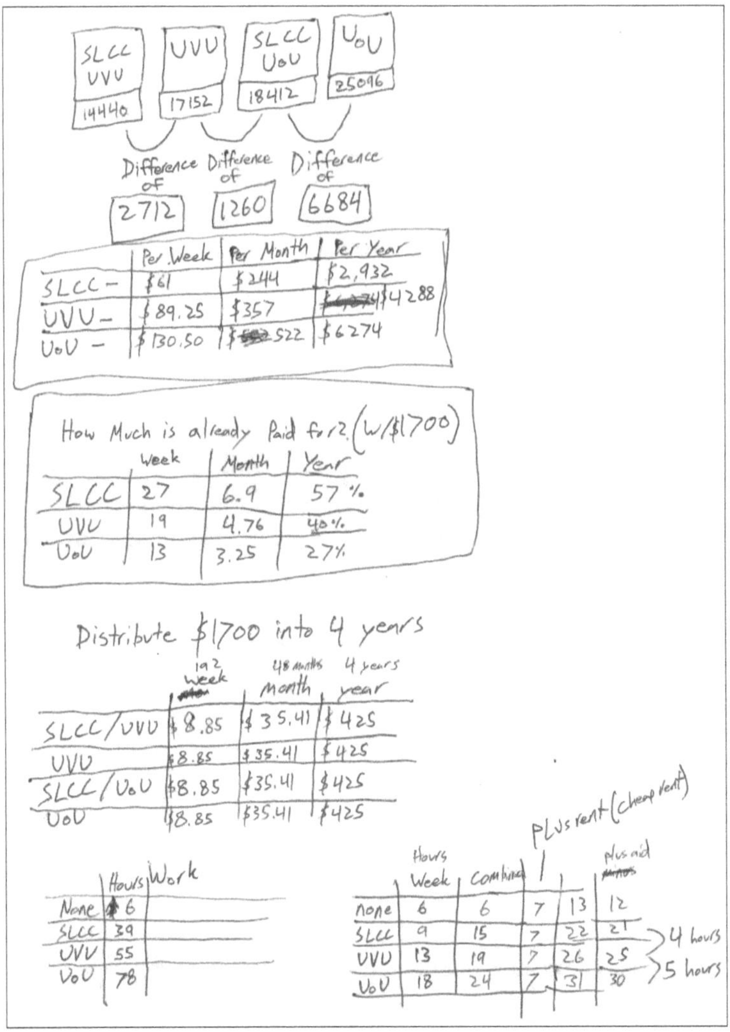

SLCC UVU	UVU	SLCC UoU	UoU
14440	17152	18412	25096

Difference of 2712 | Difference of 1260 | Difference of 6684

	Per Week	Per Month	Per Year
SLCC –	$61	$244	$2,932
UVU –	$89.25	$357	$4288
UoU –	$130.50	$522	$6274

How Much is already Paid for? (w/$1700)

	Week	Month	Year
SLCC	27	6.9	57%
UVU	19	4.76	40%
UoU	13	3.25	27%

Distribute $1700 into 4 years

	192 week	48 months month	4 years year
SLCC/UVU	$8.85	$35.41	$425
UVU	$8.85	$35.41	$425
SLCC/UoU	$8.85	$35.41	$425
UoU	$8.85	$35.41	$425

	Hours	Work
None	6	
SLCC	39	
UVU	55	
UoU	78	

Plus rent (cheap rent)

	Hours Week	Combined			plus aid
none	6	6	7	13	12
SLCC	9	15	7	22	21
UVU	13	19	7	26	25
UoU	18	24	7	31	30

4 hours
5 hours

THIS IS WHAT EDUCATIONAL DECISION MAKING looks like for many community college transfer students. Nathan Lacy crunched these numbers in 2011, when he was eighteen years old. Neither of Nate's parents had gone to college, and if he went, he knew he'd have to pay for it himself while working full-time to keep a roof over his head, food in his fridge, and gas in the car he'd need to travel between jobs, classes, and home. SLCC, UVU, and the U were the three public institutions within commuting distance of the apartment he shared with roommates. Like many students along the Wasatch Front, Nate was comparing not just individual colleges and universities, but the *combinations* of institutions that would give him the lowest overall tuition and the greatest flexibility relative to his work schedule.

Nate chose to enroll at SLCC, and, after three years of taking courses part-time while working nights as a security guard at a pharmaceutical manufacturing facility, he transferred to the U and decided to major in WRS. I met Nate in my Writing as Social Practice course in spring 2015. Over the next three years, although he rarely enrolled full-time and was therefore ineligible for most scholarships or the Undergraduate Research Opportunity Program, Nate was a key member of the team of transfer students who co-researched and coauthored this book. He often came to our meetings off a night shift, bleary-eyed but quick with a joke. Nate finished his bachelor's degree in spring 2017 and went on to complete our department's master's program in 2020. As he was packing up his apartment after graduation, he found his younger self's tongue-in-cheek budget and showed it to me, rightly thinking I'd find it meaningful. When I asked, he allowed me to put it in this book.

I open Part II with Nate because he, and students making calculations like his, are the reason composition studies must account for and to two-year colleges. Although the term "two-year college" risks reproducing normativities about how long a degree should take, it is the nomenclature used by TYCA, and it denotes a specific set of institutional spaces and professional structures. Those spaces include public and private "junior" colleges, access-oriented branch campuses of public universities, many technical colleges, and comprehensive community colleges. In addition to transfer curricula, community colleges provide access to a variety of additional learning opportunities: noncredit community education courses, worker retraining and vocational certifications, and various "precollege" programs. Those programs include adult basic education, GED preparation, courses for learners of English as an additional language, and "developmental" courses, as well as other forms of academic support, such as writing centers and supplemental instruction. Many community colleges also oversee dual or concurrent enrollment programs for area high schoolers, and some now offer bachelor's degrees in "applied" and/or high-demand fields.

As of 2017, there were 1,108 community colleges in the United States. These institutions enrolled 7.2 million students in credit-bearing courses, accounting for 41 percent of all US undergraduates (American Association of Community Colleges). Nationwide, two-year colleges teach roughly half of first-year composition courses and most basic/developmental writing and reading (Hassel and Giordano, "Occupy"). Nearly 40 percent of postsecondary English faculty are employed at two-year institutions (Bureau of Labor Statistics). Two-year colleges are also major points of access for groups historically underrepresented in postsecondary education:

- 56 percent of Native American, 52 percent of Latinx, 43 percent of Black, and 40 percent of Asian and Asian American or Pacific Islander undergraduates attend two-year colleges.
- 56 percent identify as women.
- The average student age is twenty-eight; 49 percent are twenty-two or older.
- 36 percent are first-generation college students.
- 17 percent are single parents.
- 12 percent have documented disabilities.
- 7 percent are not US citizens.
- 62 percent attend college part-time.
- 63 percent are employed full-time. (American Association of Community Colleges)

Community colleges are also the most common point of postsecondary access for DACA and unDACAmented students (Perez; Jain et al., *Power*). And although there are few national data about the sexual identities of community college students, studies suggest these institutions provide important educational access for LGBTQIA+ students, particularly those who are also low-income, working class, and/or students of color (J. Taylor; Zamani-Gallaher and Choudhuri). As of 2019, 41 percent of designated minority-serving institutions (MSIs) were two-year colleges, including:

- 202 (41 percent of) Hispanic-serving institutions (HSIs).
- 49 (44 percent of) predominantly Black institutions (PBIs).
- 48 (36 percent of) Asian American, Native American, and Pacific Islander–serving institutions (AANAPISIs).
- 19 (56 percent of) tribally controlled colleges and universities (TCUs.)
- 15 (37 percent of) Native American–serving nontribal institutions (NASNIs).
- 12 (28 percent of) Alaska Native and Native Hawaiian–serving institutions (ANNHSIs).
- 11 (11 percent of) historically Black colleges and universities (HBCUs).

Given these demographics, anyone interested in the relationships between literacy instruction and racial inequities in the United States must recognize the significance of two-year colleges.

Since the Truman Commission launched the modern community college movement in 1947, these institutions have embraced a rhetoric of democratic opportunity (Sullivan, *Economic*). Two-year college composition faculty have famously called them "democracy's open door" (Griffith and Connor) and "democracy in action" (Pickett). Advocates tout community colleges as engines of economic mobility: the average student who completes an associate's degree at a community college will earn $5,400 more per year than a student who drops out (Belfield and Bailey).[7] All of us who work in these spaces have met students who would have been unable to attend college without a locally accessible, affordable option. However, critics also identify ways in which these institutions contribute to social stratification.

Sociologists of education have argued that community colleges provide the illusion of equal access to the middle class but actually function to *divert* students—particularly working-class students and students of color—into low-status institutions dominated by vocational programs, thereby reducing their likelihood of completing a bachelor's degree and their long-term earnings and social status (e.g., Clark; Pincus; Karabel; Brint and Karabel). In these analyses, community colleges perform a "cooling-out function," lowering students' aspirations (Clark 569). They serve as a social "safety valve," letting off the steam of lower-class ambitions while maintaining the elite status of universities and fulfilling capital's need for semiskilled labor (Brint and Karabel 208). Those who work in two-year colleges are often aware of these critiques: Holly Hassel, Mark Reynolds, Jeff Sommers, and Howard Tinberg describe cooling out as a specter "haunt[ing] two-year college faculty, staff, and administrators who embrace the mission of open-door higher education as uniquely democratic and socially ambitious" ("Editorial" 324). While such critiques have been contested, even sympathetic researchers observe that the democratic function of these "contradictory colleges" is undercut by competing missions and policy mandates (Dougherty) and chronic underfunding (Beach; Harbour; Sullivan, *Economic*).

Since the 1990s, scholars both in and beyond composition studies have also observed a pervasive neoliberalism driving community college administration and policy. They suggest that community colleges exacerbate social inequality by facilitating economic globalization, the corporatization and instrumentalization of higher education, and the casualization of postsecondary teaching (Levin; Kroll, "End"; Harbour; Klausman, "Out"; Griffiths and Jensen; Jensen, "Political"; Hassel et al., "Editorial"; Higgins and Warnke). Over the last four decades, as neoliberal policies have led to state disinvestment in public education, per-pupil funding disparities between two- and four-year institutions have worsened (Beach; Harbour).[8]

In recent years, as the latest wave of neoliberal "accountability" movements has reshaped the policy landscape, reform-minded critics and megaphilanthropies have focused on the comparatively low degree-completion rates at community colleges. Responding to these critics, Patrick Sullivan ("Measuring"; *Economic Inequality*) cautions readers to recognize the distinctive motivations, levels of commitment, resources, and life circumstances shaping community college students' academic trajectories. Not all students who enroll at community colleges intend to earn a degree or transfer to a four-year institution. Some change their initial goals as they gain experience with college coursework, and many of the factors undermining the persistence of those who would stay are beyond the control of colleges or instructors—they must be addressed through expansion of financial aid and the social safety net. On the other hand, the federal government's traditional metrics for "success" undercount part-time students who take longer to finish their degrees, as well as those who transfer without completing a credential (Toth et al., "Dubious"). Recent changes to federal metrics demonstrate that, when part-time students are included over an eight-year time horizon, 60 percent of those who enroll at community colleges either earn a degree or transfer. At the alternative promoted by advocates of privatization—for-profit colleges—that rate is 39 percent (Carey).

While neoliberal "reformers" often fail to account for the distinctive missions and student populations at community colleges, the transfer figures should still give faculty at two- and four-year institutions pause. While 81 percent of entering community college students say they aspire to a bachelor's degree, only 33 percent transfer to a four-year institution within six years (Jenkins and Fink), and just 16 percent earn a bachelor's degree (Shapiro, et al., *Completing College: A National View of Student Attainment Rates—Fall 2010 Cohort*). There are racial disparities in these transfer rates. Nationally, 33 percent of Latinx students and 26 percent of Black students who enroll at two-year colleges earn any kind of credential within six years; that figure is 45 percent for white students and 44 percent for Asian and Asian American students. Furthermore, only 11 percent of Latinx students and 9 percent of Black students who begin at two-year colleges eventually complete bachelor's degrees, compared to 19 percent of white students and 23 percent of Asian and Asian American students (Shapiro, et al., *Completing College: A National View of Student Attainment Rates by Race and Ethnicity—Fall 2010 Cohort*).[9] Higher education researchers call this phenomenon the *racial transfer gap*: Black and Latinx students are significantly less likely to transfer successfully between two- and four-year institutions than their white and Asian and Asian American counterparts (Crisp and Nuñez). Gaps within these broad racial categories—for example, among different Latinx and Asian American communities and at the intersections of identities like gender, class, age, sexuality, and disability—also appear in locally specific ways.

These inequities are real, and, throughout this book, I resist what William DeGenaro calls the "dangerous" tendency to romanticize two-year colleges ("Social" 129). However, I will also resist the tendency of university-based critics to dismiss community colleges without considering the material realities in which students like Nate make decisions about postsecondary education. As Sara Goldrick-Rab demonstrates, federal financial aid has failed to keep up with increased costs of college attendance in the United States. With lower tuition and flexible course scheduling, two-year colleges are often the *only* affordable option for working or rural students, as well as students who are unable to apply for federal financial aid.[10] For those students, the choice is not between an open-admissions two-year college and a selective-admissions university. Particularly for those who are unable to relocate because of family, finances, work, and other personal or cultural commitments, the choice is frequently between the local two-year college and no college at all, or a for-profit institution more likely to leave them in greater debt, often without a degree or improved prospects for employment (Toth, et al., "Dubious").

Another critique of two-year colleges revolves around labor practices. In an age of neoliberal austerity, the relative affordability of these institutions has been purchased in no small part through the exploitation of adjunct faculty, who now make up 70 percent of the community college instructional force (Cohen et al.) and teach 58 percent of courses (Center for Community College Student Engagement). There are pay disparities by institution type: for example, first-year-writing faculty at the U are paid twice as much per course as at SLCC. These labor structures undermine the professionalization of two-year college faculty and of postsecondary writing instruction more generally (Kroll, "End"; Klausman, "Two-Year"). However, two-year colleges serve the least affluent students with far less per-pupil state subsidy than public four-year institutions (Harbour). They also have the least wealthy alumni base for fundraising. It is unjust to expect low-income and working-class students to shoulder the cost of fairly compensated faculty when the wealthiest taxpayers won't. Ultimately, *all* of us who work in US postsecondary education are complicit in a system that exploits part-time faculty labor and pushes students who are already structurally disadvantaged into underresourced institutions where they are less likely to complete degrees. I believe those who benefit most from that complicity in terms of pay, job security, and professional status—namely, *tenure-line university faculty*—should take responsibility for our roles in that system.

Taking responsibility means moving from social critique to social action. As an institution type, two-year colleges are unlikely to disappear any time soon. If they do, it will be because policymakers decide it is no longer worthwhile to use taxpayer dollars to provide educational access for students who "didn't succeed the first time"—i.e., in high school (Toth, et al., "Dubious"). That punitive mentality would be fueled by raced, classed, and gendered notions of *who* is benefiting from such educational "welfare." If two-year colleges were to go away or begin seriously restricting admissions, it is hard to imagine that most universities would find the resources or the institutional and pedagogical will to offer the same relative affordability, accommodation for student work schedules and family responsibilities, and commitment to supporting students from diverse educational trajectories that two-year colleges at least attempt to provide. Eliminating two-year colleges would not produce a more equitable postsecondary system. Rather, it would foreclose access to that system in ways that would reflect, reinforce, and deepen existing social inequities.

This is educational reality at the start of the century's third decade, a period of social upheaval fueled by the digital revolution and a globalizing economy; income inequality; demographic shifts toward urbanism and greater racial, ethnic, and linguistic diversity; white backlash; and the COVID-19 pandemic. Generations of young and no-longer-young people are trying to forge their futures in the wreckage of mass incarceration and racialized police violence, the opioid epidemic, regional declines in manufacturing and farming, inaccessible or inadequate healthcare, environmental racism and classism, gentrification, decades-long war, an enraged patriarchy, persistent heterosexism and transphobia, pervasive ableism, and the cruelties of US immigration policy. Climate change is redrawing water sources, forests, and shorelines, and thus economic and demographic maps. People will need second, third, and fourth chances at postsecondary education, with high-quality teaching for information literacy and political action. If composition studies has any hope of addressing those demands, open-admissions two-year colleges are going to be the major point of access. The challenges of the coming decades require us to work across institution types to expand opportunities for two-year college students making calculations like Nate's.

FROM NATE, AN ADJUNCT INSTRUCTOR AT SALT LAKE COMMUNITY COLLEGE, IN 2021:

The characters in this book, which was written over the course of my BS and MA programs, include some of the closest friends I've ever made, colleagues I admire and have traveled across the country with, incredible people who have shared with me some of my fondest memories. It's weird to see a receipt of your twenties printed among the pages of someone's bid for tenure. As sentimental as reading this text makes me feel, as I consider the start of my potential career in academia, I find myself in a familiar state of anger about money and labor conditions.

I believe that community colleges have great potential to create social change and help restructure positions of power to be more equitable for the communities they represent. I'm concerned, however, that if we don't find a way to address the pay of faculty, adjunct or otherwise, we risk further exploitation of all faculty members, as well as of our students, which could contribute to broader social inequities. This doesn't seem like a problem we can solve as individuals, nor within our own institutions, but something we might be able to address collectively. If postsecondary institutions were financially equipped to hire adjunct faculty as full-time employees with benefits (likely with state or federal assistance), we'd have greater bandwidth to help our students succeed. Without such structural change, we risk further exploitation of already overburdened educators and will not create the institutional changes necessary to help our students meet their various educational and professional goals. To support a more diverse student population, we need to constantly be learning and adjusting our pedagogies. I worry that, left unchecked, schools will look to standardized, corporate, neoliberal solutions to generate more tuition money from students rather than offering their instructors financial security. We need to hold our systems accountable for the sake of our students, ourselves, and our communities.

Now if you'll excuse me, I need to crunch some numbers to figure out which combinations of schools I'll need to adjunct at in order to pay the bills this year.

2

A Discipline Worth Being

COMPOSITIONISTS HAVE EMBARKED on a multigenerational bid for "professionalized academic disciplinarity" (Horner, "Rewriting" 451) with what Bruce Horner assesses as "at best tenuous" success ("Grounding" 52). John Trimbur describes this pursuit as fraught with "intellectual ambivalence and conflicted emotions" (5), and Steven Parks expresses misgivings about seeking to "ma[k]e ourselves legitimate in a system premised on exclusion and elitism" (*"Opportunity"* 208). Professionals have historically used disciplinary expertise to exert authority—to subordinate knowledges—rather than enact "solidarity" with "everyday people" (Trimbur 2). In their CCCC Chairs' Addresses, Gwendolyn Pough and Malea Powell warn that narrow investments in disciplinarity can marginalize the knowledges of communities of color and the transdisciplinary insights of scholars in critical race, ethnic, and gender studies. Powell and her co-speakers describe their embodied experiences being "disciplined" in rhetoric and composition, reminding listeners of the patriarchal, heteronormative, racist, classist, and ableist colonial epistemologies from which academic disciplinarity has emerged. Asserting that "it's bigger than comp/rhet," Pough calls on the field to be "undisciplined," to refuse to "police its borders" (305–6).

Across these critiques, I hear persistent concerns that pursuit of disciplinary respectability distracts scholars from, and sometimes actively undermines, the work that "really matters in the world" (Maher 166): laboring with students and communities to co-produce and circulate what Trimbur calls *socially useful knowledge*, "redistributing rather than consolidating professional expertise" (*Solidarity* 49). I share these concerns. Disciplinarity as traditionally conceived can and often has undermined solidarity with two-year college colleagues, whose academic trajectories, transdisciplinary roles, and commitments to educational access may depart from university-centric norms.

Trimbur, who began his own academic career at a community college, identifies three categories of structural difference that produce professional stratification: differences in "the provision of writing instruction based on institution type," in "access to opportunities for research and development," and in the "production of scholarship" (74–75). The inequitable distribution of resources along these categories can create a profession of "insiders" and "outsiders" (76). With their heavier teaching loads and uneven institutional support for professional engagement and publication, two-year college faculty are the least advantaged in all these categories and therefore the most stigmatized by those invested in the hierarchies of university-based academia. As Cynthia Lewiecki-Wilson and Jeff Sommers observe, composition's "entire discussion of disciplinarity assumes a single, common institutional space—the research university—which, we would remind readers, is only *one kind* of higher education space" (460). For me, the university-centrism of professional academic disciplinarity and the consequent marginalization of two-year colleges is a problem not just as a matter of equity among composition faculty, but because it can further constrain educational opportunities for the least advantaged students in the postsecondary educational system.[11]

The 2018 volume *Composition, Rhetoric, and Disciplinarity*, edited by Rita Malenczyk and colleagues, signals that composition studies is at a(nother) key juncture regarding its disciplinary status. In "Mapping the Turn to Disciplinarity: A Historical Analysis of Composition's Trajectory and Its Current Moment," Kathleen Blake Yancey posits that composition is undergoing a "disciplinary turn," a shift from a loose field to a recognizable discipline marked by "four recurring themes" (16):

> (1) a renewed research agenda, including research into and theory about transfer of writing knowledge and practice; (2) the development of projects consolidating what the field has

> established as knowledge; (3) the continuing development of the major in Rhetoric and Composition; and (4) the changing location of Writing Studies within institutional structures. (17)

This book is unavoidably situated within that turn. It is grounded in composition scholarship and empirical study of transfer between SLCC and the U. Much of our work has focused on transfer into the U's WRS major, which has a curriculum shaped in part by "knowledge consolidation" projects like Linda Adler-Kassner and Elizabeth Wardle's efforts to crowdsource disciplinary threshold concepts (*Naming*; *(Re)Considering*). These developments have enabled us to strengthen disciplinary relations across institutions. We created bridge experiences to support SLCC students' writing transitions to the U, and SLCC launched an associate's degree in writing studies that transfers into the U's WRS major. These collaborations, authorized by local recognition of "writing studies" as an academic discipline, positioned our departments as leaders when national reform movements put transfer "pathways" on the Utah System of Higher Education agenda. That position enabled us to engage pathways reform on something closer to our own terms.

As embedded as this book is within the disciplinary turn, it also emerges from my concerns about how bids for disciplinary status can marginalize two-year college faculty and students. These concerns are not dispelled by *Composition, Rhetoric, and Disciplinarity*. The collection includes an important chapter by Shelley Rodrigo and Susan Miller-Cochran, former community college instructors now at the University of Arizona, about the disciplinary contributions of two-year college faculty. As they write, "the scope of the influence of community college scholars in Rhetoric and Composition is vast, yet their work is not always recognized and valued either by their institutions or by their discipline," in part because of "how Rhetoric and Composition has historically defined 'scholarship,' which tends to exclude important scholarly work from many faculty in a variety of positions, institutions, and locations" (53).[12] However, other essays in the collection—most notably, Kristine Hansen's "Discipline and Profession: Can the Field of Rhetoric and Writing Be Both?" and "Editors' Conclusion: Where Are We

Going and How Do We Get There?" (Malenczyk et al.)—seem unable to square disciplinary investments in specialization with the transdisciplinary demands and deprofessionalizing material conditions of two-year college composition.

My goal in this chapter is not to elide these tensions, but rather to understand their emergence, identify the competing values and interests involved, and consider how they might inform conversations about what composition studies could be and do. I have strategic investments in the recognition of composition studies as a discipline and of two-year college writing instruction as a "distinct and significant" profession (Reynolds and Holladay-Hicks, Introduction ix). However, one lesson I've learned in Salt Lake is that the students moving between our institutions are more important than either disciplinary identities or professional status. Students are making enrollment decisions on the assumption that two- and four-year institutions are working together to deliver on the transfer promise community colleges make. That promise is that anyone can take advantage of the affordability and local accessibility of these institutions, institutions where they will experience high-quality instruction relevant to their goals that offers a clear path to completing a bachelor's degree, securing meaningful employment, and using their education to contribute to their communities.

Here is the argument I aim to make in Part II of this book: All composition professionals participate in a hierarchical system of postsecondary education, of which two-year colleges are an integral but often underacknowledged part. We therefore all have a responsibility to work together to deliver on the promises that system makes to community college students. Those of us at universities are, by and large, not yet meeting this responsibility, and our failures contribute to structural inequities. To live up to the social justice commitments espoused by composition's professional organizations and much of its scholarship—to co-constitute a discipline worth being—I suggest we strive to create *transfer-conducive writing ecologies.*

This book is a case study of collaborative efforts to foster a more transfer-conducive writing ecology in the Salt Lake Valley.

Cultivating such an ecology requires reimagining community college–university relations in composition studies, which demands awareness of how this would-be discipline arrived at its current inequitable state. In this chapter, I outline these histories, endeavoring to destabilize the university-centric assumptions that have structured disciplinary relations and to foreground the presences and perspectives of two-year college faculty. As Lewiecki-Wilson and Sommers insist, the teaching of writing at two-year colleges has been "central to the historical formation and continuing practice of composition studies" (440), although university-based compositionists have not always recognized it as such.

A CENTURY OF RELATIONS

A comprehensive history of composition studies is beyond the scope of this study: I am relying on readers' familiarity with dominant narratives of composition's twentieth century, which have been told, complicated, and retold many times. Despite extensive scholarship on the discipline's formation, there has been little attention to histories of two-year college composition. These institutions receive scant mention in foundational histories of rhetorical education and early revisionist historiographies, which tend to focus on elite university contexts (e.g., Berlin; Brereton; Connors, *Composition-Rhetoric*). Even the Octalogs, with their polyvocal discussions of the politics of inclusion and exclusion in rhetorical historiography, make no mention of two-year colleges (Murphy et al.; Enos et al.; Agnew et al., "Octalog III"; Agnew et al., "Rhetorical Historiography"). This oversight is an epistemological problem with material consequences. As Thomas Miller writes, "when we center 'our' history on research universities, we tend to overlook much of our field of work, and many of our coworkers" (4).

In the last decade and a half, composition has seen a turn toward critical and revisionist historiography more attentive to nonelite and so-called minority-serving institutions (Gold, "Remapping"; see also Kates; Gold, *Rhetoric*; Donahue and Moon; Donahue; Enoch; Kynard; Ruiz). This chapter is indebted to that turn. For context, I draw on the handful of existing historical studies of two-year college composition, which have been produced by both two-year college and university-based scholars. My primary sources are scholarly writings by two-year college composition faculty over the last century, an archive that includes books, journal articles, master's theses, doctoral dissertations, conference papers and proceedings, workshop summaries, organizational reports, and policy papers. Across this archive, I have listened for two-year college voices that have been ignored or forgotten in disciplinary histories.

This method has significant limitations. Most two-year college composition teachers have not written, and still do not write, for scholarly publication. Furthermore, my efforts to compile this archive made clear that, historically, the two-year college composition faculty who have written for scholarly publication have been predominantly—although not exclusively—white full-time faculty. As Taiyon Coleman and colleagues point out, the demographics of two-year college composition faculty "did not just happen. They are a result of the cumulative legacies of violent, historical, cumulative, contemporary, and ongoing institutional exclusion and oppression" (368). The archive reflects the settler colonialism, white supremacy, patriarchy, heterosexism, ableism, and exploitative labor policies that have structured the United States and its postsecondary education system. I have sought out writings by two-year college composition faculty of color in publications in and beyond English studies, and I have endeavored to foreground their intellectual and activist contributions. However, the narrative I present reflects the reality that professional and disciplinary conversations have not included most of the people who have done the work of teaching two-year college composition over the last century.

This narrative focuses on community college–university relations in composition. I trace the development of these relations at three levels: local interinstitutional relations, relations within the profession(s), and relations in disciplinary knowledge making. Other scholars with different investments would have read for and seen other themes in these texts. I present this narrative to situate my call for reimagining community college–university relations within the century-long intellectual history of two-year college composition. Those relations have been the subject of persistent renegotiation across asymmetries of power. I offer this story with a plea for complication and retelling based on localized studies and microhistories that draw on broader archives and oral histories that include more faculty of color, more voices from minority/global majority-serving institutions, and modes of professional and political engagement other than scholarly publication.

Progressive-Era Origins

Two-year colleges and composition emerged from a similar confluence of social, economic, and ideological forces at the turn of the twentieth century. This period saw rapid industrialization, a surge in immigration, and the rise of progressive intellectual and political movements. Critical rhetorical historiographer William DeGenaro argues that "the new junior college and the new writing course at Harvard were born as gatekeepers . . . when leaders of higher education in the United States increasingly came under the influence of the vision of the research university" ("William Rainey Harper" 197). The junior college model was initially promoted as a way for universities to offload lower-division education so research faculty could focus on specialized upper-division and graduate teaching; early junior colleges were often founded as extensions of high schools, their faculty hired from secondary schools (Andelora, "Teacher/Scholar"). In this model, "lower-division teachers were constructed as . . . 'junior' member[s] of academe" (DeGenaro, "William Rainey Harper" 184–85) who blurred the distinction between secondary and postsecondary. While the communities establishing junior colleges often prioritized local access to education that would transfer to four-year institutions, the national junior college movement tended to emphasize nontransfer vocational education (Frye; DeGenaro, "Class Consciousness").

The call for junior colleges was premised on social sorting: many elite advocates saw working-class, often immigrant or first-generation Americans as "undisciplined bodies who needed to be taught taste and to assume their positions within industrial capitalism" (DeGenaro, "Class Consciousness" 500). Like the normal and industrial schools David Gold examines in *Rhetoric at the Margins,* junior colleges were characterized as suitable for those unfit for the rigors of university study or too immature to leave the moral oversight of their families and communities (DeGenaro, "Social Utility," "Class Consciousness," and "William Rainey Harper"; Ford). Many junior colleges were women-only, and at least twenty-eight Black junior colleges were founded in southern states prior to the passage of the Civil Rights Act of 1964 (Lane; C. L. Miller; Beach). Some proponents were straightforward about the "cooling-out" function junior colleges were to serve, suggesting these institutions would "soften the blow of exclusion" by gradually discouraging "less worthy students" from pursuing the baccalaureate (DeGenaro, "William Rainey Harper" 193).

From the founding of the first public two-year institution in 1901, composition "was an essential part of the junior college curriculum," with "the introductory English course . . . modeled closely on that offered in neighboring four-year institutions" (Shugrue 3). In 1931, when Walter Eells reviewed course catalog from 279 of the 405 junior colleges in the United States, 97 percent offered composition courses (491). The emergence of junior colleges coincided with the early professionalization of English teaching, which was marked by the 1911 establishment of NCTE. Junior college faculty were present at NCTE's annual convention by 1919, and, beginning in 1925, they were frequent contributors to NCTE's *English Journal* and, after its 1939 founding, to *College English.* During these decades, they also published dozens of articles in *Junior College Journal* and other education periodicals.

DeGenaro rightly urges us not to romanticize junior colleges during the interwar period ("Social Utility," "Class Consciousness," and "William Rainey Harper"). Analyzing thirteen publications by junior college composition faculty, most of which appeared in *Junior College Journal,* he argues that the pedagogies they promoted were grounded in "a deficit model, wherein the purpose of education becomes compensating for what students lack" ("Social Utility" 131). These approaches "had nothing to do with progressive politics or even active engagement in political discourse and debate. [They] were efforts to produce well-socialized, well-behaved, standardized two-year college graduates" (133). I have compiled an expanded archive of fifty-three scholarly publications by junior college composition faculty published between 1917 and 1945. Nearly half the publications were authored by women, and all writers identified themselves to US census-takers as white. This body of scholarship suggests a more complex ideological portrait than DeGenaro presents. Many of the authors express paternalistic and sometimes outright demeaning views of students, participating enthusiastically in social sorting. Others, however, demonstrate respect for students' intellectual capacities and promote responsiveness to their experiences and interests, advancing versions of what Chris Gallagher calls "pedagogical progressivism." Some describe curricula engaging directly—although not unproblematically—with issues of class, race, and gender, as well as labor struggles, global politics, and the rise of fascism.

By the early 1930s, junior college English faculty were commenting on their relations with four-year colleagues. Some defend their composition curricula by pointing to alignment with university expectations and practices. Many, however, insist open-admissions junior colleges have unique "functions": offering "preparatory" coursework for transfer to four-year institutions (Thomson 160); "popularizing" education in local communities (Thomson 161); providing nontransfer ("terminal" or "vocational") education (Richardson 30); and teaching "remedial" or "sub-freshman" courses (Cook 316). Those functions, they argue, present distinct demands that render university composition curricula "antiquated" and ineffective (Cook 313; Inlow). Although some describe turning to university faculty for curricular consultation (Himes; Rosaire), several express ambivalence about the power universities have to "la[y] down the law for the junior college" (Thomson 160). Others challenge the assumption that university faculty have greater expertise in composition than teachers at two-year colleges. As Melvin Rigg of Oklahoma City College writes,

> The teaching of composition is hard work. It requires training, experience, and enthusiasm. . . . The writer cannot help wondering what is the situation in large universities where the Freshmen are turned over to young graduate students who must in some way or other make a living while they work out their Ph.D.'s. . . . It is one of the opportunities of the junior college, freed as it is from the graduate school, to bring to the teaching of composition men [*sic*] who are especially trained and fitted for the work. (95)

In other words, two-year colleges were not cut-rate imitations of universities. They had structural advantages for the cultivation of faculty expertise in composition. In Briarcliff Junior College dean Alice Rice Cook's estimation, "the junior college has a real contribution to make in the field of the teaching of English" (313). Two-year colleges, these advocates argue, could be sites for knowledge making valuable to instructors at other types of institution.

During the interwar period, "junior" college composition faculty developed curricula with attention to what was happening at nearby universities, but their institutions also presented unique considerations, pressures, and challenges. Several themes regarding two-year–four-year relations emerge from their body of published work that become persistent discursive threads over the next seventy-five years: (1) a desire to participate in professional and scholarly spaces alongside other English faculty, but with *recognition* of the distinctive nature of composition instruction at their institutions; (2) a desire for *validation* of that work, and of junior colleges as sites of curricular and pedagogical innovation that have something to offer the English-teaching professions; (3) an interest in accessing the *resources* university colleagues and professional organizations make available, but a desire to do so on their own terms rather than through top-down mandates or condescending tutelage; and (4) a diverse and sometimes conflicting range of *ideological perspectives* on language, literacy, and education, including occasional willingness to grapple with the politics of composition instruction at open-admissions institutions.

Postwar Professionalization

The decades following World War II were a transformative period for two-year colleges. In 1947, a presidential commission released *Higher Education for American Democracy*, often called "the Truman Commission Report." This report called for the establishment of a national system of public community colleges providing vocational, transfer, and continuing education to all Americans who sought access (Sullivan, *Economic*; Kim and Rury). In 1948, there were 650 two-year colleges in the United States, half of which were public institutions. By 1973, there were 1,141, and 80 percent were public (Cohen et al. 16). Beginning with the establishment of Navajo Community College, Indigenous nations began transforming the idea of the community college to address their self-determined needs and interests. Between 1968 and 1978, when Native activists secured the federal Tribally Controlled Community College Assistance Act, eighteen tribal colleges were founded (Stein; Pease-Pretty On Top).

By the late 1960s, two-year college activists, several of them faculty of color, would become influential figures in the profession—I discuss their activities in the next section ("Profession, Politics, and the Bid for Disciplinary Respectability"). Individual census records from the mid-twentieth century are not yet available to the public, but to the best of my knowledge, all two-year college composition faculty named in the remainder of this section were white.

The period of expansive growth in two-year colleges coincided with the postwar professionalization of composition, initiated by NCTE's establishment of CCCC in 1949. Two-year college faculty were involved in the organization from the outset. They were invited to the first annual convention in Chicago (Andelora, "Professionalization"; Bird), served on that convention's general and local committees ("Founding"), and, until 1959, had four guaranteed representatives on the executive committee (Bird). Reports published in *College Composition and Communication* (*CCC*) demonstrate that, throughout the 1950s, dozens of two-year college faculty attended CCCC each year, participating in conversations that shaped the formation of the field. While lack of institutional support hindered the participation of many, CCCC "became one of the first disciplinary homes for at least a small group of two-year college English faculty" (Andelora, "Professionalization" 7–8). According to Nancy K. Bird of New River Community College, the organization soon recognized that two-year faculty, "while sharing many professional concerns with their colleagues in four-year colleges, had a group of unique problems" (86). The 1957 convention introduced an annual workshop dedicated to two-year college interests ("Teaching Composition/Communication") that continued through the early 1970s.

These workshops focused on the distinct demands of composition instruction at two-year colleges, including the unresolved question of "whether the junior college program should differ from that of the four-year college and university" ("Special" 155). At the 1959 convention, workshop participants voiced "frustration" about their "so-called 'crown colony' status, the assumed determination of the nature of composition courses by four-year colleges or universities to which some of the students transfer" ("Composition/Communication Course" 179). They argued that "junior colleges should independently determine the nature of their courses because of their peculiar problems and in order to maintain their own self-respect" (179). In a 1961 general session on the "Current Status of the Two-Year College," panelists countered widespread misrepresentations of two-year college faculty as undercompensated, underqualified, or consigned to drudgery, arguing that these institutions often attract and retain the best English teachers, in part because they "offer their faculties the free intellectual life" without "the 'publish or perish' rule" (133). The panelists called for more composition research *in* two-year college settings and *by* two-year college faculty, and they called on university-based colleagues in professional organizations to "help" support that work (133).

The initial help was not on two-year faculty members' terms. In 1963, Alfred Kitzhaber of the University of Oregon issued an NCTE/CCCC report based on a review of twenty two-year college course catalogs and syllabi—and, apparently, little or no conversation with actual two-year college faculty. The report makes sweepingly negative pronouncements on the "quality" of two-year college students and describes a professoriate "bear[ing] a closer resemblance to high school faculties than to those of four-year colleges," operating in an "unintellectual if indeed not anti-intellectual atmosphere" (15). In Andelora's estimation, Kitzhaber's report drew needed attention to the rapidly growing two-year college sector but had "a devastating impact on the status of two-year college English faculty and their programs, for years, if not decades, to come" ("Professionalization" 8). Two-year college faculty soon began countering Kitzhaber's representations with their own.

In 1965, an NCTE/CCCC committee chaired by Samuel Weingarten of Wright Junior College and Frederick Kroeger of Flint Community College published a report on their survey of 239 two-year college English instructors. They identified several structural barriers to professionalization, including "excessive teaching load," "lack of administrative encouragement" for scholarship, and "lack of arrangements for attendance at meetings of the professional organizations" (Weingarten and Kroeger xiii). What was needed, the committee argued, was better graduate preparation for two-year college teaching, more national conference activities and journal articles relevant to two-year college contexts, and the establishment of regional conferences specifically for two-year college English faculty. Even as the Weingarten-Kroeger Report argues for the social importance of educational access, it reproduces deficit discourses about two-year college students and their communities based on race, ethnicity, class, and region. However, the report was a clear call to colleagues at baccalaureate-granting institutions to listen to two-year college faculty and respond to their *self*-identified needs, rather than dictating those needs from a university-centric perspective (McPherson, "Remembering").

NCTE/CCCC responded by sponsoring the 1965 National Conference on the Teaching of English in the Junior College. This gathering of seventy-three at Arizona State University, referred to as "the Tempe Conference," included university-based professional leaders from CCCC, NCTE, and the Modern Language Association (MLA), representatives from state and federal offices of higher education, and thirty two-year college English faculty from around the country (Archer and Ferrell 128–31). The published proceedings present a portrait of good intentions but inequitable relations. Many university-based leaders were present, signaling their recognition of the meeting's importance, but the two-year college attendees were outnumbered. Only six of the sixteen scheduled speakers were two-year college faculty. Kitzhaber gave the opening address.

The three-day conference consisted of general sessions and six "seminar study groups" (Archer and Ferrell iii), each of which focused on a major issue in two-year college English. Several of those issues required collaboration between two- and four-year faculty: graduate preparation, curricula for transfer students, and "the relation of junior college English programs to four-year colleges and universities" (Archer and Ferrell iii). The latter seminar's speaker, W.O.S. Sutherland of the University of Texas, ponders the "terms" of those relations (80). Validating the "intellectual integrity" of two-year college faculty (79) and critiquing the tendency of universities to "dominate" (82), he suggests that collaborations across institution type ought to be undertaken "as equals" and at a "limited geographical level" (81). Sutherland's paper demonstrates that university faculty were capable of imagining more equitable relations with two-year college colleagues. However, with Sutherland as the conference's lone voice on this topic, universities were still positioned to set the terms.

All this organizational attention spurred the creation of professional infrastructure for two-year college faculty. In fall 1966, CCCC voted to establish the National Junior College Committee (NJCC), and the following year they passed a constitutional amendment making the NJCC ex officio voting members of the executive committee (Andelora, "Professionalization"; Bird). In spring 1967, two-year college faculty led the implementation of seven regional conferences, with NCTE/CCCC assisting with the planning, funding, and provision of keynote speakers (Andelora, "Professionalization"). These conferences were the seeds of today's TYCA regional organizations: Northeast, Southeast, Midwest, Southwest, West, Pacific Northwest, and Pacific Coast. Over the next decade, combined attendance at the regionals grew to fifteen hundred annually (Andelora, "Professionalization").

The NJCC quickly began advocating for change. In 1968, it released a statement on two-year college faculty workload (National Junior College Committee), and then, in 1971, the "Guidelines for Junior College English Teacher Training Programs" (Cowan et al., "Guidelines"). Throughout the 1970s, specialized graduate programs for two-year college English began to crop up at universities across the country, some of them developed in collaboration with two-year colleagues (Cowan, "1978 National Directory"; Sparrow and Fearing; Kroll, "(Re)Viewing"; Knodt; M. Reynolds, "Checking" and "Response 1"; Jensen and Toth). To many, these developments signaled the successful professionalization of two-year college English (McPherson, "Remembering").

In 1974, faculty in East Carolina University's Graduate Program for Two-Year College English Teachers collaborated with leaders in NJCC and the two-year college regionals to found a new NCTE journal, *Teaching English in the Two-Year College* (Sparrow; Fearing). The launch of *TETYC* was a culminating moment in two-year college faculty efforts to gain professional recognition for their "burgeoning and distinct branch of English studies" (Sparrow 14). Throughout the 1960s and 1970s, two-year college faculty also continued to publish in other NCTE journals as well as in the MLA's *ADE Bulletin* and education periodicals like *Junior College Journal* and *New Directions for Community Colleges*. They produced composition textbooks, edited collections, and guides for professional development (for example, Garrison, *Junior College Faculty* and *Teaching*; Roth and Altshuler; Bobrow et al.; Pickett and Laster; Barton and Beachner; Cowan and McPherson; Friedrich and Kuester; Gibson). Many were involved in other English studies organizations, including the MLA, the College English Association (CEA), and the College Language Association (CLA) (Shugrue; M. W. Davis).

The sense that two-year colleges were coming into their own led some to declare curricular independence. In a 1972 *CCC* article, Audrey Roth of Miami-Dade Junior College reflects on a local meeting she attended in which a university professor spoke disparagingly about the writing abilities of transfer students and insisted that "professors at his university were going to hold the line" (259). The junior college, she writes,

> has reached the point where it is increasingly able to stand up and *be* a junior college, to remove itself from the tyranny of dictatorship by universities. To be an English Department with its own integrity, answering to the community and to its own students and faculty for curricular choices rather than some four-year school the faculty doesn't know and the students won't attend. (263)

For Roth, commitments to local community transcended abstract disciplinary fidelity, including obligations to university-based faculty who neither cultivated relationships with two-year college colleagues nor valued their students. Her assertion that two-year college English had "its own integrity"—that it could and should be evaluated in terms of its own goals and values, rather than in relation to university curricula—was a recurring theme in two-year college writings during this period (see, for example, Worthen, "Implications"; McPherson, "Will" and "Where"; Friedrich and McPherson; Toth, "Getting"). Roth was part of a group of faculty who sought not just to professionalize two-year college English but also to challenge the elitist underpinnings of university-dominated academia. By the late 1960s, long-time CCCC leader Gordon Wilson considered the growing prominence of two-year college English faculty the organization's "most recent and significant" development (17). These faculty shaped what CCCC was becoming as it entered its third decade.

Profession, Politics, and the Bid for Disciplinary Respectability

By the latter half of the 1960s, two-year college English faculty began connecting community colleges' commitment to open admissions and the broader social movements unfolding across the United States. There were hints of this shift in Dick Worthen's response to Kitzhaber at the Tempe Conference. Invoking the Civil Rights Movement, rising student activism, and the "heartless competition" of capitalism ("Implications" 25), Worthen, a white faculty member at Diablo Valley College, argues that English teachers deal with "the most explosive of all bombs, one that man has always policed and exploited—the symbolic process, and . . . our discipline should be illuminating its nature so that it can be taught honestly . . . at any level and with any class" (26). Worthen asserts that two-year college faculty often operate from different values than those at the "multiversity" (24). As he comments, "[W]e have all had our moments when we wished that our colleagues engaged in scholarship would get a little more of the social vision" (27).

In the late 1960s, some two-year college faculty began to push CCCC to get a *lot* more social vision. Among the most influential figures was Ernece Kelly, a Black teacher, scholar, and activist who taught at Chicago City College's Loop Campus. When Dr. Martin Luther King Jr. was assassinated while the 1968 CCCC convention was in session, Kelly delivered a speech, "Murder of the American Dream," which called on the organization to recognize its own pervasive racism (see Smitherman, "Historical Struggle"; Sirc; Kynard for discussions of this speech). The speech was published in *CCC*; later that year, Kelly coedited a special issue of the journal foregrounding the work of Black scholars, and she published with her students in other scholarly spaces (Gabbin et al.; Kynard). Kelly went on to direct the NCTE Task Force on Racism and Bias in the Teaching of English and led the Textbook Review Committee, which produced 1972's *Searching for America*, a landmark collection challenging white supremacy in college literature textbooks. Kelly was an early member of NCTE's Black Caucus, as were Adam Casmier and Betty Pollard of Forest Park Community College, Susan B. Casmier of Florissant Valley Community College, and Vivian I. Davis, who taught at Bishop College, an HBC, and then Tarrant County Junior College and the two-year Eastfield College. (Davis served as the 1978 CCCC chair and went on to receive

NCTE's 1994 Distinguished Service Award.) Indeed, the identity-based caucuses have long been spaces where faculty work across institution types, include two-year college colleges, to pursue social justice within and beyond CCCC. (See M. W. Davis; Blackmon et al.; García et al.).

In "The Historical Struggle for Language Rights," Geneva Smitherman calls Kelly's speech "a symbolic turning point" for CCCC, when "race/Color as a central component of linguistic difference became an in-yo-face issue that the organization could no longer ignore" (14). This moment was also a turning point among some white two-year college faculty who participated in pushing the organization to address social justice issues. The most prominent figures were Gregory Cowan and Elisabeth McPherson (Parks, *Class*; Toth, "Getting"), colleagues of Casmier and Pollard at St. Louis's Forest Park Community College. In 1971, Cowan chaired the NJCC committee that produced the "Guidelines for Junior College English Teacher Training Programs." That document challenges university norms and values with a vision of politically engaged open-admissions education. The statement affirms that two-year college faculty should be grounded in academic knowledge about language and learning, but it also insists those faculty should be dedicated to the critical teaching of rhetoric and composition to *all* students; respectful of two-year college students' languages, cultures, values, and intellectual capacities; and committed to making change within and beyond the academy (see Roth; McPherson, "Remembering"; Jensen and Toth; Toth, "Getting"). With its rejection of the "academic insistence on a so-called 'standard' English for all situations" as "an unrealistic political and social shibboleth based on unsound linguistic information" (305), the "Guidelines" helped provide precedent for CCCC's 1972 Statement on Students' Right to Their Own Language (SRTOL) (Parks, *Class*).

McPherson was the first chair of the NJCC and a contributor to the "Guidelines" document. Smitherman describes her as a "crucial member" of the committee that composed SRTOL ("Historical" 17); two-year college faculty Adam Casmier and Myrna Harrison also served on the committee (see Casmier; McPherson, "Remembering"; Smitherman, "CCCC's Role"; Gilyard). In 1969, McPherson became the first two-year college faculty member to chair CCCC (Friedrich). She brought an activist sensibility to this role that helped shape the organization in the first half of the 1970s. McPherson publicized the work of Kelly's Racism and Bias taskforce (McPherson, "All God's Children"; Friedrich and McPherson) and cofounded NCTE's Committee on the Role and Image of Women in the Council and the Profession (Nilsen). In a 1971 *CCC* essay, Ray Kytle of Central Michigan University observes, "This year's [CCCC] Conference . . . was characterized, in contrast with the past meetings, by heavy student involvement, demonstrations and workshops rather than set speeches, and greater audience participation. It is no coincidence that the program director was Elisabeth McPherson, a junior college teacher" (340). Convention reports from 1971 show two-year college faculty and students spoke in a range of interactive sessions, including several focusing on issues of sexism and racism.[13]

During this period, several two-year college faculty advanced a model of professional identity that engaged public discourse. Through the late 1960s and into the 1970s, Worthen argued against instrumentalist educational policies and for critical literacy pedagogies preparing students for democratic participation (see Worthen, "Junior College English," "Junior College English and the Discipline," and "Changing World"; Worthen and Cohen). In 1971, Cowan urged CCCC to endorse the "People's Peace Treaty," a statement against the Vietnam War (Parks, *Class*). In the mid-1970s, McPherson cofounded NCTE's SLATE program, which pushed the organization's membership to take direct political action and intervene in public debates about language and literacy learning (McPherson, "Remembering"). Vivian Davis made a forceful case for public engagement in her 1978 CCCC Chair's Address, "Our Excellence: Where Do We Grow from Here?" Davis and McPherson were career-long advocates for Black language and against English-only policies in composition classrooms (see Davis, "Teachers" "Paranoia," and "Working"; Wible; McPherson,

"Language," "Then," and "Where"; McPherson et al.; Friedrich; Smitherman, "Historical Struggle"; Toth, "Getting").

In her history of the Black Caucus, Marianna Davis names other white two-year college faculty in NCTE/CCCC who were supporters of racial justice efforts, including Roth, Nancy Prichard of Shoreline Community College, and Lionel Sharp of Cazenovia College, who became chair of CCCC in 1975. CCCC workshop reports from this period name additional two-year college faculty who worked to advance racial and gender equity, including Gabriel Córdova, Francisco H. Ruiz, Bernard J. Raphael, Elisabeth Martin, and Lynn Siegel. While such figures may have been exceptional—as McPherson notes, some of the staunchest opponents of SRTOL were community college teachers ("Remembering")—two-year college faculty paid a collective price for this activism. By the latter half of the decade, what Ira Shor calls the "Conservative Restoration" had set in. Richard Lloyd-Jones, another member of the SRTOL committee, recalls that "[s]ome of the four-year college program directors grumbled about being coerced by two-year college people, by radicals" ("Writing the Resolution" 9). Writing in 1977, Bird reports: "more traditional members have expressed the opinion that CCCC went too far toward egalitarianism, even creating a new 'elite' composed of these newer groups"—that is, "junior college teachers, women, and racial minorities" (210). She observes that CCCC's activist turn was "paralleled by a 38 percent drop in membership" (210), prompting concerns about the organization's future. Between 1972 and 1981, four two-year college faculty chaired CCCC: McPherson, Sharp, Davis, and Lynn Troyka of Queensborough Community College. After Troyka, no two-year college member chaired CCCC again until 1990.

By the 1980s, the boom in new community colleges was over, and neoliberal austerity measures were being put into place nationwide that fueled adjunctification of two-year college teaching. As the number of full-time positions declined, graduate programs for two-year college English teaching dwindled (Fearing; Kroll, "(Re) Viewing"; Buck and Frank). Some were converted into a new kind of program: the PhD in rhetoric and composition (Knodt; Jensen and Toth). While these programs are often celebrated as a benchmark of disciplinary status, scholars like Parks (*Class*; "*Opportunity*"), Trimbur, and Lester Faigley observe that composition's bid for disciplinary respectability in the 1980s was purchased through alignment with elitism. A critical mass of university-based composition scholars distanced themselves from two-year college faculty, perhaps because these colleagues' prominence in CCCC undercut composition's academic stature. Figures like McPherson, who describe their pedagogies as responses to student-activists' demands for community-relevant education ("Composition"), were dismissed by powerful composition theorists as "expressivists" (Fulkerson 411).

Much of the professional infrastructure two-year college faculty built in the 1960s and 1970s functionally isolated them from the discipline in the 1980s. The TYCA regionals had become self-sustaining but were disconnected from NCTE and CCCC (Andelora, "Professionalization"). *TETYC* was valued by many two-year college faculty, but in 1984 Robert Connors described it as "frankly second-rate" ("Review" 358). That assessment apparently absolved generations of university-based scholars from including it in graduate syllabi, literature reviews, or disciplinary histories.[14]

CCC's publication patterns provide another window into the growing university-centrism of composition studies. Between 1970 and 1979, *CCC* published fifty-nine pieces by two-year college faculty, twenty-eight of them after 1974, the year *TETYC* was launched. Between 1980 and 1989, however, only twenty-five pieces by two-year college faculty appeared in *CCC*. Except, perhaps, in the subfield of basic writing (see Otte and Mlynarczyk), university-based scholars largely ignored the intellectual work of two-year college compositionists. One price of composition's ascendant academic fortunes, it seems, was a discipline that excluded two-year college faculty, their knowledge making, and the visibility and interests of their students.

Renegotiating Disciplinary Relations

In his 2007–8 *TETYC* series chronicling the professionalization of two-year college English, Andelora describes the frustrations of the renamed National Two-Year College Committee (NTCC) during the 1980s. As a committee within CCCC, the NTCC had "no revenue stream, hence no ability to develop initiatives or programs, nor did it have any strength in its bargaining position" ("Professionalization" 17). Its members "felt thoroughly disenfranchised" within NCTE, and by their broader "sense of invisibility, lack of a clear professional identity, and lack of a voice at the national level" (16). The year 1990 was a pivot point. Jane Peterson of Richland College became the first two-year college faculty member to chair CCCC in nearly a decade, and CCCC held a breakfast at the annual convention celebrating the twenty-fifth anniversary of the two-year college regionals. This gathering spurred the idea of a national organization ("Professionalization").

Andelora repeatedly characterizes the effort to establish TYCA as a separate association within NCTE as a "fight" ("Professionalization" 17; "TYCA and the Struggle for a National Voice: 1991–1993" [hereafter "1991–1993"] 133; "TYCA and the Struggle for a National Voice: 1994–1997" [hereafter "1994–1997"] 253). This fight surfaced themes present in two-year college composition since the 1930s. Two-year college leaders acknowledged CCCC as a "benefactor" that had "supported NTCC since its inception" (Andelora, "1991–1993" 134), and they recognized shared interests. They wanted to sustain relations with university-based colleagues and remain part of the larger composition community. However, as NTCC chair Helon Howell Raines of Casper College argued, they also believed two-year colleges "should occupy a place in NCTE that was equal to the other major constituents" because "although the 'issues confronting all of us in English education are similar, we also recognize that those issues manifest themselves differently at each level'" (136). Two-year college faculty needed to "'be certain that we determine our own destiny in the NCTE, rather than be assigned a place designated for us by others'" (134). They wanted to renegotiate organizational relations to gain greater recognition of their distinctive roles and contexts, validation of their work, and access to organizational resources on their own terms. This renegotiation promised reciprocal benefits. With expanded representation and resources for two-year college faculty,

NCTE might attract new members at a time when organizational membership was declining (136).

Andelora provides a detailed account of the financial and administrative negotiations that unfolded between 1992 and 1996. It was a frustrating process for Raines and her NTCC successor, Paul Bodmer of Bismarck State College, as well as the other two-year college leaders involved. When progress on negotiations slowed, some two-year college leaders talked of seceding from NCTE, their frustration exacerbated by a history of feeling ignored and undervalued within the organization ("1991-1993"; "1994-1997"). But they persisted, and at the 1997 CCCC Annual Convention, TYCA was launched as an independent association within NCTE. It is worth noting the demographics of this development. Although the TYCA leaders named in this section come from a range of socioeconomic, religious, regional, and ethnic backgrounds, and many are women, to the best of my knowledge (in consultation with senior colleagues who were involved in the formation of TYCA) all identify/identified as white.

As separate sibling organizations within NCTE, TYCA and CCCC remained what Andelora calls "friends with benefits" (Greeting). In 1997, former *TETYC* editor Nell Ann Pickett of Hinds Community College served as the sixth two-year college faculty member to chair CCCC, and Troyka was elected to be TYCA's first chair. TYCA would become an important space for cultivating CCCC leaders. Over the next two decades, John Lovas of De Anza College, Judith (Jay) Wootten of Kent State's two-year Salem Campus, Marilyn Valentino of Lorain County Community College, and Carolyn Calhoon-Dillahunt of Yakima Valley Community College would each serve as TYCA chair before chairing CCCC. These patterns of leadership mediate the complexity of composition's community college–university relations, affirming the distinct transdisciplinary "profession of English in the two-year college" (Reynolds and Holladay-Hicks) *and* the reality that composition—as a curricular category and a disciplinary community—spans two- and four-year institutions.

In the 2000s, TYCA released several position statements addressing the professional status of two-year college English, and university-based compositionists were part of their intended audience. The 2006 "Guidelines for the Academic Preparation of English Faculty in Two-Year Colleges" spoke to the persistent mismatch between curricula in graduate programs and the demands of teaching in two-year colleges. Likewise, TYCA's statement on "Research and Scholarship in the Two-Year College," passed in 2004 and revised in 2010, countered stereotypes of two-year college faculty as "teaching drones, burned-out husks of what we once were, with little time and inclination to stay up-to-date on current scholarship and research" (Tinberg, *Border Talk* vii). These position statements demonstrate that TYCA's efforts to renegotiate disciplinary relations have required contending with university colleagues' assumptions about the nature of two-year college intellectual work while challenging the university-centrism of disciplinary knowledge making.

Two-year college faculty began publishing composition scholarship in 1917 and never stopped. However, their push for professional recognition in the 1990s coincided with a surge in academic publication, much of it speaking to community college–university relations in the discipline. While pushing for the creation of TYCA, Raines wrote several scholarly essays "explaining and claiming our majority" (Nist and Raines, "Two-Year Colleges"; Nist and Raines, "Writing"; Raines). Meanwhile, Keith Kroll of Kalamazoo Valley Community College and *TETYC* editors Mark Reynolds[15] and Howard Tinberg (the latter of Bristol Community College) urged two-year college faculty to "defy the constraints of their institutional cultures and write themselves into the professional conversations," exhortations that amounted to "a campaign to recast ourselves as experienced teachers of writing whose pedagogies and programs were not only worthy of study, but were, in fact, central to the discipline" (Andelora, "Teacher/Scholar" 308; see also Andelora, "Forging"; Kroll, "Empowering"; Sommers, "Two-Year College English Faculty"; Tinberg, "Seeing Ourselves" and "We Do Theory"; Tinberg et al.; Toth and Sullivan). In his 2005 article "The Teacher/Scholar: Reconstructing Our Professional

Identity in Two-Year Colleges," Andelora assesses the 1990s and early 2000s as a period in which two-year college faculty sought to "establish ourselves as viable members of the discipline with a voice that would help shape the future of composition studies" (308). Nearly two decades later, that effort is ongoing.

Since the mid-1990s, two-year college faculty have produced a body of composition scholarship that engages disciplinary conversations but reflects their distinctive teaching contexts and professional roles. Much of this work has appeared on the pages of *TETYC*, which has become more theoretically and empirically grounded over time (Moe; Sommers, "Instructional Note"; Hassel et al., "Editorial Perspectives"), as well as in collections edited by two-year college faculty (see Reynolds, *Two-Year College English*; Alford and Kroll; Reynolds and Holladay-Hicks, *Profession*; Sullivan and Tinberg; Sullivan et al.; Sullivan, *Sixteen Teachers*) and as book-length works (for example, McGrath and Spear; Griffith and Connor; Tinberg, *Border Talk*; Tinberg and Nadeau; Ostman; Rousculp, *Rhetoric*; Sullivan, *New Writing Classroom* and *Economic Inequality*; DeLong et al.).[16] In their 2013 *CCC* article "Occupy Writing Studies: Rethinking College Composition for the Needs of the Teaching Majority," Holly Hassel and Joanne Baird Giordano observe that two-year colleges remain underrepresented in composition scholarship relative to their role in the landscape of postsecondary literacy instruction. However, the needle is moving. Two-year college faculty are increasingly invited to contribute to special issues and edited collections on a range of composition-related topics. They continue to publish articles in "flagship" NCTE journals such as *CCC* and *College English*, as well as disciplinary journals like *Writing Program Administration*, the *Journal of Basic Writing*, *Basic Writing E-Journal*, *Computers and Composition*, *Kairos*, *Across the Disciplines*, *Pedagogy*, *Praxis*, *Composition Forum*, and the *Journal of Writing Assessment* (see Rodrigo and Miller-Cochran). Under the editorship of Steven Parks, CCCC's Studies in Writing and Rhetoric series has foregrounded two-year college literacy studies.

Two-year college composition faculty publish in other areas of English studies, as well as in education, in applied linguistics, and in critical transdisciplinary fields like ethnic, gender, and disability studies. Those who are professionally engaged beyond their institutions frequently attend conferences and hold organizational memberships across multiple disciplinary communities and professional roles (Toth et al., "Distinct"; Toth, "Unmeasured Engagement"). As Tinberg suggests, community college faculty often do not have the same investments as university faculty in patrolling disciplinary boundaries (*Border Talk* and "Teaching English"; see also Reynolds, "Intellectual Work" and "Two-Year College Teachers"; Madden; Toth et al., "Distinct"; Toth, "Unmeasured Engagement"; Griffiths, "Reinventing the Spiel"). That is partly because of hiring practices and professional expectations in two-year college English departments, but also because composition studies has not always produced scholarship that serves two-year colleges well. Its knowledge making often fails to account for the students, institutional missions, material conditions, and faculty roles of the "teaching majority" (Hassel and Giordano, "Occupy Writing Studies"; see also Lovas; Toth and Sullivan; Toth et al., "Two-Year College Teacher-Scholar-Activism"; Giordano and Hassel). Many university-based scholars do not read scholarship by two-year college faculty (Rodrigo and Miller-Cochran), and this "intellectual blind spot" (Lovas 274) results in obliviousness to two-year college contexts in their research (see also Hassel and Giordano, "Occupy Writing Studies"; Toth et al., "Dubious"; Toth and Sullivan; Larson; Jensen, "Political Turn") as well as misrepresentations of "the field" in graduate programs (Jensen and Toth; see also Jensen, *Tilting*; Toth and Jensen; Griffiths, "Professional Autonomy"; Griffiths and Jensen). In the 2010s, these longstanding frustrations converged with national pressures for educational reform to produce calls for another round of renegotiations in community college–university relations in composition studies.

The Teacher-Scholar-Activist (Re)Turn

On March 16, 2017, at the opening session of the CCCC Convention in Portland, TYCA Chair Jeff Andelora delivered a cheeky greeting to the assembled profession:

> Good morning, CCCC. It's time we had that talk again. You know, about our relationship. No, it's nothing you did. In fact, as usual, it's me more than you. First, I want you to know that you've been great from the beginning. Planning that first chilly April 1 meeting in Chicago in 1949, you made sure to invite junior college faculty from ten midwestern states. And by 1956 we were actually on the program—sessions by and for junior college faculty. And then, when the 1960s hit and all hell broke loose with almost five hundred new junior colleges opening their doors . . . you helped sponsor seven regional conferences and the National Junior College Committee. By 1967 we even had voting members on the CCCC Exec Committee! And things were good for a long time—over twenty years of relatively smooth sailing. We were genuinely happy. But then—you know this story—we got a little restless, that twenty-year itch, and I wanted to be more than just a committee. And so after almost five years of "figuring it out," we came up with TYCA—an Association in NCTE . . . . With TYCA, we officially became friends with benefits! . . . But that inaugural was twenty years ago. I'm starting to feel restless again, and I think it's time we take our relationship to the next level. While I'm not sure exactly what that means, this I know: if we strengthen our ties, unite our voices, grow our collective membership, and cultivate new capacities—together—well, that should serve both of us well, at least for another twenty years.

By 2017, many in two-year college literacy studies were experiencing the restlessness Andelora described. From our various positions and commitments, we were trying to figure out what it would mean to take community college–university relations to "the next level"—to work together across institution types to expand educational access and opportunities, particularly with students and communities most threatened by the outcome of the 2016 presidential election. For the TYCA Executive Committee, "the next level" meant establishing a national TYCA conference in conjunction with the annual CCCC convention. The first was held in Pittsburgh in 2019, the fulfillment of a dream dating back to the 1980s (Andelora, "1991–1993"). For me and several of my Salt Lake colleagues, "the next level" meant collaborating across institutions to support transfer student writers, efforts documented in this book (see also Toth et al., "Traveling Together"; Ruffus and Toth; Ruffus et al.; Toth et al. "Bridging Literacies"; Toth, "Not Quite a Love-Letter-Manifesto"). Two months after Andelora made his remarks, SLCC professor Andrea Malouf and I began team-teaching our first summer bridge course for transferring WRS majors, WRTG 3030: Writing across Locations, with Nate Lacy and Cassie Goff as in-class transfer mentors.

That summer, I would also draft an article with Calhoon-Dillahunt and Patrick Sullivan of Manchester Community College arguing for reconstructing the "disciplinary matrix" of composition (Toth et al., "Two-Year College Teacher-Scholar-Activism"). It was a call for university-based colleagues to enact solidarity with two-year college "teacher-scholar-activists" in disciplinary, professional, policy-making, and institutional contexts. The article grew out of a conversation in two-year college literacy studies that had been unfolding since at least 2012. That year, Kroll published a manifesto in *TETYC* titled "The End of the Community College English Profession." It was a dire warning about the impact of neoliberalism on the professional status of two-year college faculty and the need to take political action. In 2013, Andelora penned a response to Kroll titled "Teacher/Scholar/Activist" calling on two-year college English faculty to become public intellectuals, appending the term "activist" to his well-known "teacher/scholar" construct (302). While combining the words "teacher," "scholar," and "activist" was not new, particularly among faculty in ethnic studies, pairing those terms with "two-year college" was.

In 2015, Patrick Sullivan published a *TETYC* article titled "The Two-Year College Teacher-Scholar-Activist," which takes up the term in greater depth, offering an expansive vision of what such a professional identity might entail. The challenges at the end of the Obama administration included neoliberal policies reducing education to instrumentalist job training, community college reform movements that failed to involve faculty in decision making, extreme and growing socioeconomic inequality, and the threats these forces posed to the democratic principle of open admissions ("Teacher-Scholar-Activist"; see also Sullivan, *Economic Inequality*). Sullivan identifies building "commonality and solidarity with four-year institutions" as a necessary part of this activist work, stating the need to "explain . . . to our colleagues at four-year institutions which issues we have in common (so that we can work together on them) and which issues are unique to the two-year college (so that our colleagues at four-year colleges can understand these issues and why they need to care about them)" ("Teacher-Scholar-Activist" 341). Sullivan's essay made community college–university relations a central part of the conversation about two-year college teacher-scholar-activism.

That conversation was galvanized by the 2016 special issue of *TETYC* on the two-year college and national trends/developments in higher education. Particularly powerful was the article "The Risky Business of Engaging Racial Equity in Writing Instruction: A Tragedy in Five Acts," by Taiyon Coleman, Renee DeLong, Kathleen DeVore, Shannon Gibney, and Michael Kuhne. This article bears painful witness to the consequences of white dominance in two-year college English departments and conference spaces. It made clear that teacher-scholar-activism requires interrogating and challenging racial inequities not just in two-year college classrooms, but also within departments and the various professional spaces of the discipline, including organizations like TYCA. My misguided attempt to advance that work through a proposed edited collection on race and two-year college composition demonstrates that community college–university relations are fraught with risks of appropriation and colonization, particularly when white, university-based researchers fail to maintain awareness of how our positionality is shaping our professional interactions (see DeLong et al. 2–4).

Two-year college English faculty are, as Sullivan observes, "heirs to a robust activist tradition" ("Teacher-Scholar-Activist" 327). The term "teacher-scholar-activist" gives name to work that has been going on since at least the 1960s. There has always been an activist element to two-year college faculty members' fight for recognition in composition's hierarchical, normatively four-year disciplinary structures, and this fight has, at some junctures, been in explicit solidarity with broader social justice movements. During his 2001–06 tenure as *TETYC* editor, Tinberg fostered an activist scholarly sensibility that his successors Jeff Sommers (2006–16), Holly Hassel (2016–2020), and now Darin Jensen have continued to cultivate (see Hassel; Hassel et al., "Editorial Perspectives"). Since the late 2000s, TYCA itself has been moving toward an increasingly public orientation (see Calhoon-Dillahunt, "Finding"; "We've Come a Long Way") visible in its 2015–2016 white papers on developmental education reform (Hassel et al., "TYCA White Paper") and on placement assessment (Klausman et al.), as well as in its 2017 guidelines for graduate preparation (Calhoon-Dillahunt et al.; see also Johnson). Each of these documents calls for solidarity from university-based colleagues and resources from shared professional organizations.

While teacher-scholar-activism is not new, the term has proved useful to some working toward institutional, organizational, and disciplinary change. Since 2015, it has appeared as a key concept in two-year college-related conference presentations and *TETYC* articles. Under Jensen's leadership, *Teacher-Scholar-Activist* became the title of a blog featuring essays by writing faculty across educational sectors. The term has surfaced in scholarly publications beyond *TETYC*, framed a special issue of *Basic Writing E-Journal*, and made its way into the call for proposals for the 2019 National TYCA Conference. In an echo of Kelly and McPherson's commitments to foregrounding student perspectives, Sullivan has published community college student-authored writing alongside his calls for teacher-scholar-activism (*Economic Inequality*, "Meet My English 93 Class", and *Sixteen Teachers*).

Calhoon-Dillahunt, Sullivan, and I describe this phenomenon as a "teacher-scholar-activist turn" in two-year college literacy studies. Considering the histories I have reviewed in this chapter, I now think it might be better understood as a *re*-turn, one Jensen situates within a broader "political turn" in composition studies fueled by the 2016 presidential election ("Political Turn"). I have been a participant in the collective effort to think through what this (re)turn might mean for the wider discipline, labor that has shaped my unsteady efforts to become what I would consider a university-based professor worth being. I cannot disentangle my participation in these national conversations from the local work I have been doing with students and faculty at SLCC.

BRINGING DISCIPLINARY HISTORIES HOME

Here are the guiding insights for reimagining community college–university relations I draw from these histories as I have been reading, reconstructing, and living them over the last decade—insights that have shaped this book and the programmatic work it documents:

- Community college–university relations must proceed from a recognition of the distinctive nature of two-year college composition: its complex institutional histories, contexts, and missions; the evolving transdisciplinary professional roles of its faculty; the ever-changing local diversities of its students; and the material conditions in which those students strive to learn and their faculty to teach. Two-year college composition must be understood on its own terms, rather than through university-centric disciplinary lenses.
- Community college–university relations must be built on validation of the democratic ideal of open admissions, as well as an appreciation for what makes two-year colleges distinct. These relations must recognize that, while institutional differences can present challenges for two-year college faculty and students, they also provide unique intellectual and pedagogical possibilities. Two-year college contexts offer affordances, relationships, local knowledges, and academic freedoms to which university-based faculty might not have access, and from which they stand to learn.
- Validation does not mean romanticization. No one should suspend critical awareness of the roles two-year colleges and two-year college composition instruction have played

and continue to play in reproducing racial and other social inequities. Likewise, no one should forget that four-year institutions and their faculty have always been complicit in these hierarchical systems and contributed in the inequities that result. Recognizing disparities should provide an impetus for working together across institution types to challenge those injustices and expand opportunities for two-year college students and faculty.

- Community college–university relations must proceed from a recognition that resources are not distributed equally across institution types. Faculty and students at two- and four-year institutions have access to different kinds of resources, knowledges, and opportunities, all of which are valuable. However, university-based faculty often have access to money, time, professional development opportunities, research infrastructure, and institutional authority two-year college faculty might not. We can and should work to share resources across institutions on terms established through mutual negotiation and grounded in common commitments to the students who attend two-year colleges, particularly students of color and students from low-income and working-class backgrounds.
- Following teacher-scholar-activists like Kelly, McPherson, and Sullivan, we should involve two-year college students in collaborative knowledge making, organizational work, and interinstitutional partnerships. They know what learning opportunities they want for themselves and for their communities, and they can help make sure faculty enact disciplinarity in ways that center students' interests and wellbeing. They are the primary reason for—and, to a significant degree, the mediators of—interinstitutional relations. They are the future of our respective professions, shared discipline, and communities. They are essential collaborators in making knowledge that "really matters in the world" (Maher 166).

In their closing chapter, the editors of *Composition, Rhetoric, and Disciplinarity* ask readers to consider "what kind of discipline we are and want to be" (Malenczyk et al. 331). I am perhaps among their more recalcitrant readers: suspicious of expertise as a form of dominance, terrified to my bones that the academy, in all its coloniality, is not so different from the military in which I grew up. And yet, five years into helping build a freestanding WRS department that attempts to structure community colleges into what it is and does, I find myself in cautious agreement with those editors. They assert that composition studies can more effectively take responsibility for challenging literacy-related social injustices—and better position itself to influence higher education policy and faculty labor conditions—if its embraces an "open, networked, and continuously emergent" model of disciplinarity (Reid and Miller 96) rooted in values like inclusion, access, difference, social interaction, rhetorical production, and amplifying nondominant voices (Wardle and Downs, "Understanding"). That sounds a lot like the discourse of writing ecologies. Like Rodrigo and Miller-Cochran, I believe that composition studies can only enact those values if we co-construct a discipline that accounts to and for two-year colleges, the faculty who teach in them, and the students who attend them. To me, that is the only kind of discipline worth being.

Interstitial III:

Claudia's Theory of Writing

REFLEXIÓN

THIS MORNING AS I WHINED about having to get up, I swiped the "dismiss" icon on my phone's alarm and got on it to check Facebook, as usual nothing new since I checked last night, just a game invite to Candy Crush from my distant uncle. I began to look for any excuse to stay in bed, so I started looking through my profile pictures to relive all the likes and hearts, the "You're so cute!" and "Fiu" from my now-forgotten friends in Mexico. Then, I caught her looking at me, the moment our gazes met it was like the past was looking at the future and there wasn't an in between, like the span of time hadn't passed and I traveled in a time machine from 2011 to 2016 skipping all the years in between—there she was a stranger in the past watching me through the screen today.

Time travels faster than neurons can blast electric signals that tell my fingers to type, although it's almost instantaneous writing to me always seemed like such a drag. Nothing in High School had ever inspired me to write, in fact I have been avoiding writing papers at all costs, and even attempted to get through Community College without writing an essay but of course I couldn't get away with it. The writing process always was: Spend as little time as possible on this dreadful task,

accidentally indent your paragraphs twice,
make the font size 12.5 slightly bigger than 12,
press enter twice to leave more space on a new page,

leave two spaces between words, utilize an abundance
of utterly pretentious and inadequate lexicon, do anything
except write, fill up five pages of empty thoughts.

Every time I had a new assignment, my personal time machine autopilot would take over, writing from point A to point B, just getting things done, and in the dead air of time I was never able to find out what I was capable of writing. Writing about this now I wonder how long has the autopilot been writing for me, and why did I let it take over?

Claudia, 1997, Querétaro, México

Ahí estoy, tengo cinco años brinco en la cama, y me gusta jugar a las escondidillas. Me gusta ir a el kindergarten porque tengo muchos compañeros, y estoy aprendiendo el alfabeto en ingles y español. Estoy sentada esperando a que nuestra maestra de ingles pase a nuestro salón, todos mis compañeros están sentados muy callados y bien portados pero al entrar la maestra mi piloto automático se encendió, comencé a gritar "FUERA! NO ME GUSTA TU CLASE", y de repente había un salón lleno de mocosos echando a la solloza maestra de ingles, que salio escabulléndose, jamas la volvi a ver. Pero el tiempo pasa, y ahora estoy en el tercer grado de primaria, siempre me saco el primer lugar en los exámenes de mi salon, me encanta leer y jugar con mis cotorritos australianos, son mis mejores amigos. Ahora mi relación con la escritura es leer libros de historia prehispánica y ya puedo leer instrucciones de mi tarea sin ayuda.

Llegó al cuarto año escolar, pero ya no estoy en casa ahora estoy en Coper jills elementari y no se hablar, escribir, ni leer Inglish-pikin-glish y ya no hay necesidad de read mis libros favorite. I suddenly became illiterate, I couldn't understand what anyone was saying, just the few words I learned when I was five and all of the things I had learned about reading and writing in Spanish didn't matter anymore, the stories I loved, the songs I cherished, and finally I understood how overwhelmed that girl must have been at that moment when her sprouting world froze in time, the autopilot stayed on to help her get by, and has been writing her storyline since.

OFF THE WALL

Self-portraits by Claudia, 2014.

There were only two things I understood how to do, draw pictures and color, that was the only thing in my new fourth grade class that got me first place to anything. So every day after school I would come to a house stuffed with three families, and retreat to the empty basement of my aunt's house, where I would spend my time with my sketchbook, drawing pictures of made-up characters who became my new friends; it was my new way of writing and reading. Meanwhile as time passed I learned English and tried every day to erase my "Mexican" accent because having an accent meant I would be alone.

Ironically, I learned English even better than my shamed kindergarten teacher. Quickly I mastered this elitist language and its incoherent grammar, much faster than my peers who still had to take ESL through Jr. High. Reading the English dictionary became my new hobby, to learn impressive words proving I was just as good as everyone else, and by now when someone notices my skin tone then follows it up with this remark: "You're Mexican? You speak English very well! You don't even have an accent!" I took pride in hearing these comments, but what did I know? At the time all I wanted was to be the same. In a way I never stopped playing hide and seek, but the game turned to only hiding, so I stayed in the basement writing poems:

Itzel

I am born from
Debris of volcanic stone from el Cerro de Culiacán
Out of buried pyramids of the Otomí and Mexica
Once bathe by Laja

I am from
An adobe house, blessed by los campos
Where the
Nahuatl of my great grandmothers made us atole
And the work of my great grandfathers gave us Elote

I am from
The longing of mi mama to have a whole family
And the ventures of mi papa to have enough to provide
I am from the survival of the desert
As my sisters held my hand

I grew from
"Tienes que aprender Inglés"
Or
You won't make it

I am from the resilience of past generations
As I stumble to stand

Claudia Sauz Mendoza wrote this essay in December 2016, the end of her first semester at the U. It was her final assignment in WRTG 3020: Write4U, an upper-division writing course our research team designed for incoming transfer students. We were piloting that course the semester Claudia enrolled. "Reflexión" was the last of three revisions to a "theory of writing" statement students drafted in the first weeks of the term—an assignment adapted from the Teaching for Transfer (TFT) curriculum in Kathleen Blake Yancey, Liane Robertson, and Kara Taczak's book *Writing across Contexts: Transfer, Composition, and Sites of Writing*. In her accompanying reflection on the final version of this statement, Claudia wrote, "I attempted to embody my theory of writing instead of saying it." This embodiment expanded my conception of the critical work this assignment, the course, and our transfer programs could perform.

In her reflection, Claudia stated, "I really enjoyed the flexibility of this assignment and used it to broaden my scope of what writing can be." When I read her essay, I am moved by how powerfully she transferred—*transformed*—far more than school-based English literacies, struck by how she gazes from the page with steady eyes: theorizing writing on her own terms, confident academic readers should be the ones to blink. Claudia's intellectual labor is not a one-way importation of "skills" learned at the community college, not a function of "articulation agreements" or a shared "framework for success," not the product of a singular transfer "pipeline" or "pathway." Nor is it a rehearsal of "key terms" from writing studies, although many of the disciplinary concepts we discussed that semester—discourse, identity, language ideology, genre, meta genre, multimodality—are embodied in this text. Her theory is situated and material, adapting and repurposing many kinds of knowledge gained across an array of literacy experiences, in and out of school, across times, places, languages, genres, technologies, and modalities.

In Chapter 1, Claudia poses questions that haunt me: "Why does academia need to validate experiences? What evidence should I include to convince you my experiences are real?" As Dimpal

Jain and colleagues observe in *Power to the Transfer*, a core tenet of critical race theory is "the centrality of experiential knowledge," often presented in narrative forms. They assert that "the actual lived experiences of students of color through the transfer process matter and should be included in order to make socially just changes in a transfer receptive culture" (23–24). "Reflexión" suggests how inadequate a narrow, deficit-oriented construct of "academic preparedness" is when accounting for the range of writing knowledges students can transfer to the university, and how those knowledges might change institutional and disciplinary ecologies.

Claudia seemed to enjoy thinking, talking, and writing about writing the way we did in WRTG 3020. In Spring 2017, she declared a WRS major, joined the transfer research team, and became a coauthor of this book. Over the next two years, she was an essential partner in developing the transfer programs emerging from our research. She was in-class transfer mentor for WRTG 3020 in fall 2017, and in spring 2018 she became our first Co-Coordinator of Transfer Initiatives, a paid undergraduate position she created and held until she graduated in spring 2019. In that capacity, Claudia connected dozens of SLCC students with our summer programs and other transfer resources. In collaboration with Writing Studies Scholars Joseph Moss and Kelly Corbray, she created a free textbook lending library and experimented with models of peer-led writing support that would provide transfer students, particularly students of color, with an alternative to the university's writing center (Castillo et al.). In 2018, she developed a peer-led bilingual writing studio that now accompanies our SLCC bridge courses each summer.

Claudia's activist work extended beyond our transfer initiatives. In fall 2017, she and Nic Contreras led a series of community write-ins pressing elected officials to support Dreamers. A year later, she became the department's first WRS Dream Center Fellow, a position she developed in collaboration with the U's Dream Center staff to provide individualized writing assistance to DACA and unDACAmented students and their families in locations where they were comfortable meeting. I name Claudia's efforts here not to take credit for her work—it is hers, and hers to write about if she chooses—but to recognize her labor, which has transformed my own. Claudia's labor spans institutions and communities in a way only that of a transfer student with her experiences, knowledges, identities, and rhetorical capacities could.

Since Claudia graduated, several students have taken up the positions she created and reimagined those roles through their own experiential knowledges. Jose Loeri, Adi Tolentino, and Jem Ashton have each been in-class transfer mentors for WRTG 3020. As co-coordinator of transfer initiatives, Kimberly Gamarra expanded our social media presence and online recruitment activities, and her successor Jem reimagined our out-of-class events and designed a WSS peer-mentoring program. Cristina Guerrero Perez ran the bilingual summer writing studio, and she and Stef Zavala further developed the WRS Dream Center Fellowship in collaboration with SLCC's Dream Center in West Valley City; Jessica Begay adapted this model to provide on-location writing support for students at the U's American Indian Resource Center. Heather Graham piloted an online writing studio to support WSS students taking remote classes during the COVID-19 pandemic. Our transfer programs continue to change with each wave of students who make those programs what they need in their moment. In an ecology, change is inevitable, but Claudia's refusal of "the autopilot" and the knowledge she contributed to our local instantiation of academia will always be real to me.

FROM CLAUDIA IN 2021

Here I am reflecting on my reflection again. In case you were worried, I'm happy to say that I've retired the autopilot and no she's not a stranger anymore. My first instinct was to critique "Reflexión" but I refuse to pick apart my writing from five years ago and although I can point out syntax and punctuation "errors," I won't do it. I wonder what it was like for you to read it. Were you able to look beyond the grammar and see the person who wrote it? Ultimately it comes down to two things: acceptance and honoring. Accept students into the classroom as they are. Create curriculum that will allow students to honor their own knowledges as a foundation to acquire new academic knowledge and not lower their grades based on grammar.

Lastly, I've answered my own angst-ridden questions: "Why does academia need to validate experiences? What evidence should I include to convince you my experiences are real?" It doesn't; I don't need nor do I want academic validation. I know my experiences are real and that's enough. It wasn't the grades or the conferences we presented at or this book even, it was the confidence that grew as the result of being accepted and honored through this project and all my professors who saw me struggle with deadlines but worked with me anyway, met with me outside the classroom when I couldn't stand Rancière, and believed in my ideas. Being shown that humanity and kindness is what helped me believe myself when I say "I am a writer."

3

Toward Transfer-Conducive Writing Ecologies

In 2020, Dimpal Jain, Santiago Bernal Melendez, and Alfred Herrera published *Power to the Transfer: Critical Race Theory and a Transfer Receptive Culture*, the culmination of a decade of work developing their titular concept. Historically, the onus to "prepare" students to transfer to universities has been placed on community colleges, which are blamed for low and inequitable transfer rates. Throughout the 2010s, Jain and colleagues wrote a series of articles arguing that two- and four-year institutions have a *shared* responsibility for creating conditions that facilitate transfer (Herrera and Jain; Laanan and Jain, "Advancing"; Jain et al., "Developing"). Universities, they argue, must make "an institutional commitment . . . to provide the support needed for students to transfer successfully" (Jain et al., "Critical Race Theory" 253). Grounding their arguments in tenets of critical race theory, they assert that honoring this commitment requires challenging ideologies of meritocracy and race neutrality that mask structures of privilege and oppression in postsecondary education.

Transfer-receptive culture is not the only framework available for theorizing universities' responsibilities for transfer. Jain and colleagues identify two concepts in the higher education literature similar to transfer-receptive culture: "transfer affirming culture" (Handel) and "a transfer student receptive ecosystem" (Strempel).[17] Despite some conceptual overlap, they observe that "a critical examination of race is absent from both frameworks—and not just of the racialized experiences that students of color may face, but also the historical and contemporary racial legacy that often exists between universities and their community college partners" (*Power*,

36). A transfer-receptive culture, they argue, "is explicitly guided and anchored by critical race theory and centers transfer students of color in its analysis and application" (36). Colorblind transfer research and initiatives fail to address—and may reinforce—racial inequities.

Jain and colleagues identify five elements that contribute to transfer-receptive culture at universities, including (1) establishing "transfer of students, especially nontraditional, first-generation, low-income, and underrepresented students" as an institutional priority; (2) partnering with community colleges to provide extensive pretransfer outreach that "complement[s] the community college mission"; (3) developing "distinct" financial and academic support for transfer students whereby "they are stimulated to achieve at high academic levels"; (4) valuing students' "lived experiences" and the important roles their communities and families play in their education; and (5) creating "appropriate and organic frameworks from which to assess, evaluate, and enhance transfer receptive programs and initiatives that can lead to further scholarship on transfer students" (Jain et al., "Critical Race Theory" 258). Crucially, a transfer-receptive culture rejects deficit discourses about transfer students, believing instead that "students will be successful *because* they are transfer students" (253) who bring academic, experiential, and community knowledges that make important contributions to the entire campus (see also Jain et al., "Developing"; Jain et al., *Power*; Pérez and Ceja; Urias et al.; Castro and Cortez).

Jain and colleagues' model for transfer-receptive culture encompasses systemic changes to business as usual at universities, including recruitment and admissions practices, credit articulation, housing policies, and institutional research, as well as student services, financial aid, and academic support. Beginning in 2015, our transfer research team sought to understand how *writing* factors into the inequities Jain and her colleagues challenge, and how WRS might contribute to creating a more transfer-receptive culture at the U. Over the next three years, we put what we learned from the higher education literature in conversation with composition scholarship, local research on transfer student writing experiences, and our emerging theorization of Salt Lake's writing ecology. In 2018, we began experimenting with the phrase *transfer-conducive writing ecologies* to describe the kind of interinstitutional disciplinary relations we sought to cultivate. In this chapter, I develop the idea of transfer-conducive writing ecologies: not as an alternative to Jain and colleagues' concept of transfer-receptive culture, but as a discipline-specific, writing-focused framework aimed at advancing a transfer-receptive culture in local contexts.

First, I introduce concepts from the higher education literature on community college transfer that inform how we imagine transfer-conducive writing ecologies. Then, I review the composition literature regarding transfer students that has shaped our imagining. Finally, I present select findings from the mixed-method study of transfer student writing experiences we conducted in 2015–16. This local study provided a snapshot of how transfer students were experiencing our interinstitutional writing ecology and what changes would better support their transitions. I suggest the discipline's surge of interest in the transfer of writing knowledge—what the Elon University Research Seminar calls "critical transitions" (Moore and Anson 3)—demands attention to transfer *students*. As we discuss in Chapter 1, these writers are always emplaced, embodied, and historically situated. The conditions in which they are adapting writing knowledge are always material as well as social and academic, and many face structural disadvantages that must be countered with intent. However, they are also uniquely positioned to develop rhetorical meta-awareness and contribute to disciplinary knowledge making *because* they are transfer students. Meeting disciplinary responsibilities to these students might require composition studies to undertake some critical transitions of its own.

FROM TRANSFER-RECEPTIVE TO TRANSFER-CONDUCIVE

One of the most cited concepts in the higher education literature on transfer students is *transfer shock*, which refers to a temporary dip in grade point average during a transfer student's initial term at a four-year institution. This literature suggests that, while some community college students experience transfer shock, the effect is not universal, is usually temporary, and is often associated with specific courses or fields of study. On average, community college students who transfer to four-year institutions complete bachelor's degrees at rates similar to or higher than those of their nontransfer peers (Bahr et al., "Review"). Contrary to elitist assumptions, transferring from a community college does not necessarily mean a student will struggle at a university. Nonetheless, the higher education literature documents barriers and challenges many transfer students face. In the following pages, I discuss three critical concepts from this literature that inform our conceptualization of transfer-conducive writing ecologies: *racial transfer gaps*, *(transfer) capital*, and *transfer stigma*.

Racial transfer gaps. Nationally, 81 percent of entering community college students say they aspire to a bachelor's degree, but only 33 percent transfer to a four-year institution within six years (Jenkins and Fink) and just 16 percent earn a bachelor's degree (Shapiro et al., *Completing College: A National View of Student Attainment Rates—Fall 2010 Cohort*). The term "racial transfer gap" (Martinez-Wenzl and Marquez 6) refers to racial disparities in those already troubling figures. One in four Asian and Asian American and one in five white students who start at two-year colleges complete a bachelor's degree within six years, compared with one in ten Latinx students and one in twelve Black students (Shapiro et al., *Completing College: A National View of Student Attainment Rates by Race and Ethnicity—Fall 2010 Cohort*).[18] These are compounding inequities: Black and Latinx students are both *more* likely than white or Asian and Asian American students to attend community colleges and *less* likely to transfer successfully to four-year institutions (see Wassmer et al.; Pérez and Ceja; Martinez-Wenzl and Marquez; Crisp and Nuñez; Castro and Cortez; Laanan and Jain, "Advancing"; Jain et al., "Developing").

Thus community college transfer students may be as academically successful as nontransfer peers "on average," but those figures only include students who transfer, and that group is disproportionately white. Writing assessment scholars like Asao Inoue, Mya Poe, and Norbert Elliot have argued for the importance of disaggregating multiple forms of outcomes data to identify and counter racial inequities (Inoue, "Racial Methodologies" and *Antiracist Writing Assessment Ecologies*; Inoue and Poe; Poe and Inoue; Poe et al.; Poe and Cogan; Elliot), and this principle extends to transfer students (Laanan and Jain, "Advancing"; Jain et al., *Power*). Working toward transfer-conducive writing ecologies requires disaggregating data to identify whether transfer rates are inequitable and determine how different groups fare post-transfer. Those disaggregated data can and should include outcomes related to writing.

As Inoue observes, racial formations are a function of "local diversities" (*Antiracist Writing Assessment Ecologies,* 68), and local studies can reveal transfer gaps for specific racial, ethnic, and tribal communities obscured by broad racial categories in national data. For example, research team member Joanne Castillo notes that the broad category "Asian" obscures potential transfer disparities affecting students from Salt Lake's Southeast Asian communities. Similarly, as Nic Contreras and Claudia Sauz Mendoza point out, the categories "Hispanic" or "Latinx" lump together communities in the valley with distinct identities, histories, and privileges. Furthermore, transfer experiences are intersectional: race, ethnicity, and/or Indigeneity can intersect with class, gender and sexual identities, language background, nationality, documentation status, cultural and religious factors, age, disability, and/or veteran status to produce local transfer gaps (Jain et al. *Power*). In transfer-conducive writing ecologies, institutional agents work together continuously to identify and close these gaps.

<u>(Transfer) capital</u>. Until recently, the dominant theoretical framework in the literature on transfer students has been *integration*—transfer students' sense of academic and social belonging at four-year institutions—and associated behaviors, often discussed in terms of *involvement* or *engagement* (Bahr et al., "Review"). Studies employing these frameworks suggest that social integration is typically less important to transfer students than academic integration. Traditional university social activities

often don't appeal to transfer students, who typically live off campus and are pursuing education alongside work and other life responsibilities. Instead, transfer students tend to develop social connections through engagement in the classroom and through co-curricular activities associated with their academic interests and professional goals (Townsend and Wilson, "'A Hand Hold'" and "Academic"; Reyes; Bahr et al., "Review").

These frameworks focus on what students do—whether they "integrate" or "get involved"—and highlight the importance of creating opportunities for transfer students to engage in ways that are accessible and relevant to their goals. However, Peter Bahr, Kathryn Thirolf, Johanna Massé, and I have sought to move the frame to theories of *capital*, which have

> the potential to shift the analytical focus from students' behaviors to the ways in which *receiving four-year institutions* might privilege cultural knowledge and social connections that students from nontraditional or underrepresented backgrounds (who are overrepresented among community college students) are less likely to possess. (Bahr et al., "Review" 491, emphasis mine)

Theories of capital foreground how the inequitable distribution of social and material resources can constrain students' opportunities; they encourage scrutiny of the *institution's* structures and choices rather than student behavior. Pierre Bourdieu argues that educational systems reproduce social inequities in part through differences in knowledge, attitudes, manners, values, and *habitus*—that is, habitual ways of using language, moving one's body, dressing, and behaving in social contexts—that mark class distinctions. Ways of knowing and being associated with the dominant group—in the United States, affluent white people—are often privileged in academic and professional settings (Inoue, *Antiracist Writing Assessment Ecologies*). These ways of knowing and being constitute a kind of wealth, or capital, that is not equitably distributed. What some higher education researchers call *transfer student capital* (Laanan et al.), or "accumulated knowledge about how to negotiate the transfer process" (Bahr et al., "Review" 493), might be understood as a form of cultural capital, one that some families and communities—often, those that are white, middle-class, and US-born—possess in greater quantities. Differences in cultural capital can contribute to racialized transfer gaps.

In Bourdieu's work, cultural capital is linked to social capital: the network of acquaintances into which one is born or to which one can gain access through social, educational, and professional connections. These networks are ecological, in the sense that they are social, material, emplaced, and emergent. Information and other resources circulate through these networks, and the denser one's social connections, the greater access and potential mobility one has. It is important to recognize that transfer students *do* possess important cultural and social capital (Urias et al.; Castro and Cortez; Jain et al., "Developing"; Jain et al., *Power*), some of which might not be valued in university spaces but is central to their relationships, identities, and lives as whole people. However, not all transfer students have equitable access to the capital that might help them navigate the transfer process, engage the full range of resources and learning opportunities at the university, and secure post-graduation employment that aligns with their goals. Universities offer but do not guarantee access to forms of capital on which social mobility can depend. In transfer-conducive writing ecologies, such capital accrues to *all* students, and the knowledge and relationships transfer students bring are recognized, valued, and invited into their writing.

Transfer stigma. The term *transfer stigma* describes the consequences of negative social perceptions of community colleges and the students who attend them (Alexander et al.; Bahr et al., *Transition Processes*). Grounded in the work of sociologist Erving Goffman, *stigma* refers to the social disapproval or marginalization resulting from disjunctures between the *virtual* identity—that is, the ideal characteristics and qualities—of an individual in a social setting and that individual's *actual* identity (Goffman; Bahr et al., "Review"). If the virtual identity of "university student" is someone who enrolls at a selective-admissions residential four-year institution right after high school, community college transfer students may be stigmatized, with negative effects on their well-being and access to opportunities.

Experiences of stigma often come through transfer students' interactions with peers at the four-year institution, who may view transfers as "back-door" admits who have circumvented the competitive admissions process (Alexander et al.). Stigma might also be perpetuated by university admissions staff, advisors, and faculty who communicate negative assumptions about transfer students' academic preparation or ignore their presence entirely, thereby signaling that transfer is not a normative academic trajectory. Members of our research team point out that stigma is also communicated through popular culture and its representations of college life, as well as the ways community colleges are talked about among students' families and friends, high school personnel, and other people in their communities. Transfer stigma is an ecological phenomenon emerging from interrelated forces within and beyond the university, and countering it requires ecological change. Transfer-conducive writing ecologies disrupt rather than reproduce transfer stigma.

Jain and colleagues refuse to frame discussions of transfer students in terms of "a remediation model or a deficit narrative" (Jain et al., *Power* 48). They urge readers to understand community colleges as "centers of diverse scholar production," and to "conceptualiz[e] transfer students as scholars" who are "essential to the fabric of academia" (48). They describe their programs as fostering *transfer pride* (see also Jain et al., "Developing"). Thus, transfer-receptive culture shifts the terms of debate away from the stigmatizing focus on whether community colleges adequately "prepare" students for the university. Instead, it confronts universities' failures to create institutional environments that support transfer students, particularly low-income and working-class transfer students of color. Transfer-conducive writing ecologies embrace this antideficit orientation and shared responsibility for supporting equitable transfer (see Urias et al. 25 for further articulation of this "antideficit, institutional responsibility" approach). Writing is part of academic structures that oppress many transfer students, but writing also offers means for confronting and potentially changing those structures.

Why propose *transfer-conducive writing ecologies* as a distinct term? For me, this shift has three purposes: (1) decentering the university, (2) foregrounding composition's discipline-specific stakes in interinstitutional transfer, and (3) recognizing how transfer relations and responsibilities are co-constituted with locations. The word "receptive" calls necessary attention to universities' unmet responsibilities to transfer students. However, "conducive" foregrounds the *multidirectional* flow of discourses and ideas, forms of capital, and physical bodies between community colleges, universities, and the communities in *and lands on* which they are situated. Fostering transfer-conducive ecologies requires recognizing existing disciplinary, professional, and pedagogical relations, as well as the mutual, emplaced responsibilities those relations entail. It requires cultivating relations that are more conducive to students' agentive movements across the physical and bureaucratic structures of institutions: densifying, diversifying, and demystifying networks to create more conductivity. It demands an explicit commitment to countering transfer stigma and forging relations that increase transfer and close local transfer gaps. Transfer-conducive ecologies create opportunities for more *critical* transfer of writing knowledges across institutions and communities. To theorize the kinds of ecological change that might be conducive to such transfer, I turn to the composition literature.

TRANSFER STUDENTS IN COMPOSITION STUDIES

No higher education studies focus on how reading, writing, and negotiating language differences factor into community college students' post-transfer transitions, but there are hints in this literature that academic literacies play an important role (Bauer and Bauer; Laanan, "Making" and "Studying Transfer Students: Part I" and "Part II"; Townsend; Castro and Cortez). In her qualitative study of transfer student "survival" at a large public research university, Barbara Townsend found that "[e]ight of the nine students indicated that university faculty required more writing, both for assignments and for tests, than did community college faculty. As one student said, 'I have found that the key to doing well at the university is being able to write'" (183). Yet composition studies has been slow to address the writing experiences of transfer students. I have located only four publications focusing primarily on the writing experiences of community college transfer students (Mathison; Goldblatt; Alexander; Gere et al.).

In recent composition scholarship, the term *transfer* has been used to discuss how students "boundary-cross," "remix," "repurpose," "generalize," "integrate," "adapt," or "transform" writing knowledge across contexts ("Appendix A" 347–50). One might expect this wave of research, which Yancey positions at the heart of the "disciplinary turn" (17), to view transfer between two- and four-year institutions as a central concern. To date, however, the transfer literature has reflected the pervasive university-centrism of composition studies. As Holly Hassel, Mark Reynolds, Jeff Sommers, and Howard Tinberg point out, the landmark collection *Critical Transitions: Writing and the Question of Transfer*, does not include a single reference to community colleges, despite the fact that two-year college faculty produced several foundational studies of writing transfer (Hassel et al., "Editorial Perspectives"; see also Hassel and Giordano, "Transfer Institutions"; Giordano and Hassel; Fallon et al.; Blaauw-Hara; Tinberg, "Reconsidering"). Transfer students have appeared in several studies of writing transfer (Jarratt et al.; Nowacek; Cleary; Yancey et al.; Baird and Dilger), but their transfer status is treated as incidental rather than as a phenomenon worth studying in its own right. Applications of Yancey and colleagues' teaching for transfer (TFT) curriculum in two-year college contexts are beginning to appear (Tinberg, "Teaching for Transfer"; Andrus et al.). However, I know of only two published studies discussing how students transfer writing knowledge *across* two- and four-year institutions, neither of which was designed primarily as a study of knowledge transfer: research at the University of Michigan (Gere et al.) and this book's examination of transfer at the University of Utah.

The earliest study focusing on transfer student writers is—not coincidentally—also situated at the U. This 2003 chapter, "Making Rhetoric Explicit: Demystifying Disciplinary Discourse for Transfer Students," was written by Maureen Mathison, long-time director of UWP and a major force behind forming an independent WRS department.[19] Mathison describes an upper-division Writing In the Disciplines (WID) course for transfer students that she developed in the mid-1990s titled "Ways of Knowing in a University Setting," part of a short-lived program for transfer students called Horizons of Possibilities (HOP). The course was "designed to assist [transfer] students . . . by making explicit some of the tacit demands of thinking and writing that students will be expected to learn and produce in their respective majors" (55). Through a series of projects aimed at "studying disciplinary practices," the course sought to "train students to be student-researchers in their classes, and in doing so, to help them develop an understanding of academic practices as they are lived in a research institution" (55).[20]

Mathison explores the affordances of this curriculum through the case study of one transfer student, "Liz," an older/returning white woman "from a traditional family that seemed more concerned with her welfare as a wife than as a student" (56).[21] For her culminating project, Liz combined disclosures of her personal history with an analysis of women's authorial voices in the introductions of scholarly articles in anthropology. In Mathison's estimation, Liz "learned to write with a degree of authority as she pursued her own intellectual interests and placed them within the concerns of a larger community. In this sense the personal and the academic were made compatible and . . . relevant to others" (60). While HOP did not survive, Mathison and Liz's intellectual work has rippled into the present. Their feminist approach to this transfer course was an important influence on the curriculum we developed for WRTG 3020: Write4U.[22]

Maureen's course was premised on the assumption that transfer students often experience challenges with disciplinary writing when they arrive at the university. As a graduate student, I helped conduct a study at the University of Michigan that provides empirical evidence for this premise (Gere et al.). While disaggregating outcomes data for UM's upper-level writing requirement (ULWR) courses, we found that transfer students had lower average course grades than nontransfer students. Through an initial study in 2012 and a follow-up study in 2014–15, we interviewed a total of twenty-nine students who had transferred to UM from two- and four-year institutions across the United States. We identified five common—although not universal—writing-related transitions:

- *Adjusting to workload*: At UM, many transfer students experienced a "significant increase in the volume and complexity of the reading and writing they were expected to do outside of class" (Gere et al., 340). This jump included longer and more complicated writing tasks—sometimes multiple projects that needed to be completed simultaneously—that often required more extensive revision than transfer students had undertaken in their previous coursework. Likewise, students reported being assigned more reading at UM, with a greater emphasis on primary academic scholarship. For some, the increased reading and writing load created unanticipated time-management challenges.
- *Navigating instructional differences*: For community college transfer students, moving to UM required "learning to manage large class sizes and relatively impersonal relationships with faculty teaching lecture courses" (341). They described difficulties figuring out whom to approach for help when their teachers included not just professors but lecturers, graduate student instructors, and/or course graders.
- *Understanding expectations*: Most transfer students indicated that UM instructors' expectations for writing were different than those at their prior institutions. Those expectations "related to depth of thinking and reasoning and the length and complexity of assignments, as well as for mechanics and style" (341). Some interpreted their instructors' expectations as personal preferences, while others described them in terms of discipline and/or genre, suggesting variability in transfer

students' awareness of how disciplinarity and genre shape writing expectations. For some transfer students, failing to meet UM instructors' expectations was "their first experience with missing the academic mark—a (transfer) shock to their sense of themselves as students and as writers" (342).

- *Negotiating peer relationships*: While many students described receiving feedback from family, friends, or classmates that helped them transition to writing at UM, others found that "forming . . . connections with peers was difficult because [of] differences in age, life experience, or perceived class background" (342). Some struggled to break into well-established social networks among nontransfer peers, including classmates who could have been valuable sources of writing support.
- *Identifying resources*: Many transfer students were unaware of or unsure how to access writing-related resources on campus. Several described orientation as "too much, too fast; they received so much information about different aspects of campus and academic life that they often did not understand or remember the full range of resources available to them" (343). The writing center and UM's research librarians could be valuable resources, but faculty provided little guidance about how to access those services, perhaps because they assumed that upper-division students were already familiar with them.

Based on these findings, the UM research team developed a one-credit writing course for transfer students—Writing 350: Excelling in Upper-Level Writing—which was designed to be taken concurrently with ULWR courses. Writing 350 "foreground[ed] the discipline-specific nature of upper-level writing expectations by using reading and writing from students' other courses as the basis of workshops and discussions" (344). The course sought to create a supportive space to navigate instructional differences and get feedback on writing projects, forge peer relationships, and learn about institutional resources. UM also developed a directed self-placement (DSP) process aimed at inviting incoming transfer students to assess their own preparation for upper-division writing and presenting the opportunity to take Writing 350. These pilot efforts had mixed results. Students who took Writing 350 described it as a valuable learning experience that supported their transition to UM, but enrollments were low, perhaps in part because few transfer students were completing the labor-intensive DSP process (Gere et al.).

My involvement in the UM study informed our transfer research and program development at the U. Those five writing-related transitions became key sensitizing concepts in the U study, and UM coauthor Anna Knutson drew my attention to the strategies and resources transfer students brought to bear during these transitions. She encouraged me to see how transfer students' "experiences with writing and studenting across a range of institutions were a valuable asset, not a liability" (Gere et al. 353), an insight aligning with the antideficit orientation of transfer-receptive culture.

While I acknowledge these intellectual debts, our transfer research at the U diverged from UM on two principles. First, the article I coauthored with the UM team, "Mutual Adjustments: Learning from and Responding to Transfer Student Writers," was inattentive to the roles race and ethnicity play in transfer students' experiences. I conducted the interviews in our initial 2012 study, and I think those students' embodied identities mattered. For example, one community college transfer student was quoted as saying, "My papers have been destroyed" (342). What the article does not note is that he was also Asian American. His racial presentation and surname could have factored into the instructor's inclination to "destroy" his paper. Likewise, the student quoted as saying, "I just feel, I don't know, X'ed out" (341) was not just a community college transfer student: she was a Black woman and first-generation college student. The feelings she described likely emerged from the intersections of her transfer status with race, gender, and class. We invoked the concept of transfer-receptive culture in the article's literature review, but we did not note its grounding in critical race theory or its explicit challenge to meritocratic ideologies that function as "colorblind racism" (Bonilla-Silva). I regret these elisions of race, and I have endeavored not to reproduce them at the U.

Second, the U research sought to challenge university-centrism. At UM, we called our approach *mutual adjustments*: "Instead of the one-directional expectation that transfer students adapt to our institutional environment, we recognize that the university also has a responsibility to make research-based adjustments to become more receptive to transfer students" (336). While I agree that universities have a responsibility to change, and that change should be informed by local research, I no longer believe "adjustments" are adequate to address the structural inequities that cool out working-class and low-income community college students, particularly those who are students of color. I think university-based faculty need to get much more critical about the barriers our institutional cultures, professional hierarchies, and disciplinary practices present for transfer students, and how those barriers are contributing to racial transfer gaps. To co-constitute transfer-conducive writing ecologies, we must work across institutions toward what Carolyn Calhoon-Dillahunt, Patrick Sullivan, and I call "mutual transformation" (Toth et al., "Two-Year College Teacher-Scholar-Activism," 107).

Two other composition publications focusing on transfer students offer important insights into the kinds of interinstitutional collaboration that might foster such mutually transformative ecologies. In *Because We Live Here: Sponsoring Literacy beyond the College Curriculum*, Temple University's Eli Goldblatt describes his work with colleagues at the Community College of Philadelphia (CCP). In the early 2000s, 45 percent of transfer students at Temple were failing to complete bachelor's degrees, and graduation rates were worse for students from CCP (50 percent) than for those transferring from suburban community colleges (58–63 percent) (89–91), signaling race- and class-based transfer gaps. Goldblatt suggests that acting on these data must be a collaborative effort:

> The most pressing business involves making connections across programs and departments at the partner schools to assure that students really get the preparation they need to

> succeed in upper level courses and the support they need to graduate with a bachelor's degree. Writing is a key competency for transfer students, and [writing program administrators] bear responsibility for understanding the journey students make across these boundaries and smoothing the transition for them. (83)

Goldblatt describes his efforts to sustain "collective conversation" with CCP colleagues as a process of *deep alignment*, which he defines as "a connection between institutions that goes beyond articulation agreements and the automatic acceptance of course equivalencies" (96) and works toward "a shared understanding of students' needs that would encourage common approaches and sequential coursework across the 2-year/4-year college divide" (84). Temple and CCP faculty embarked on a series of joint meetings in which they compared assignments from composition courses across the two institutions and discussed what the similarities and differences might mean for CCP students' writing experiences at Temple.

Goldblatt makes several important observations that inform my thinking about transfer-conducive writing ecologies. The first is that community colleges and universities have a shared responsibility to transfer student writers that they are not meeting, and university faculty in particular often carry "attitudes toward transfer students that don't particularly help those students succeed" (85). Goldblatt suggests that countering these stigmatizing attitudes requires sustained, dialogic relationships across institutions geared toward mutual understanding:

> We wanted to promote deep alignment not by having the university faculty dictate what the community college instructors would teach, but by fostering a true dialogue that could make courses on both sides of the divide better. . . . Both sides must be willing to listen and to reevaluate their own practices and goals in light of what they learn in the dialogue. (96–98)

In Goldblatt's vision of deep alignment, university faculty do not set the terms, nor is the university's writing curriculum assumed to be the standard or beyond reproach. This orientation is essential for fostering transfer-conducive writing ecologies.

I share Goldblatt's commitment to interinstitutional "connections," "partner[ship]," and "dialogue," but I resist his language about transfer student "preparation" and "need." This deficit discourse risks devaluing students' educational experiences at community colleges, which may be different from what the university offers but are potentially more relevant to their lives and communities. Indeed, Goldblatt states that discussions between CCP and Temple led him to reflect on whether his university's first-year writing curriculum, in which the "concept of introducing students to academic discourse has been an article of faith," had perhaps "gone too far in ushering students into 'our' culture, that we had put the prized conceptions of literacy in the research setting above the interests of students in writing classes" (117). Engagement with community college faculty pushed Goldblatt toward critical recognition of problems with centering academic literacies to the exclusion of literacy practices in students' alongside-school communities. It disrupted the university-centrism dominating composition studies.

In 2016, Jonathan Alexander took a dialogic orientation toward interinstitutional collaboration several steps further in his essay "Queered Writing Assessment." Reflecting on his work as writing program administrator (WPA) at the University of California, Irvine, Alexander describes using conventional program assessment to tell the university "very informed 'straight' stories about what our courses do and do not accomplish": stories that made the case for revising curricula, creating a writing center, and establishing professional development workshops for faculty. It was work, he writes, that made him feel at once "strangely powerful and oddly fraudulent" (203). As a queer theorist, he valued "alternative trajectories, pursuing other possibilities" (202) and understood that "deviations from the straight and narrow . . . often stigmatize" (203). He thus found himself "worried over a piece of data, something that queered the story for me—*the writing of some transfer students.* It seemed that in some cases, and not always consistently, our transfer students weren't writing as well in upper-division WID courses as our 'homegrown' students" (203).

Sidestepping suggestions to set up a placement test for transfer students or impose additional coursework to get them "'up to speed"' (204), Alexander invited faculty at regional community colleges for a series of dialogues. His aim was "to have a broad set of conversations about what writing is, what we wanted our students to understand about writing, and . . . what our students could teach us about writing from their perspectives" (204). Like Goldblatt, Alexander knew "the development of professional and personal relationships" was essential to this process (204). Soon, faculty were sharing curricula across institutions, setting up workshops and summer institutes on writing pedagogy, presenting together at conferences, and collaborating on professional development for graduate students interested in two-year college careers. As Alexander writes,

> [W]e queered our campuses together in blurring the boundaries between two- and four-year schools. Surely one of the goals here was to ease transfer from one segment to another. But I also became convinced that it wasn't right to try to force our transfer students to stick to the story everyone else was telling. Their knowledges about writing that they brought to campus needed to be honored, not just corrected. I wanted our four-year writing folks to be exposed to what faculty on the community college campus were up to, what *they* knew about writing, and how they honored the many disparate paths students take toward a college degree. (204–5)

Alexander's experiences suggest the real "need" might not be improvements to transfer students' "preparation," but rather efforts to pluralize how universities value languaging, literacies, and paths through postsecondary education. This move toward "blurring" community college–university divides, to learning from *students* as well as from one another as faculty—to being mutually transformed by collective reconsiderations of what writing is and could be—resonates with our emergent vision for transfer-conducive writing ecologies in Salt Lake.

An ecological framework helps us see we are already related across our institutional and professional divides. The boundaries have always been porous, and students have always been crossing them, although not always in ways that are equitable or just. In the following pages, I present findings from a study of transfer student writing experiences we conducted at the U in 2015–16. Like Alexander, we found ourselves resisting institutional pressures to tell a "straight," university-centric story about SLCC students' "preparation" for academic writing. Instead, we used the findings to inform our efforts to enact ecological change. I won't claim we have been mutually transformed: I can't speak for my SLCC colleagues. However, our interinstitutional collaborations and the knowledges transfer students bring have indisputably shaped what WRS is becoming, and they have transformed me as a scholar and teacher.

CO-CONSTRUCTING A LOCAL PORTRAIT

Transfer is always situated within local histories and diversities, social geographies, and institutional structures. Any efforts to support transfer students should be grounded in local research, drawing on multiple sources of data disaggregated to identify systemic inequities. To construct a local portrait of transfer students' writing experiences and hear their ideas about writing-related resources they would find beneficial, we undertook a mixed-method study that combined institutional data, student surveys, and interviews with transfer students across a range of educational trajectories and major programs. The design of this study was similar to UM's, but with three intentional differences: (1) transfer students were co-researchers and co-designers of the supports we developed based on our findings; (2) we paid explicit attention to the experiences of *community college* transfer students, with an eye toward issues of racial equity as well as first-generation college student status; and (3) we shared findings with SLCC colleagues and sought their collaboration in expanding writing-related opportunities for transfer students.

In spring 2015, SLCC professor Andrea Malouf introduced me to several SLCC transfer students who became the first instantiation of our research team. That team included Shauna Edson, an MA student who had transferred to the U as an undergraduate; Davor Simunovic, a transfer student approaching graduation; Nate Lacy, who was in his third semester at the U; and Wes Porter, Nic Contreras, and Sandra Salazar-Hernandez, all of whom were preparing to transfer in fall (see Chapter 1). Justin Whitney, a PhD student who had also transferred from a community college, contributed to data collection and analysis. During the fall semester, we developed a survey instrument and interview protocol, secured IRB approval, collected and analyzed survey data, and conducted semistructured transfer student interviews. Through winter and spring 2016, we analyzed the interview transcripts and generated ideas for supports we might develop.

Insights from Institutional Data

Our investigation of local transfer gaps is grounded in the demographics of Utah, particularly Salt Lake County. The student populations of both the U and SLCC are two-thirds white, which is somewhat lower than in the overall population of the state (see Table 1). However, SLCC's student body more closely reflects the racial and ethnic makeup of Salt Lake County than does the U student body. SLCC enrolls a higher percentage of Latinx, Black, Pacific Islander, and Native American students, all of whom are underrepresented at the U relative to their presence in Salt Lake. The U enrolls a slightly higher percentage of Asian and Asian American and multiracial students than the population of Salt Lake County or the state of Utah. Salt Lake has been a refugee resettlement city since the 1970s and is world headquarters for the Church of Jesus Christ of Latter-day Saints. In recent decades, the valley has seen waves of immigration from Southeast Asia, the Pacific Islands, Eastern Europe, Latin America, the Middle East, and East Africa. If the broad racial categories used in institutional reporting were further disaggregated, we would likely see differences in how the valley's refugee, immigrant, and second-generation communities are represented across SLCC and the U.

Table 1. Salt Lake County racial demographics compared to U and SLCC enrollment

	% Population of Utah (2018)	% Population of Salt Lake County (2017)	% SLCC Enrollment (Fall 2017)	% U Enrollment (Fall 2017)
White	78	71	67	67
Latinx	14	18	18	12
Asian and Asian American	3	4	4	6
Two or more races	3	3	3	5
Black	1	2	2	1
Native Hawaiian or Other Pacific Islander	1	2	1	<0.5
Native American or Alaska Native	2	1	1	<0.5

Source: Data for SLCC and U enrollments from the National Center for Education Statistics College Navigator (nces.ed.gov/collegenavigator/).

Note: The table excludes NCES figures for students who were classified as "non-resident alien" or did not report their race or ethnicity.

Demographic data on transfer students provided by the U's Office of Budget and Institutional Analysis (OBIA) reveals local transfer gaps (see Table 2). White students are overrepresented in the U's transfer population relative to their percentage of the entire undergraduate population, suggesting they benefit disproportionately from transfer as a "pathway" to the U. Among SLCC transfer students, white, Asian and Asian American, and multiracial students are overrepresented and Latinx, Pacific Islander, and Native American students are underrepresented relative to their percentages of the SLCC student population. In other words, white, Asian and Asian American, and multiracial students at SLCC are more likely to transfer to the U than their Latinx, Pacific Islander, and Native American peers. However, Latinx, Black, and Pacific Islander students are also overrepresented among the SLCC transfer population relative to their percentages in the overall undergraduate population at the U. Transfer from SLCC is thus a disproportionately important path to the U for students from these groups. Without the mechanism of community college transfer, Latinx, Black, and Pacific Islander students would be even more underrepresented in the U's undergraduate population than they already are.

Table 2. Races/ethnicities of 2017–18 SLCC transfer cohort

	% SLCC Transfers to U (2017–18)	
	N	%
White	673	68.4
Latinx	162	16.5
Asian and Asian American	51	5.2
Two or more races	40	4.1
Black	19	1.9
Native Hawaiian or Other Pacific Islander	5	0.5
Native American or Alaska Native	1	0.1

Source: University of Utah Office of Budget and Institutional Analysis.

Over the last decade, the SLCC transfer population at the U has become less white and more Latinx (see Figure 1). In 2010–11, white students constituted 80.7 percent of incoming transfer students from SLCC, whereas in 2018–19, they were 67.1 percent. Conversely, in 2010–11, Latinx students constituted 8.4 percent of transfer students from SLCC; in 2018–19, they had grown to 19.6 percent. This shift is a function of the county's changing demographics as well as concerted efforts by community members and leaders in SLCC's Office for Diversity and Multicultural Affairs to better support transfer among Latinx students. Throughout the 2010s, the representation of other racial groups in the transfer population remained relatively flat. However, even as undergraduate enrollment at the U increased by nearly 1,400 during this decade, the number of SLCC students transferring to

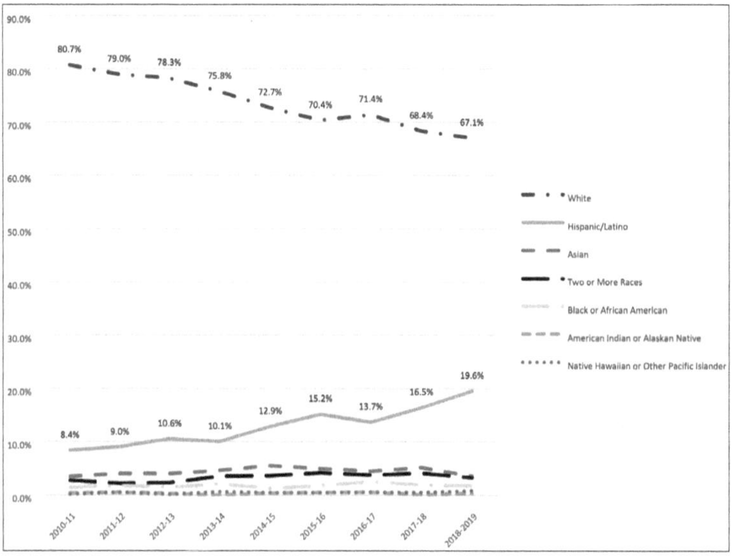

Figure 1. Salt Lake Community College transfer student demographic change 2010–19. (Data are from the University of Utah Office of Budget and Institutional Analysis.)

the U declined from 1,371 in 2010–11 to 848 in 2018–19. Given that transfer constitutes a disproportionately important path to the U for Latinx, Black, and Pacific Islander students, those numbers are cause for concern. To me, these figures suggest a need for more intentional efforts by departments and major programs across the university to connect with SLCC students—particularly students of color—prior to transfer. Such pretransfer outreach is a crucial element of transfer-receptive culture.

Degree completion rates among transfer students at the U demonstrate racial disparities in post-transfer outcomes. Among SLCC transfer students with an associate's degree admitted between 2010 and 2014, 69.2 percent earned a bachelor's degree within four years. White and Asian/Asian American students were more likely to complete their degrees within four years of transfer than Latinx, multiracial, and Black students, and far more likely than Native American and Pacific Islander students. White and Asian/Asian

American transfer students were also more likely than their Latinx, Black, multiracial, Pacific Islander, and Native American peers to complete degrees within two years of transfer. That additional time to bachelor's degree completion—what Eric Lichtenberger and Cecile Dietrich call "the community college penalty"—represents more years of lost earnings potential (i.e., greater opportunity cost) for many BIPOC transfer students.

To gain a sense of how academic literacies play into post-transfer writing outcomes, we examined OBIA data on transfer students' grades in communication and writing (CW) courses. To earn a bachelor's degree, all U students must complete a course that carries the CW designation. CW courses are upper-division, writing-intensive, and disciplinary in focus; transfer students' grades in these courses offer one metric of success with U writing. The CW data counters stigmatizing assumptions that community college transfer students are inherently "underprepared" for upper-division writing. Transfer students from SLCC had virtually identical average CW course grades (3.4) and completion rates (93 percent) to those of students who entered the U as first-year students.

When we disaggregated CW data, however, we saw evidence of race- and class-based inequities among both first-year admits and transfer students.[23] White and Asian/Asian American students had the highest average CW course completion rates among first-year admits. Multiracial and Latinx first-year admits completed at slightly lower rates, and Black, Native American, and Pacific Islander students—those groups most minoritized at the U—showed even greater disparities. There were similar patterns in completion rates among SLCC transfer students, with white and Asian/Asian American students completing CW courses at higher rates than those who were Black, Latinx, Pacific Islander, and Native American. While SLCC transfer student writers perform as well in CW courses as their first-year admit peers on average, BIPOC transfer students complete CW courses at lower rates than white transfer students.

It is important to interpret these numbers in local context. Many U transfer students are from white, middle-class Latter-day Saint families that expect children to pay for their own postsecondary education. For religious/cultural reasons, these students often start families at younger ages, and they tend to be debt-averse. These individuals use SLCC and other access-oriented state institutions as an economical path to a U bachelor's degree. Their transfer experiences matter, but they are also, in many ways, systemically privileged. Rather than adopting the common refrain that "transfer students do as well or better at the university than nontransfer students," it is important to identify groups whose writing experiences might be obscured by aggregate outcomes data at a predominantly white institution. It is equally important to ask who never makes it into the U's institutional data to begin with. The U appears to lose a disproportionately high percentage of Latinx, Black, Pacific Islander, and Native American students prior to transfer.

Insights from Surveys

In fall 2015, we sent an online survey to a representative sample of 2,185 currently enrolled transfer students who had been at the U between one and six semesters. We incentivized participation with a drawing for a $50 gift card to the campus bookstore. We received 269 responses, a 12 percent response rate. While those who responded may not be representative of the overall transfer population at the U, their responses did enable us to make comparisons within groups in the sample: 36 percent of respondents had attended only four-year institutions before arriving at the U, and 48 percent had attended SLCC. The survey responses provided additional evidence countering transfer stigma: 63 percent of all respondents *and* 63 percent of those transferring from SLCC said their pretransfer experiences had prepared them fairly or very well for writing in their major. However, these responses also suggest the U required some not-always-anticipated shifts in reading and writing practices, and those shifts might be more dramatic for students transferring from SLCC than from four-year institutions.

Table 3. Literacy transitions among transfer student survey respondents

	All Respondents	4-Year-Only Respondents	SLCC Respondents
Volume of reading at U (somewhat, fairly, or very surprised)	44%	24%	57%
Volume of writing at U (somewhat, fairly, or very surprised)	33%	26%	39%
Kinds of reading at U (fairly or very similar to previous institution)	39%	44%	39%
Kinds of writing at U (fairly or very similar to previous institution)	42%	49%	38%
Understanding of U writing expectations (arrived understanding fairly or very well)	56%	67%	48%
Preparation[24] for research writing at the U (arrived fairly or very prepared)	56%	65%	47%

These responses suggest that many transfer students experienced continuity in academic literacy practices between their prior institutions and the U. However, a subset from *all* originating institution types were finding reading and writing at the U to be a departure from their prior experiences, and the disjunctures were greater for respondents transferring from SLCC than for those transferring from four-year institutions. A majority of SLCC respondents indicated surprise at the volume of reading at the U, and less than half felt they had arrived understanding their professors' expectations for writing or prepared to undertake the kinds of research required for their writing assignments.

Our research team took three insights from these survey responses. First, we should not assume that all transfer students struggle with reading and writing. However, some transfer students might benefit from more support for their transitions to academic literacies at the U. Specifically, we might provide opportunities for incoming transfer students to learn about the genres, research practices, and workload they were likely to encounter at the U. To gain a more nuanced portrait of transfer students' writing experiences and the supports they believed would be useful, we turned to interviews.

Insights from Interviews

On the survey, we asked respondents to indicate whether they would be willing to participate in a one-time interview about their writing experiences and receive a $20 gift card to the campus bookstore, and 195 respondents marked "yes" or "maybe." We initially selected interview participants representing a range in ages, racial and ethnic backgrounds, gender identities, originating institution types, and major programs, but when response rates to our requests for interviews were low, we decided to reach out to all survey respondents who had expressed willingness to participate, and we interviewed everyone who agreed to meet. We asked participants to bring a recent piece of their writing to the interview, and a portion of the protocol was document-based.

We interviewed forty-five students from a range of prior institutions. Twenty-one of those participants had attended SLCC at some point in their educational trajectory, eleven had attended another two-year college, and three who had attended a two-year college had also spent time at another four-year institution before they transferred to the U. Seven interview participants were WRS majors, four of whom had attended SLCC. The students on the research team, all IRB-certified and trained in interview methods, conducted a total of thirty-two interviews: graduate students Shauna and Justin conducted ten interviews and undergraduate researchers conducted twenty-two. I conducted the remaining thirteen.

Because we were particularly interested in the experiences of community college transfer students, we focused our analysis on the twenty-seven interview participants who had attended SLCC and/or another two-year college. These participants were less diverse than we had hoped: twenty-two (81 percent) were white, and twenty-one (78 percent) had grown up in households where only English was spoken. Five participants were students of color: three self-identified as Hispanic, Mexican, or Latina, one identified as Tongan American, and one was an international student from Indonesia. All five students of color grew up in multilingual or non-English-speaking homes, and one disclosed that they were undocumented. Sixteen participants (59 percent) identified as female and eleven (41 percent) as male. We did not ask about disabilities, neurodivergence, or LGBTQIA+ identities, but one student described themselves as having attention-deficit disorder and three disclosed histories with mental health challenges. No students disclosed LGBTQIA+ identities. Of the twenty-three participants who provided information about their parents' educational backgrounds, ten (37 percent) were first-generation college students. Our recruitment methods yielded a group of participants who were weathering their transition to the U; struggling students could have been less likely to respond to our surveys or requests for interviews. These dynamics might have contributed to the disproportionately high number of white and continuing-generation participants.

Fifteen participants (56 percent) had grown up in Utah, nearly all in the Salt Lake area. The other domestic students came from California, Oregon, Washington, Idaho, New Jersey, and Tennessee; four had grown up in families that moved frequently because of military or other employment. We did not ask directly about religious identities, but ten participants (37 percent) indicated that they grew up in Latter-day Saint households, and three others self-identified as coming from Christian families without specifying denomination. The participants ranged in age from early twenties to late forties, with fifteen (56 percent) between the ages of twenty-four and thirty. Six (22 percent) were parents. Their majors included photography, film studies, WRS, English, linguistics, communication, African studies, political science, geography, psychology, anthropology, social work, education, engineering, computer science, mathematics, and accounting.

All interviews were transcribed and uploaded into qualitative coding software. Working through a sample of eight interview transcripts, Shauna and I developed an initial codebook using an iterative process of open and axial coding. We then collaborated with undergraduates on the team to code the remaining transcripts. We met weekly to discuss the coding-in-progress and make additions or adjustments to the codebook as necessary. Here, I discuss the themes that informed the supports we went on to develop: *recognizing rhetorical capacities, transferring writing knowledge, identifying challenges, accessing U resources/opportunities,* and *suggesting change.*

Recognizing rhetorical capacities. The students we interviewed were active readers and writers across a range of contexts. In addition to assigned coursework, they all read outside of school, with interests spanning fiction, narrative nonfiction, journalism, reviews, blogs, social media, religious or spiritual texts, academic books and articles, and reading for work. Eleven described engaging in various kinds of workplace writing, including emailing and instant messaging, grant writing, blogging and web design, paralegal activities, and news reporting. Seventeen were involved in non-work-related writing outside of school, such as emailing and letter-writing with friends and family, writing for activism or volunteer activities, blogging or social media, journaling, and faith-related writing. Eleven aspired to write books in the future, and six said they were regularly composing poetry, fiction, or song lyrics. Three had already written books, three had worked as freelance journalists, and one had owned and operated a small-town newspaper before coming back to school.

While some said the demands of school prevented them from reading and/or writing as much as they wanted, these students were participating in a range of literacy activities beyond academics spanning multiple discourses, genres, media, and sometimes languages. These practices were deeply entwined in their alongside-school communities. The older students brought years of experience writing across contexts, and eight commented on the value of greater experience, maturity, confidence, sense of purpose, or appreciation for learning that came with age. Likewise, five of the six multilingual students stated that knowing a language other than English made positive contributions to their reading, writing, and academic performance. Participants' alongside-school social networks also provided support for their school-based writing: eighteen described seeking feedback on writing from friends, siblings, parents, or partners. These knowledges, experiences, and relationships constitute rich rhetorical capacities—what some theorists might call resources, assets, forms of capital, or wealth—that transfer students draw on as they move across and beyond institutional contexts.

Much of what students said about their transfer experiences countered deficit discourses. Twenty-four participants spoke positively about their community college writing experiences. Eighteen identified first-year writing courses as important sites of learning, eight described memorable learning experiences at writing centers, and two emphasized how much they had learned from working on *Folio*, the SLCC literary magazine. Twenty identified community college courses in other disciplines—English literature, creative writing, history, philosophy, psychology, business, and engineering—where they gained important writing experience. Eight saw few differences between the writing they were doing at the community college and the U, and eleven stated that their transition to writing at the U had been smooth. Five found writing at the community college to be more challenging than at the U, and four said the biggest surprise of transfer was that they had expected U courses to be harder.

Thirteen participants noted aspects of the learning environment at the community college they valued relative to the U. Recurring themes included small class sizes, an institutional culture that accommodated students' life and work demands, flexible course options and scheduling, parking availability, more approachable instructors, faculty's connections to the work world, and, overwhelmingly, the lower cost of tuition and ability to fund one's education without resorting to student loans. Cost was a particularly pressing issue for the undocumented student who was not eligible to apply for federal financial aid. Seven participants—all women, students of color, older/returning students, and/or first-generation college students—noted that they valued the diversity of their community college classmates, something they missed at the U.

On the other hand, three interview participants—all white and continuing-generation—spoke dismissively of their community college experiences. One described SLCC as an "extension of high school" and said she had "phoned it in" for most of her classes. Another called SLCC writing assignments "busywork." These participants spoke disparagingly of their classmates at SLCC. One stated, "The biggest difference I notice between those two [schools] is the intelligence of the students. I felt like all the people at Salt Lake Community College were subpar and not really trying to excel in life and school." This assessment, issued by a white male student with ambitious professional goals, seems freighted with classism and potentially racism. All three of these participants stated they had learned little about writing at SLCC.

These students might have been expressing what our team came to call *internalized transfer stigma*, or a belief held by a transfer student that community colleges are a nonnormative and undesirable educational path. Internalized transfer stigma may lead some students to devalue their own educational experiences and desire not to be associated with other transfer students. These three interview participants may have sought to distance themselves from a stigmatized identity, particularly in conversation with institutional representatives who they believed might doubt their academic abilities. All three came from college-educated white families for whom meritocratic ideologies and classed, raced, and immigration-related stigma associated with community colleges might have posed a threat to their sense of themselves as intelligent or successful. While internalized transfer stigma is a function of broader ecological forces, these participants were enacting classist and racist educational hierarchies, and their time at the U appears to have affirmed rather than challenged that stance. We cannot know whether these participants devalued their writing experiences at the community college because they had learned little or whether they learned little because they had been primed to devalue their community colleges and classmates.[25]

Transferring writing knowledge. As we coded the data, we saw extensive evidence that students were adapting prior knowledge to writing contexts they encountered at the U. Demonstrating what Susan Jarratt and colleagues call "pedagogical memory," twenty-five were able to recall writing-related insights or practices they had learned through specific assignments, interactions, or experiences at their community colleges. Although they rarely used recognizable key terms in composition studies (Yancey et al.), nearly all the interviewees displayed the kinds of writing knowledge Anne Beaufort identifies in *College Writing and Beyond.* Twenty-three articulated writing-process knowledge (e.g., describing invention or planning strategies, approaches to drafting, seeking/working with feedback, revision strategies). Seventeen displayed rhetorical knowledge by talking about how their writing would be understood and valued by a particular audience and described their rhetorical choices in terms of audience needs and expectations. Sixteen demonstrated knowledge of disciplinary writing, describing their rhetorical choices with reference to discipline-specific practices, conventions, or ways of knowing. All twenty-seven articulated forms of genre knowledge, in the sense that they named and distinguished expectations for different genres, described specific genre features, and/or discussed drawing on prior genre experiences or models to enact a particular genre. Given this depth of memory and knowledge, we began to wonder if the experience of transfer—of moving across institutions in the middle of one's postsecondary journey and needing to adapt to a new writing context—might offer a unique opportunity for fostering rhetorical awareness.

Identifying challenges. While participants brought a range of rhetorical capacities and were adapting their prior writing knowledge to the U, they also described writing-related challenges that resonated with findings of the UM study. Eighteen participants described a significant jump in their academic workload after they transferred, including longer and more difficult reading assignments, more required writing, and longer and more complex writing assignments. Twenty-four experienced shifts in faculty expectations and pedagogical approaches surrounding writing, including more open-ended assignment prompts; less scaffolding of assignments; greater reliance on students' prior knowledge and willingness to seek out resources; increased expectations for depth and type of analysis or integration of academic theory; expectations for more extensive research using academic sources; greater attention to discipline-specific formats and citation practices; more scrutiny of "grammar" or mechanics; and/or a general sense of higher standards or tougher grading.

All participants "survived" their initial transfer transition, but that transition was rockier for some than others. Five described receiving lower grades or more negative feedback from instructors on their writing than they had anticipated, experiences that took an emotional toll but from which they learned and recovered academically. Two students, however, described failing writing-intensive courses during their initial post-transfer semester. Notably, both students were women of color who had moved away from their families to attend university. Both described their struggles as a combination of difficulty understanding the professor's expectations for a large end-of-semester writing project and broader emotional challenges that affected their academic performance. Both stopped out after that initial semester, adding time and expense to their pursuit of a bachelor's degree. While most community college transfer students weather the initial transition to university writing, some do not, and those failures can reinforce race-, class-, and gender-based inequities. The consequences of failure, while not insurmountable, can have harmful effects on students' mental health, their academic self-conceptions, and their access to material resources like financial aid and scholarships.

For some participants, the increased time demands were unanticipated. Their challenges weren't a matter of inadequate "time management strategies" (Gere et al. 341), but rather a function of the strained material conditions under which many transfer students pursue their education. Twenty-three participants worked the entire time they were in school, and twenty-one had little or no financial assistance from family. The sudden increase in study time required at the U coincided with the logistical demands of adapting to a new institution: figuring out new commutes and parking; piecing together upper-division major course schedules that were less flexible than general education courses; learning to navigate the geography of an unfamiliar campus; and planning for childcare and/or time with partners while juggling school and work. At community college, participants may have achieved a balance between credit load, hours worked to pay their bills and tuition, and personal time. However, the combination of increased academic workload, getting to and from campus, and the ratcheting cost of attendance at the U threw off that balance. Several interview participants described stressful decisions to withdraw from already-paid-for courses and/or cut their hours at work during their first semester. Our research team came to call this phenomenon *workload shock*.

Accessing resources and opportunities. As in the UM study, most U participants were not accessing campus writing resources. None reported hearing about the UWC during transfer orientation. Most now knew it existed, but only three had ever gone. Two described positive experiences at the UWC, but one—a woman of color who had failed a writing-intensive course during her first semester—described being turned away when she sought help on that assignment because she didn't have a draft. Some noted the logistical difficulties of attending in-person consultations. One thought the UWC was only for "ESL" students; another believed UWC staff were unable to help with writing in engineering. Participants were much more likely to seek feedback from faculty, TAs or lab instructors, classmates, or their social networks.

While these networks were important resources, they could also reproduce race- and class-based inequities. Several participants described getting feedback from college-educated parents, siblings, or partners, but first-gen students often have fewer college-educated people in their networks. We needed to make accurate representations of the UWC and its services more available to incoming transfer students and ensure those services were accessible and equitable. As Claudia Sauz Mendoza would observe (Castillo et al.) and faculty colleagues Romeo García and Clint Gardner continue to research, university writing centers might not affirm the identities and experiences or address the interests and preferences of community college transfer students, particularly students of color.

As our research team analyzed the interview data together, I began to consider how differences in cultural and social capital might cost transfer students opportunities for writing engagement through co-curricular experiences. None of the participants described writing for nonacademic campus activities. However, three said they learned a lot about writing through on-campus undergraduate research positions. Working with students on the transfer research team created openings for me to hear about their challenges and help them find institutional support. Research suggests that transfer students, especially transfer students of color, benefit from high-engagement, mentored co-curricular opportunities like research assistantships (Reyes; Townsend and Wilson, "Academic and Social Integration"). However, they face barriers to accessing such opportunities at the U. Some of these barriers are institutional. Many co-curricular opportunities at the U are designed for "traditional" students without work or family responsibilities, and accessing these opportunities depends on relationships with faculty few transfer students have been at the U long enough to form. Some barriers are material. Transfer students often cannot afford to exchange long-term off-campus jobs for an on-campus opportunity that pays less and will only last a semester. Transferring to the U, we saw, does not necessarily provide equitable access to the full range of writing and learning opportunities the institution offers.

Suggesting change. At the end of each interview, we asked for suggestions about how we might better support transfer students' transitions to writing at the U. Participants offered a range of ideas. Several stated that providing more scholarships or otherwise lowering the cost of attendance would enable them to work fewer hours and put more time into their reading and writing. Some suggested improvements to information provided at transfer orientation and called for more online writing resources. Four noted ways community college and U faculty could take responsibility for supporting transfer students. They called for more extensive feedback on student writing, before and after transfer; more opportunities to read and write in their major discipline or areas of professional interest prior to transfer; and clearer expectations for upper-division writing assignments that do not assume students are already familiar with U resources.

When we asked whether they would have considered taking a U writing course specifically for transfer students, two participants had a strong negative reaction, insisting they were only willing to pay for courses required for their major programs. Eighteen expressed some degree of support for the idea, albeit with caveats. One participant insisted such a course should *not* be required of all transfer students. Four suggested the course should be upper-division, and nine stated it should fulfill an existing bachelor's-degree requirement. Five stated such a course should focus on students' major or professional interests. Participants also suggested the class should be small and supportive and the instructor personable and accessible. They said the class should help students understand assignment expectations, approach difficult readings, and apply for scholarships. Finally, most participants became more enthusiastic when we floated the idea of offering the course to SLCC students *prior* to transfer, particularly when we presented it as an opportunity to get a head start at earning upper-division U credits while building connections with U faculty and future classmates.

TOWARD A MORE TRANSFER-CONDUCIVE LOCAL WRITING ECOLOGY

Review of scholarship on transfer, our local study of transfer-student writing experiences, and feedback from students on the transfer research team and faculty colleagues at SLCC led us to several conclusions. First, we should create resources to support the writing transitions of *all* transfer students at the U, but we should devote specific resources to students from community colleges. While we should work to support all community college transfer students, we needed to pay particular attention to those who are first-generation college students and/or students of color. Finally, we should develop resources for students who had already arrived at the U but also work across institutions to connect with students *before* transfer. These efforts should have the twin goals of (1) providing opportunities for students to anticipate the academic workload they would encounter at the U, and (2) creating opportunities for SLCC students to make social connections that would support them after they arrived at the U. Before and after transfer, the resources we created should be tied to students' academic and professional goals: i.e., their majors. If course-based, those opportunities should fulfill bachelor's degree and/or major requirements.

Second, our efforts should be grounded in an antideficit approach that counters transfer stigma. We should seek to communicate to students that we want them at the U *because* they are transfer students—because we value the knowledges and experiences they bring, and because we know they have had opportunities beyond the U that will help them achieve their goals and change the U for the better. We should refuse to talk about the resources we developed in terms of whether students are "prepared" to "go up to the U," and instead frame transfer between institutions as a lateral movement across contexts. We should recognize and make use of the transfer experience as a unique opportunity to reflect on one's prior writing experiences, cultivate critical awareness of disciplinarity, and exercise rhetorical adaptability.

Third, we should be thinking about how the resources we developed might counter systemic inequities related to transfer students' identities, material conditions, and access to social capital. In addition to supporting transfer students' writing transitions and introducing them to the UWC and library, we should be working to connect them with the range of resources on campus that would support their social, emotional, and material well-being, as well as units that could help them gain access to post-graduation opportunities. We should create opportunities to connect with faculty in their major areas of study who could become mentors.

Finally, we should seek to lower students' cost of attendance at the U. In addition to helping them apply for existing scholarships, we should *generate* scholarship funding for transfer students and create opportunities for them to earn upper-division course credit for low or no tuition. Over the next four years, we channeled these insights into the creation of our transfer bridge programs, a story I tell in Chapter 4.

When I look at those distant-yet-converging demographic lines in Figure 1, I consider how every fraction of a point Latinx transfer students have gained at the U represents the hard-won accomplishments of writers like Nic, Claudia, and Sandra, three of our interview participants, and many students in our bridge programs at SLCC, which is now designated as an emerging Hispanic-serving institution. These students have had to fight too hard to carve paths through a postsecondary system that is not built for them, that fails to recognize the knowledges they bring, that requires them, in Claudia's words, to "leave" so much of themselves "at the door." Those who are undocumented have done it without access to federal financial aid; those who do not have DACA status and did not attend a Utah high school must pay out-of-state tuition no matter how much they and their families have contributed to the state's economic growth.

Co-constructing a postsecondary system that recognizes these students amid transfer data dominated by white experiences and literacies—cultivating a system that is conducive to transfer on something closer to students' own terms—requires ecological change. In Chapter 4, "Pathways and Ecologies," I discuss how we drew on the findings of our study to enact such change: through the creation of two writing courses for transfer students, the development of a comprehensive bridge program for SLCC transfer students entering WRS, and advocacy for transfer students beyond our departments.

Interstitial IV:

Joanne's TYCA-West Keynote

THE WORK BEYOND ACCESS

FEBRUARY 19, 2017, FOUND ME JOBLESS. I began to wonder if going back to school after ten years was a mistake. I had thought getting a writing certificate at the local community college would be a helpful academic credential, and that accomplishment might help my declining mental health. However, midway through my first class, my job loss meant I might have to have to quit school again because I wouldn't have the money to complete the classes required for the certificate. Nevertheless, I was determined to finish this class well—even if it didn't mean anything to anyone else. That night, after a lot of crying and a glass of wine, I pulled myself together and prepared to complete my reading assignment. I opened my online portal and saw that my memoir paper had been graded. Clicking on the notification, I nervously waited for the page to load, unsure whether I could handle any more bad news that day. The score of 100 percent surprised me, but my professor's comments floored me. "You did a great job editing this down. The story comes alive with the dialogue and imagery. This is definitely one of the best memoirs I've ever read by a student. Nicely done! May I use this as an example? (I can either leave or remove your name.)" Never in a million years had I believed that anyone other than my parents would want to read anything I wrote—much less have other students read my work as a genre model. As far as I was concerned, I was a failed STEM major. I enjoyed writing for myself, but I loved the sciences. Besides, most people couldn't make money writing, right? Twenty years in corporate America had beaten the idealism out of me and replaced it with capitalistic pragmatism.

But this vote of confidence over a piece of nontechnical writing by a professor I'd only known online allowed me to perceive my abilities and strengths differently.

On March 27, 2017, I was flourishing in Dani's class. My time in the workforce had taught me useful strategies I employed as I worked with my professor through some elements I found difficult within the course. To me, finishing this class well meant I could actually excel in the academic world, no matter what my past told me. That sunny spring day, I received an email from my advisor, Sidney Brown, telling me about the Writing Studies Scholars Program that would not only allow me to continue learning but would assist me in getting back to the University of Utah—the institution that I had failed out of . . . twice. I was skeptical about my abilities, but Dani's statements gave me the courage to look into this opportunity. A week later, on April 4, I met with Christie for the first time. In that short meeting, I recognized that this experience could potentially be different from the previous times I'd claimed the title "student" at the U. If I made it through the summer class and back onto that campus, I was determined not to leave again without a degree.

The first day of WRTG 3030 was May 17, 2017, and I waited nervously outside of that third-story classroom at the South City Campus of Salt Lake Community College. My insecurities about my ability to handle the requirements of an upper-division writing class reached a fever pitch. The first assignment involved reading forty pages, and the sheer amount of what seemed to be theoretical gobbledygook was beyond daunting. Andie Malouf from SLCC let some of us into the classroom, and I was comforted that one of my teachers would be from a place I trusted a little more than the School on the Hill. At this point, Christie was still an unknown quantity to me. Though my meeting with her on the Hill had showed me she was different, I still had questions. But she began that class with these words: "You each have valuable experiences and knowledges that I will never have, and I'm excited to learn from you and your writing this semester." While I leaned heavily on Andie for supplemental sources for my research projects and as a sounding board for some of my ideas, both instructors adhered to the ethos of that sentiment. Watching them back up their words with actions built a trust I'd never had with higher education. That trust slowly transformed the way I perceived my position in academic spaces, my potential for contribution, and the possibilities available to me to do this work of learning. That statement created a unique atmosphere where I as a whole individual was valued. This simple but powerful difference helped me to see my history as a resource and not "baggage."

On May 14, 2018, I parked my car behind the Administration Building of SLCC's Redwood Campus. I couldn't help smiling at the difference a year made. I sat in Clint Gardner's office in the Student Reading and Writing Center and waited for Christie and PhD Candidate Charissa Che to join us. I was co-teaching WRTG 3030 with them that semester. As a member of the second generation of what we called "The Transfer Team," I felt like part of a community that was assisting students like me. I had leveraged the autoethnography I had begun in this class the previous summer into a paid research opportunity that continued through this summer. And I was still jet-lagged from a research trip to South Korea assisting then-Department-Chair Jay Jordan, an opportunity made available to me because of the relationships established in that 2017 summer class. The rhetorical strategies I had learned in WRTG 3030 allowed me to observe largely hidden rhetorical situations and use my positionality to activate change using writing. I was eager to show the students at SLCC that the resources they carry with them were incredibly valuable, that there were ways of writing that would inspire them, and that there were many possibilities writing could unlock.

Faculty members, you never know whom you are addressing in your classes. You never know what confidences you are unlocking with your words, and you may never realize what life trajectories you will change. I'm sorry that you don't always know the impact of the work you do. But I am evidence that your words—spoken or written—have power. For me, your words helped launch me into an adventure I thought had passed me by long before. What successes and victories I attain right now are due largely to the words of a two-year college faculty member, and I am so grateful that she chose to share them with me.

◈◈◈◈

In October 2018, SLCC hosted the annual TYCA-West conference with the theme "The Big Picture: Transfer, Threshold Concepts, and the Two-Year College." I co-delivered the keynote address with Arizona State University's Duane Roen and several of my transfer student colleagues: Nate Lacy and Cassie Goff—SLCC transfer students who had majored in WRS as undergrads and entered our master's program in fall 2018—as well as undergraduates Kelly Corbray, Margarita Lafarga, and Joanne Castillo. Joanne had been in the first group of SLCC students to take WRTG 3030: Writing across Locations, our transfer bridge course for prospective WRS majors. In that course, she wrote a powerful autoethnography examining what it meant to live "the hyphen between 'Filipina' and 'American.'" At the U, she turned that autoethnography into a funded Undergraduate Research Opportunity Program study of intergenerational Filipina/Filipina American rhetorics. During her final semester at the U, she remediated these projects into an autoethnographic dance she performed live at the 2019 CCCC convention in Pittsburgh. That dance was a fitting capstone to her time in the WRS major, during which she drew on her expansive rhetorical repertoire to leave her mark on our department and the discipline.

Joanne remembers me launching WRTG 3030 with the words, "You each have valuable experiences and knowledges that I will never have, and I'm excited to learn from you and your writing this semester." My learning from Joanne extended far beyond that summer semester. She became—and remains—an essential intellectual collaborator. Her two years in WRS and on the transfer team were the same period I was struggling to produce a full manuscript of this book while co-coordinating the rapidly evolving WSS bridge program. Without her feedback on each chapter—and her insistence on its importance when I felt inadequate to the task—I suspect the book would never have materialized.

Justin Whitney, Claudia Sauz Mendoza, Nate Lacy, Cassie Goff, Joanne Castillo, Kelly Corbray, Charissa Che, and Nic Contreras at TYCA/CCCC 2019. Photo credit: Nic Contreras.

A lifelong journaler and scrapbooker, Joanne was an assiduous chronicler of her experiences in WSS. While in the program, she wrote about the difficulties of her journey through postsecondary education in multiple genres for a range of audiences: personal statements for scholarships; emails to leaders across campus; speeches for student competitions and advocacy events; proposals for undergraduate research opportunities; conference presentations for Watson, TYCA, and CCCC. As she approached graduation in spring 2019, I asked if she would be interested in including one of those pieces in this book. She agreed and offered several options. Her primary goal in her TYCA-West keynote was to present a version of her story that validated two-year college teaching and showed how interinstitutional partnerships could expand educational access for students like her. We decided this public-facing composition, which she delivered in person before a two-year college audience, was appropriate for a book about community college–university relations.

In her speech, Joanne describes how these interinstitutional partnerships enabled her to forge a different relationship with the U at the age of thirty-seven than she'd had as a seventeen-year-old STEM major juggling school and her family's gendered cultural expectations, or as a twenty-seven-year-old returning student isolated in a predominantly white, male STEM program. In her third attempt at earning a U degree, Joanne was determined to change her academic trajectory. Throughout her four semesters in WRS, she also worked to change the university so other students like her—transfer students, older/returning students, women of color, multilingual children of immigrants—would have access to those opportunities on something closer to their own terms. She and I joked that she was "the revenge of the statistic": a woman of color driven from STEM who was back at the university, this time with a meta-aware rhetorical toolkit, an ear for institutional discourses she could appropriate, and a fierceness born of experience and the example of her ninety-year-old Nanang, who once punched a noncompliant water buffalo in the face so her adult grandchildren could ride it around the family's Ilocos Norte courtyard. "Punching the water buffalo" became a guiding metaphor Joanne invoked when taking on institutional gatekeepers (see Castillo).

Joanne certainly faced material challenges to completing her degree. She commuted daily from her parents' home in Sandy. Having exceeded her lifetime federal financial aid eligibility, she struggled term by term to meet the cost of attendance. Through a rhetorical tenacity that combined carefully crafted emails with attendance at every campus event where she was likely to meet university leadership—skills she learned during her years in the workforce—Joanne scraped together enough scholarship funding each semester to get through. In the process, she found allies among administrators far above my pay grade. She pushed them to address the structural barriers transfer students face and to listen to students: not as objects of research but as collaborators in program development who should be paid for their labor. Her efforts led to the creation of a team of transfer student consultants in the Office of Undergraduate Studies who provide feedback on the U's transfer processes and services. Joanne graduated in May 2019. Around her neck were a dozen cords and stoles, visible honors she wore to make her accomplishments legible to her family. Among them was a teal WSS stole—her idea—embroidered with a motto chosen by students in the program: *Rewriting the Ecology*.

No student should have to work as hard as Joanne did to gain and sustain access to postsecondary education. As she notes, her personality, age, years of corporate experience, cultural and family influences, and history with the U motivated her to fight. However, when no one else was watching, I got glimpses of what those fights cost her emotionally. She was doing what she had to do to survive, even when her pushback rankled faculty colleagues and other students. The toll on those relationships was another cost she bore. Not all transfer students can or want to take on such fights. Nor, as Claudia Sauz Mendoza reminds me, should students have to shoulder the labor of combating institutional racism and classism. For many, it's hard enough just to keep coming back to campus and surviving a system designed to exclude them (see Castillo et al.). Without romanticizing Joanne's journey or taking credit for what she's achieved, I want to acknowledge the labor she put into developing WSS, advocating for our young and imperfect department, and doing everything she could to change the U.

One of Joanne's first acts after graduation was to establish the Caridad G. Andres and Divina A. Castillo Summer Scholarship, named after her grandmothers and nicknamed the Water Buffalo Punching Scholarship. It was funded through a collaboration with the Clever Bean, the Sandy coffee shop where she did much of her writing. She plans to write a memoir about her educational journey. In her TYCA-West speech, I think she achieved her purpose of demonstrating that our local efforts to foster more transfer-conducive writing ecologies have expanded opportunities for students—creating transfer "pathways" and even paths *back* to the university—that were not previously available.

FROM JOANNE IN 2021:

Post-graduation life started with so much promise. I relaxed a bit before heading out to a family reunion in Vegas where I met another hundred or so family members for the first time. Summer weddings in California and New York allowed me to reconnect with family I had largely neglected during my quest to punch water buffalo while deepening friendships I made at the U. Upon my return to Salt Lake City, those connections allowed me to find work with a company associated with the U. Teleworking options in summer 2019 meant I could officially be *that* person as I rhetorically analyzed teaching modules and websites for cultural nuances that might not be understood or mean something different internationally. I chose a coffee shop in the southeastern end of the Salt Lake Valley called the Clever Bean because it was close enough to walk to. There, I analyzed modules for the company and gave feedback on the manuscript you are reading. Secretly, I hoped the little notifications Christie got throughout the day would encourage her, would let her know that I valued what was in the manuscript and that someone not as lucky as me would find it valuable too. #shareddocrhetorics. Life was good.

The community at the Clever Bean buzzed with something beyond caffeine-induced energy. This small business seemed intent on connecting with the immediate local community and on giving back to the community in many ways. They offered to help me with the Water Buffalo Punching Scholarship I established specifically for WSS scholars who needed to go to school in the summer. It was a need I faced that wasn't met by university policy. The Clever Bean developed two drinks for me, and a portion of the proceeds of those drinks went to the scholarship. They hosted an open mic night where I invited friends and faculty from Salt Lake Community College and the University of Utah to read some of their work. I still smile as I remember how folks who rarely make their way to this end of the valley interacted with one another as colleagues, how writers from that end of the community did (or didn't) interact with them. I looked forward to doing something similar again in the next year.

But then COVID happened. I was already prepped to work from home, and the company I worked for was finalizing the changes I had suggested for their respiratory sedation online learning modules. As demand for these learning modules increased, my team and I realized we had done our jobs well—too well. My role switched from content analysis to customer service as it was deemed that I was best equipped to address the flood of emails coming in from all over the world. The flood turned into a stream, and it is now a trickle. I am still working for them, but my hours were cut back severely. I am back on the job market where I am simultaneously overqualified for some positions and lacking in experience for others. Instead of focusing on embarking on my own entrepreneurial journey or writing a book about my experiences punching the water buffalo, I find myself looking at applying for jobs that hurt my soul. I find myself doubting whether my experiences or what I learned from them will even be viable in a mid- or post-pandemic university environment. The Clever Bean hasn't reopened, and funding for the scholarship has dried up. I'm not sure what the future holds for me. I hope 2021 holds better things.

4

Pathways and Ecologies

IN 2015, HIGHER EDUCATION RESEARCHERS Thomas Bailey, Shanna Smith Jaggars, and Davis Jenkins published *Redesigning America's Community Colleges: A Clearer Path to Student Success*. The authors lay out their "Guided Pathways model," which they describe as "comprehensive reform" (217) to the structure of community college education. They attribute low and inequitable degree completion at these institutions to what they call the "cafeteria-style, self-service model" (3). Community colleges, they assert, offer a bewildering array of courses and programs that require students to make too many choices with too little guidance. This model has the most negative impact on students with the most limited knowledge about higher education and the greatest nonacademic pressures on their time: low-income students and first-generation college students, often students of color. The "redesign" Bailey and colleagues propose "engage[s] faculty and student service professionals in creating more clearly structured, educationally coherent program pathways that lead to students' end goals" (3). Those reforms encompass changes to curricula, advising, student-support services, and relationships with transfer institutions and employers.

By the late 2010s, most two-year colleges were impacted by reforms associated with Guided Pathways. Those impacts often included changes to developmental education and course placement that were already underway (see Hassel, Klausman, Jeff, et al.; Klausman et al.). Many faculties were also tasked with redesigning degree programs. Under Guided Pathways, students enter focused programs of study called "metamajors" that enable them to explore interests and choose a degree program aligned with their goals. Metamajors have clear degree maps, integrated curricula, and scaffolded learning outcomes. These curricular changes are paired with most extensive orientation and advising, including intervention when students seem to be going off course. Such reforms promise to make more efficient use of financial aid, maximize transfer credit, and lead students to "careers that pay a family-sustaining wage" (Klempin and Lahr 4).

The Guided Pathways model aims to improve student persistence, degree completion, transfer rates, and employment outcomes, and, in more recent iterations, to close equity gaps in each of those areas. Those goals are shared by most two-year college composition faculty. In fact, many changes proposed in *Redesigning America's Community Colleges* align with recommendations by composition scholars like Mike Rose (*Back* and "Reassessing") and the faculty who developed the Accelerated Learning Program at the Community College of Baltimore County (Adams et al.). Despite overlapping concerns and similar proposals, however, many two-year college composition faculty have met Guided Pathways initiatives with ambivalence.

Some of their misgivings are ideological: The discourse of Guided Pathways is unmistakably neoliberal. It conceptualizes education, particularly in community colleges, as in uncritical service to the existing economic order. It seeks to make students competitive for a limited pool of jobs that pay "a family-sustaining wage" rather than pushing for policies that would require all jobs to pay such wages. It serves employers, emphasizing "career readiness" to the exclusion of other pedagogical goals—community, civic, intellectual, artistic—further instrumentalizing community college education (see Rose, *Back,* and "Reassessing"; Blankenship et al.; Sullivan, *Economic Inequality*; Griffiths and Jensen; Higgins and Warnke). TYCA leaders Cheri Lemieux Spiegel (Northern Virginia Area Community College), Darin Jensen (SLCC), and Sarah Z. Johnson (Madison Area Technical College) characterize Guided Pathways as "one of the most recent reforms in the conservative restoration and one that can significantly narrow curriculum and student choice"

(14). Bailey and colleagues also fail to challenge the exploitative labor structures at community colleges that work against the kind of programmatic coherence they seek (see Higgins and Warnke). Indeed, they suggest that Guided Pathways can address systemic inequities with little additional permanent funding. *Redesigning America's Community Colleges* seems to make a selling point of its capitulation to neoliberal austerity.

These ideological suspicions are compounded by faculty fatigue with community college reform implemented through top-down decision making by college administrators, statewide mandates, and infusions of temporary grant funding from megafoundations (see Blankenship et al.; Adler-Kassner; Tinberg, "Idea"; Giordano and Hassel; Griffiths, "Reinventing"). Such reforms often marginalize faculty, their local knowledge, and their disciplinary expertise. As Brett Griffiths of Schoolcraft College writes, "[T]he problem with college redesign is that it advocates for interventions in . . . writing . . . instruction without attending to decades of existing pedagogical research on literacies instruction, language ideology, or learning theories" ("Reinventing" 91). Guided Pathways initiatives often either ignore disciplinary knowledge necessary to counter inequities or co-opt approaches developed in composition studies and disconnect those practices from essential critical theoretical grounding (Toth, "Directed Self-Placement"; Higgins and Warnke; Jensen et al.)

Pressures for redesign have led some two-year college faculty to become what Anthony Warnke and Kirstin Higgins of Green River College call "critical reformers" (363). As they write:

> The critical reform position attempts to live out the disciplinary values and underappreciated instructor values that have underpinned the most progressive work with regard to basic writers, two-year college students, and underserved populations in higher education. This position, we argue, involves taking up the teacher-scholar-activist mantle to its fullest extent to act both within and beyond the classroom. Critical reformers, we suggest, make it their business to engage with the structural consequences of reform. (364)

Critical reformers recognize the structural inequities Bailey and colleagues document and concur that change is necessary, but they remain skeptical of the neoliberal paradigms driving reform movements underwritten by corporate profits, and they advocate for "careful, structurally aware engagement" (368). Higgins and Warnke invoke the work of critical race theorist Derrick Bell to suggest that such engagement can make strategic use of "interest convergence" between neoliberal reform movements and critical composition scholarship to redress educational inequities (10; see also Warnke and Higgins). They call on colleagues to "fight for principled reform" (Warnke and Higgins 363) with "flexibility, adaptability, and an unwavering commitment to students" (Higgins and Warnke 10).

Guided Pathways has created opportunities for strategic engagement regarding transfer. Bailey and colleagues conclude *Redesigning America's Community Colleges* by suggesting community college faculty "build partnerships with transfer destination program faculty," stating:

> To guarantee that program maps will articulate with key transfer destination programs, community college faculty need to build relationships with their counterparts at each transfer destination. Faculty may give priority to building strong transfer pathways with those destinations that serve transfer students effectively, and that themselves have strong labor market and education outcomes for their students. (207)

This statement leaves me ambivalent. On one hand, Bailey and colleagues' highest value is alignment with the labor market, with no recognition of educational, creative, or activist goals composition faculty and students might bring. On the other hand, the authors suggest community college faculty can use their partnering capacity to exercise power. By prioritizing programs that collaborate as colleagues and do right by transfer students, community college faculty can incentivize universities to foster transfer-receptive culture. This can be an opening for principled reform.

Our local opening materialized when pathways discourse entered the Salt Lake writing ecology. In 2016, SLCC began institution-wide Guided Pathways reforms (see Blankenship et al. for faculty members' discussion of their ambivalent but good-faith participation in this effort). In 2018, USHE began putting pressure on the U to prioritize "transfer pathways," pressures soon felt by colleges, schools, and departments. By then, WRS had already established its transfer initiatives with SLCC's English Department. Being ahead of the mandates enabled us to develop partnerships on something closer to our own terms. By 2019, U leaders were holding WRS up as a model, creating opportunities for us to influence initiatives in other units on campus. My SLCC colleagues were, in turn, able to use the *Principles for Partnership* we had articulated (see Part III) to push for more equitable relations with other departments at the U that came calling (Ruffus et al.).

In this chapter, I narrate the first three years of WRTG 3020: Write4U and WRTG 3030: Writing across Locations, the two transfer "bridge" courses at the heart of our partnerships. The curricula and support structures in these courses emerged through the research presented in Chapter 3, iterative collaboration with SLCC and U faculty colleagues, and the contributions of SLCC transfer students. Our efforts at principled partnership catalyzed ecological changes I did not anticipate in 2015. Those changes suggest it is possible to harness composition's disciplinary turn to enact a professional competency identified by the National Junior College Committee back in 1971: "to work within the academic system in order to change the academic system . . . through a process of mutual development undertaken cooperatively with students and colleagues" (Cowan et al., "Guidelines" 306). Interinstitutional collaboration can be more than paving "pathways" to individual financial success amid the scarcities of late capitalism. Collaboration can become mutual transformation rooted in shared commitment to equity for students and faculty. The ecological changes we have experienced in Salt Lake offer hope that pursuing disciplinarity is not just a bid for status within research universities. Rather, it can advance our collective efforts to do the "work that really matters in the world" (Maher 166).

A TALE OF TWO COURSES

In WRS, we have a broad responsibility to support transfer students across the curriculum. We also have specific responsibilities to students entering our major, minor, and certificate programs: to support their transitions into upper-division study of writing and rhetoric; to connect them with peer networks, mentorship, and co-curricular opportunities; to assist them materially and see them through to graduation and beyond. Taking up these responsibilities with an explicit commitment to closing local transfer gaps is part of co-constituting transfer-conducive writing ecologies.

Here, I chronicle our interinstitutional efforts to address these responsibilities. Those efforts began as course development. In spring 2016, members of the transfer research team—Nic Contreras, Nate Lacy, Sandra Salazar-Hernandez, Wes Porter, Davor Simunovic, Shauna Edson, and Justin Whitney—contributed to initial conversations about what the courses should be. In summer 2016, most of these team members plus transfer interns Emily Beck and Stephanie Weidauer attended a daylong workshop with SLCC faculty Stephen Ruffus, Andrea Malouf, Clint Gardner, Justin Jory, Jennifer Courtney, and Lisa Bickmore. Our team shared research findings and floated our initial ideas for two "bridge" courses for transfer students. The negotiations during that meeting were foundational for the program development that unfolded over the next five years. Throughout the intertwined narratives of these courses, I endeavor to trace the emplaced ecology of people, campus units, material resources, policy, and knowledges—academic and otherwise—that shaped what our programs became.

These narratives have been composed through my own memories and those of students on the transfer team, aided by review of documents compiled through the first three years of program development: research team meeting notes and emails; course materials;[26] and interview transcripts, fieldnotes, and student compositions from IRB-approved course pilot studies. I chose to foreground insights that might be useful to readers seeking to support transfer student writers. I structure the discussion of each course in three parts: *iterative implementation*, *evolving curriculum*, and *critical reflections*.

Responsibilities to All Transfer Writers

Based on findings from our 2015–16 study, we took several immediate actions to better support transfer student writers across the disciplines. First, we sought to make existing writing resources at the U more visible to transfer students. We created flyers for the UWC and began tabling at transfer orientations and welcome events. We added a new page to our department website providing information on writing resources for transfer students. We began communicating regularly with transfer advisors in the U's Academic Advising Center and in the Center for Equity and Student Belonging (CESB) Transfer Program. The centerpiece of our efforts, however, was WRTG 3020: Write4U, a communication and writing (CW) course designed for upper-division students who are new to the U.

Iterative Implementation. WRTG 3020 focuses on providing transfer students with opportunities to develop critical awareness of disciplinary discourses in their majors. Many transfer students make the transition to writing at the U with little or no difficulty, and we did not seek to implement WRTG 3020 as a required or "remedial" course. Rather, we aimed to develop a challenging upper-division writing-intensive course that would

- value students' multiple and intersectional identities, prior educational experiences, and wide-ranging linguistic and rhetorical capacities
- invite students to investigate reading and writing practices in their major disciplines
- provide opportunities for critical analysis of disciplinary discourses and genres in relation to issues of access, gatekeeping, privilege, and social inequities

- connect transfer students with campus resources, peer and faculty mentorship, and co-curricular professional-development opportunities
- contribute to students' progress toward completion by fulfilling bachelor's degree requirements

We designed WRTG 3020 as a three-credit course that carries both humanities exploration (HF) and (CW) general education designations. The HF is a statewide general education requirement typically completed through lower-division coursework as part of an associate's degree. The CW is a U-specific upper-division bachelor's degree requirement that cannot be offered by community colleges, which makes this designation particularly useful for transfer students.

In fall 2016, we piloted WRTG 3020 as a course for already-matriculated transfer students. Emily, Stephanie, and WRS major Oti Langi worked with me that summer to create recruitment flyers, web content, and a robust online site for course management. WRS advisor Lisa Shaw helped us communicate with advisors across campus to raise awareness of the WRTG 3020 course among incoming transfer students. Throughout the summer, we tabled at U transfer orientations to connect with prospective transfer students in person.[27] We have offered WRTG 3020 for incoming U transfer students every fall since, and it has consistently enrolled between fifteen and twenty-five students from a range of originating institutions, the majority from SLCC. I taught the 2016 pilot section with Nic as in-class co-researcher; from 2017 to 2019 it was taught by a rhetoric and composition PhD student working with an undergraduate transfer mentor. In fall 2017, Justin co-taught the class with Claudia Sauz Mendoza, followed by Nina Feng with Kelly Corbray in 2018 and Nkenna (Kenna) Onwuzuruoha with Adi Tolentino in 2019. Each year, these graduate student–transfer mentor teams infused the curriculum with their expertise and experiential insights.

I initially imagined WRTG 3020 as a course for already-transferred students at the U. However, students on the transfer research team urged making it available at SLCC for those preparing to transfer—our interviews suggested some students would be more likely to take the class if it were presented as a pretransfer opportunity. Figuring out how to do that took some negotiating. Initially, SLCC colleagues were eager to offer WRTG 3020 as an SLCC course that could be listed in their catalog and appear on students' SLCC transcripts. That would have allowed students to apply the credits toward their associate's degree requirements and cover tuition with SLCC financial aid. When I was hauled into a meeting with U administrators, I realized I'd stumbled into a longstanding struggle: allowing SLCC to offer 3000-level courses was a line the U refused to cross.[28] However, changing WRTG 3020 to a 2000-level course that could be offered by SLCC would mean losing several distinctive benefits. CW courses are upper division, so the course would not be able to carry that designation. Furthermore, many transfer students arrive at the U with a surplus of lower-division credits; what they need are courses that count toward the forty upper-division credits required for a U bachelor's degree. Ultimately, we turned to a model developed by the U's Department of Communication, where Natasha Siegert ran a one-credit "Transfer Interest Group" (TIG) for prospective Comm majors at SLCC. The TIG is offered through the U's continuing education (CE) program, which provides community education and college-credit courses in locations across the Salt Lake Valley.

CE has several affordances useful for a transfer bridge course. CE courses can be taught at SLCC campuses, and students do not need to be admitted to the U to take a CE course. If a course is an approved part of the curriculum for regularly enrolled U students, nonmatriculated students can take a CE section and the credits appear on their official U transcripts once they matriculate. Finally, CE allows departments to set course tuition at any rate, as long as CE receives a $50-per-student fee. Whatever tuition is charged above that $50 goes to the department administering the course. Offering a transfer bridge course through CE enables students to earn upper-division credits at a significantly reduced tuition rate. We started out offering WRTG 3020 at SLCC (Write4U@SLCC) for $450, the same tuition as a three-credit SLCC course and a third of what the course costs matriculated U students.[29]

Unfortunately, students cannot use SLCC financial aid for CE courses, and, as nonmatriculated students, they cannot apply for federal financial aid through the U. However, that problem was not insurmountable. Each time we offered Write4U@SLCC between 2017 and 2019, we were able to raise enough funds through small institutional grants and external donations to provide full scholarships for all students who said they had financial need.[30] Beginning in summer 2019, we also offered the course tuition-free to any SLCC students associated with TRiO (a federal program for first-generation college students) or programs in Office of Diversity and Multicultural Affairs (ODMA).[31]

We first piloted Write4U@SLCC in spring 2017, with me as lead instructor, Kelly as in-class co-researcher, and Wes as in-class transfer mentor. To connect with prospective students, we put up flyers around SLCC, sent recruitment emails and social media messages through SLCC advisors and faculty, and visited classes associated with SLCC's writing certificate. However, enrollments were disappointing. Only six students signed up—all prospective WRS majors, all white and US-born—and only three stayed beyond the first few weeks. They were all older/returning women students: two were first-generation college students and two were parents. We were happy to connect with these students. Two went on to take WRTG 3030, transfer to the U, and become Writing Studies Scholars, as did one of the students who had to drop the course. But these enrollments did not achieve our goal of connecting with a racially, culturally, and linguistically diverse group of SLCC students across a range of majors. We soon realized the low enrollment and low persistence were partly an issue of credit load. Because Write4U@SLCC is a U course, it does not count toward students' SLCC courseload. Some students must be enrolled at SLCC full-time to get financial aid and/or complete their associate's degree requirements on their desired timeline, which makes it difficult to add writing-intensive upper-division coursework on top of their SLCC workload. Likewise, the days, times, and location we selected—midday on Tuesdays and Thursdays at SLCC's Redwood campus—was likely inaccessible for some.

I was discouraged, but SLCC colleagues wanted to give Write4U@SLCC another shot. After the initial success of WRTG 3030, discussed below, we decided to try Write4U@SLCC again in 2018, this time as a summer course co-taught by me and transfer mentor Katherine Allred, a WRS major who had taken Write4U@SLCC and WRTG 3030 in 2017. Once again, we put up flyers, sent email and social media messages through advisors and faculty, and visited SLCC classes. By this time, Claudia had become co-coordinator of transfer initiatives. She set up times for us to table in central locations at multiple SLCC campuses. She found opportunities for us to speak to student groups associated with ODMA, and we developed strong connections with SLCC's Amigos Mentores program, which serves Latinx students. We compiled a list of interested students and sent them a survey to determine what days, times, and campus locations would work best. The most popular option was Tuesday and Thursday evenings at SLCC's Redwood campus.

Enrollments were higher in 2018's Write4U@SLCC experiment. Sixteen students signed up, fifteen of whom completed the course. Sixty percent were students of color and almost three-quarters identified as women. Nearly half were older than twenty-four, and two-thirds were first-generation college students. Again, a surprising number of prospective WRS majors enrolled in the course, with eleven students enrolling in *both* WRTG 3020 and 3030,[32] but eleven were considering majors in English, linguistics, communication, psychology, special education, social work, nursing, chemistry, engineering, or music. Although we were still not reaching as many non-WRS majors as we had hoped, we considered that summer's Write4U@SLCC a success.

We offered Write4U@SLCC again in summer 2019. This time, it was taught by Kenna, who has extensive experience working in Salt Lake's community writing centers and has been an adjunct writing instructor at SLCC. Her in-class transfer mentor, Jose Loeri, was a WRS major and linguistics minor who had taken Write4U@SLCC and WRTG 3030 in summer 2018. We conducted another early-spring survey of interested students about days, times, and campus locations; midday on Tuesdays and Thursdays at Redwood received the most votes. Enrollment numbers were lower—eleven signed up and eight completed the course. Among those eight, half were students of color, and all identified as women. Three-quarters were first-generation college students, and more than a third were older than twenty-four. This time, only two prospective WRS majors signed up. Students were considering majors in business, English, philosophy, anthropology, psychology, nursing, and engineering.

Although the classes were small, comparing the broad racial and ethnic identities of those who completed the summer Write4U@SLCC courses with local demographics suggests that the course connected with some groups that have been underrepresented at the U, most notably Latinx and Black students. Fifty-five percent of students were immigrants, and 23 percent were the children of immigrants. However, we failed to reach Pacific Islander and Native American students, two of the groups most minoritized and most subject to transfer gaps in our context.

Based on her experiences in WRTG 3020 and her conversations with other transfer students, Claudia identified a need to provide more individualized out-of-class support for the summer courses, particularly for multilingual students. So, in summer 2018, she piloted the peer-led Summer Writing Studio, which offered drop-in times in SLCC's Student Writing and Reading Center (SWRC) and by-appointment meetings. Many students in Write4U@SLCC and WRTG 3030 visited the Summer Writing Studio, with several coming in multiple times a week. For some, Claudia's ability to converse in English and Spanish was helpful for working through discussions of complex theoretical concepts and ideas for their projects. This pilot was so successful that Claudia led the Summer Writing Studio again in summer 2019, with Jose, Joseph Moss, and Cristina Guerrero Perez—all of whom had taken Write4U@SLCC and/or WRTG 3030 in summer 2018—providing additional assistance. Based on the success of their efforts, we made the Summer Writing Studio a permanent part of the summer bridge programs.

Table 4. Summer Write4U@SLCC racial/ethnic identities

	% Population of Salt Lake County (2017)	% SLCC Enrollment (Fall 2017)	% U Enrollment (Fall 2017)	% WRITE4U @SLCC (Summer 2018-Summer 2019)
White	71	67	67	45
Latinx	18	18	12	35
Asian and Asian American	4	4	6	5
Two or more races	3	3	5	5
Black	2	2	1	10
Native Hawaiian or other Pacific Islander	2	1	<0.5	0
Native American or Alaska Native	1	1	<0.5	0

Source: Data for SLCC and U enrollments from the National Center for Education Statistics College Navigator (nces.ed.gov/collegenavigator/).

Note: The table excludes NCES figures for students who were classified as "non-resident alien" or did not report their race or ethnicity.

By fall 2019, we had concluded that Write4U@SLCC works best and most equitably under the following conditions:

- The course is offered in the summer, preferably in the evening.
- Students are recruited through Department of English, Linguistics, and Writing Studies (ELWS) faculty, SLCC advisors, *and* programs serving first-generation college students, students of color, immigrants, LGBTQIA+ students, and students with disabilities.

- Full-tuition scholarships are provided for students associated with those programs as well as any other students who would be unable to take the course without financial assistance.
- Linked peer-led multilingual reading and writing support is provided so students have multiple options for assistance based on what they find most comfortable and beneficial.

Evolving Curriculum. WRTG 3020 is a challenging three-credit upper-division writing course. The workload is comparable to what students encounter in any CW course, but it provides more scaffolding for reading and writing assignments, as well as metalevel discussion of disciplinary writing and the various transitions transfer students experience. Channeling insights on transfer-receptive culture, one of the central goals of WRTG 3020 is to value students' educational paths and the writing experiences and rhetorical knowledges they bring to the U. The course aims to build on those capacities and the opportunity of the transfer experience to cultivate what Shannon Carter calls *rhetorical dexterity*: "the ability to effectively read, understand, manipulate, and negotiate the cultural and linguistic codes of a new community of practice" (14), in this case their major disciplines. The course encourages transfer students to adapt their prior writing knowledge to rhetorical contexts they are entering at the U while critically interrogating how dominant disciplinary discourses, language ideologies, epistemologies, and writing practices interrelate with systemic inequities.

Influenced by cultural studies scholarship on antidisciplinarity (e.g., Kristensen and Claycomb; Claycomb and Riedner), I came to think of this approach as "writing-in-and-against-the-disciplines," a term that reflects self-conscious ambivalence about the gatekeeping function of all specialized academic discourses. The course is structured around three units. Each unit introduces a set of threshold concepts in writing studies adapted from Linda Adler-Kassner and Elizabeth Wardle's *Naming What We Know* collection.[33] These concepts provide a frame for understanding and critiquing discourses in students' major disciplines (including, potentially, writing and rhetoric studies). The threshold concepts themselves are presented as open for critique, as well: What distinguishes a threshold from a gate, and for whom? Each unit is anchored by a major writing project that goes through multiple rounds of drafting, peer and instructor feedback, and revision.

The first unit focuses on academic communities of practice—the notion that all writing, including disciplinary writing, is social practice. We read and discuss scholarly texts that present writing as situated and tied to identities and experiences, foregrounding critical perspectives on linguistic diversity and standard language ideologies. In the U version of the course, this unit is anchored by the *expert interview* project, which invites students to identify and interview a U faculty member in their major. Students read at least two publications by that faculty member and interview them about writing practices in their discipline using a flexible protocol the class develops collaboratively. The purpose of this assignment is to understand disciplines as geographically diffuse communities of human beings engaged in knowledge-making practices that shape and are shaped by specialized discourses. Students learn about the range of writing practices faculty engage in and how their academic literacies interact with their life histories and identities. This project also provides an opportunity for sustained conversation with a potential faculty mentor.

In the Write4U@SLCC course, faculty interviews are logistically unfeasible. Many SLCC students are not yet certain about their majors. Some are intimidated about approaching faculty, a difficulty compounded by the unavailability of many faculty during the summer months. Instead, we ask students to compose a profile of a specific U faculty member in their potential major based on information on the U website and a review of several publications. This low-risk approach reduces the barriers to completing the assignment, though it does not offer the same opportunities to connect with potential mentors. But both versions help students identify faculty whose interests and identities are aligned with aspects of their own. Both enable students to deepen their understanding of university faculties' teaching, research, and service. The goal is to humanize academic writing, which can often seem depersonalized and remote from what students value.

The second and most difficult unit focuses on genre. This unit draws on the work of rhetorical genre theorists (Bawarshi, "Ecology"; Devitt et al.; Devitt; Bawarshi, *Genre*; Bawarshi and Reiff; Reiff and Bawarshi; Clark and Hernandez) and the Teaching for Transfer (TFT) curriculum in *Writing across Contexts: Transfer, Composition, and Sites of Writing* (Yancey et al.). After an introduction to the rhetorical concept of genre, students embark on a scaffolded *critical genre analysis*. First, they collect six to eight peer-reviewed academic journal articles in their discipline. Using a set of heuristic questions adapted from Devitt, Reiff, and Bawarshi ("Materiality"), students analyze the articles, first focusing on identifying genre features, then developing a critical argument about the disciplinary values and epistemologies those features reveal. During our initial semesters, we asked students to accomplish both objectives in the same essay. In summer 2018, we broke this assignment into two separate papers: an analysis that focuses on identifying genre features and articulating how those features relate to disciplinary values and ways of knowing, and a second paper developing a critical argument about the *social consequences* of those disciplinary genre features.

This assignment sequence accomplishes several goals. First, the process of locating genre samples introduces students to the resources of the U's research library, including its databases, discipline-specific research guides, and subject librarians. As students locate and analyze articles, they gain a clearer understanding of the research methods used in their disciplines, the vetting mechanisms built into academic publication, and how scholars evaluate the credibility of sources in their field. The genre analysis helps students become stronger *readers* of primary academic scholarship in their discipline, and it is also an opportunity to engage in extended, iterative writing processes. For many students, it is a difficult assignment, different from anything they have undertaken before. Most experience some confusion and even frustration, but nearly all manage to complete the project through several rounds of feedback and revision. We build in multiple opportunities to reflect on *why* this assignment is hard and what resources students draw on to push through the challenges.

This project invites students to see that genre conventions emerge out of disciplinary histories and evolving social practices. Such conventions serve functions in recurring rhetorical situations, and they enact the values and epistemologies of the communities that produce them. They are dynamic and ideological; they are not beyond critique. Furthermore, disciplinary genre conventions have consequences for *whose* knowledges are represented, in what ways, and how disciplinary knowledges do or do not circulate in nonacademic communities that might benefit from or critique them. These conventions have consequences for *who* survives the process of "being disciplined" to become a member of the scholarly community, and on what terms. Those presences and absences shape the knowledges the discipline produces and the genre conventions, options, and possibilities for innovation that emerge. We encourage students to use critical insights from composition studies, as well as their own prior educational experiences and community-based knowledges, to "crack the code" on disciplinary genres while thinking critically about those codes and the power structures they enact. In their projects, we invite students to subvert, challenge, and reimagine dominant disciplinary genre conventions.

The third unit focuses on *multimodality*. Students read composition studies scholarship on this topic, and we discuss how the affordances of digital publishing are changing academic writing. The anchor project for this unit is an *online metagenre*. We ask students to remediate what they have learned about writing in their discipline into a digital resource to help incoming transfer students navigate writing in their major discipline. (Over the first three years of the course, students made videos, animations, podcasts, slideshows, video games, infographics, and webtexts.) We invite them to compose in multiple languages and/or language varieties if that would be useful to their intended audience, and students have produced metagenre projects in Spanish and Nepali as well as in English. Students have the option to publish their metagenre projects in an online archive searchable by discipline. In this way, WRTG 3020 students produce *socially useful knowledge*, "redistributing rather than consolidating professional expertise" (Trimbur, *Solidarity* 49) for students who come after them.

At four points in the semester, students compose/revise a *theory of writing* statement. This project is adapted from the TFT curriculum. Yancey and colleagues argue that developing an explicit theory of writing grounded in key terms in composition studies enables students to develop rhetorical meta-awareness that promotes long-term writing knowledge transfer. Our version of this assignment invites students to articulate what they have learned about writing through their prior educational and out-of-school experiences, and then reflect on what they want to add to or change about that theory based on each unit's readings, discussion, and projects. We do not emphasize disciplinary key terms, nor do we require students to use the language of the threshold concepts we discuss. To me, Claudia's final Theory of Writing statement (Interstitial III) suggests that students can engage disciplinary concepts in ways that are more personally and culturally meaningful if invited to theorize in their own terms.

Throughout the semester, we build in opportunities for students to engage with a range of resources available at the U. These resources included the library and UWC as well as the Career and Professional Development Center, the Office of Undergraduate Research, the Bennion Center for Community Engaged Learning, and the Hinckley Institute of Politics, which has a well-funded internship program. We also connect students with support services like the Student Success Coaches, Women's Resource Center, CESB, LGBT Resource Center, Dream Center, Black Cultural Center, and Center for Disability and Access, as well as the Crimson Transfer Mentors Program and Honors Society. We make sure transfer students are familiar with the resources available through the Office of Financial Aid, including the U's scholarship database, and in some iterations of the course we have helped them apply for scholarships.

We also tell students about the challenges, academic and nonacademic, that research suggests some transfer students experience: If they encounter such difficulties, we want them to know they are not alone. We strive to communicate to students that we value them as whole people juggling alongside-school relationships, responsibilities, and commitments while they pursue their education within inequitable material constraints. Through extensive in-class small-group work, consultations with the transfer mentor, and (in Write4U@SLCC) access to the peer-led Summer Writing Studio, we encourage students to form social connections that create a sense of community at the U.

Critical Reflections. From my vantage point, WRTG 3020 was a mixed success in its first three years. It was a success in the sense that it was a "real" 3000-level writing studies course, not a deficit-oriented "remedial" course. Nor was it an academic etiquette lesson upholding the normativity of an upper-middle-class white professional habitus. The curriculum was intellectually challenging and invited students to self-consciously transfer a range of rhetorical capacities, literacy experiences, and knowledges to develop critical awareness of disciplinary discourses. We had ample evidence that the U version of the course worked well. Completion rates were high, student course evaluations were strong, and the course developed a positive reputation with academic advisors across campus. WRTG 3020 students found research assistantships, scholarships, and assistance with housing and other financial emergencies through resources they learned about in the course. It provided a supportive space in which transfer students could make sense of their transitions to the U as they were experiencing them, and at least one student each semester decided to add a double major or minor in WRS.

By year three, however, it seemed clear we had not yet devised a WRTG 3020 curriculum that worked well at SLCC. We had addressed some of the logistical challenges of connecting with students there, and our experiences teaching the summer 2018 course suggested that the "meta" curriculum appealed to SLCC students interested in WRS. However, it was less effective for many non-WRS majors. As Kenna observed, these students were less certain about what they wanted to major in or the relationships between major disciplines and career goals. With the U still an abstraction, they had less context for the concept of disciplines and the centrality of research in university contexts. Although genre is an important threshold concept in SLCC's ENGL 1010 and 2010 curriculum (see Blankenship et al.; Jory), the genre analysis project was very difficult for some non-WRS students. Likewise, the reading assignments could be daunting, and we worried that the challenging coursework might discourage some students from transferring.

After summer 2019, we decided to redesign the curriculum for Write4U@SLCC. Rather than trying to make what worked at the U function at SLCC—or settling for a curriculum that only worked well for prospective WRS majors—we needed to reimagine what Write4U@SLCC could be. We needed to do a better job of starting where SLCC students were, rather than centering the institutional context of the U and the priorities of a research university. As we considered how to make this change,[34] we turned to the successes of WRTG 3030: Writing across Locations, our summer bridge course for SLCC students entering the WRS. Over three summers of collaborative development and revision, this course was more fully enacting our goal of valuing SLCC students' community-based rhetorical capacities, prior educational experiences, and embodied differences while inviting them to engage critically with disciplinary discourses.

Responsibility for Transfer Students in WRS

Our initiatives for SLCC transfer students entering WRS were motivated by five goals:

- Recruit more students into WRS degree programs.
- Foster a racially, culturally, linguistically, socioeconomically, and age-diverse community of WRS students.
- Support SLCC transfer students academically and socially and connect them with resources and opportunities that would enable them to achieve their goals for themselves, their families, and their communities.
- Contribute to fostering a diverse community of writers—professional and otherwise—in Salt Lake.
- Contribute to creating/sustaining a more diverse and equitable community of composition professionals at two- and four-year institutions, both locally and nationally.

The point was not to "discipline" SLCC transfer students into WRS. Rather, we wanted to *use* the disciplinary structures of an independent writing studies department to facilitate transfer, particularly for students from groups subject to transfer gaps. In the long run, I hoped doing so could change the university and the discipline for the better.

Iterative Implementation. The idea of creating a summer bridge experience for SLCC transfer students entering WRS cropped up early in our research team's conversations. While bridge programs for community college transfer students are an old idea (see Ackermann; Laanan, "Making"; Martinez and Fernández; Ornelas and Solorzano), they have gained renewed visibility in the literature on transfer-receptive culture (Jain et al., "Developing"; Jain et al., *Power*). My initial vision was modest: I wanted to teach a free summer course for prospective WRS majors at SLCC so we could connect with students in a space where they were comfortable, provide them with an opportunity to earn upper-division major credits at no cost, and get them connected with departmental advising and other U resources. However, when we shared this idea with SLCC colleagues in summer 2016, they pushed back on the idea that U faculty would swoop in and teach a writing studies course on their campus. At issue was the perception that university faculty were claiming disciplinary authority. Several SLCC colleagues suggested that such a course should be co-developed and team-taught by SLCC and U faculty. They were right. I immediately saw how sustained pedagogical collaboration around the bridge course could be mutually transformative. I just had to figure out how to pay for it.

The answer emerged from unanticipated ecological interactions precipitated by the 2016 presidential election. The outcome of that election threw me into a dry-heaving panic, not least because I was frightened about what it might mean for some of my students and their families. I had been watching the research team burn their candles at both ends for a year and a half as they worked to pay tuition, scrambled to make it to classes, tended to their relationships, and still somehow cared enough to contribute to our transfer projects. I wanted a way to support them beyond hourly wages and letters of recommendation. That February, I was scheduled to give a talk about transfer at the University of Illinois, Urbana-Champaign, for which I would receive a $1,000 honorarium. I had promised the team that any money that came to me through our collaborative work would go to benefit transfer students, so we decided to use that check as seed money for a scholarship for SLCC transfer students in WRS.

When I raised the idea with my chair, Jay Jordan, he set up a meeting with Lindsay Kite, a College of Humanities development officer. That meeting took place in December. I don't remember much about it, but I must have given Lindsay an earful about the need for dedicated funding for transfer students because, in addition to setting up our little scholarship, she suggested we ask local foundations to fund the bridge course we were developing for WRS majors. I wasn't optimistic that prospective U donors would find community college collaborations glamorous enough to support. However, with input from the research team, I assembled a dream budget for a full-fledged bridge program and sent it to Lindsay.

In January, the College of Humanities submitted a one-year, $10,000 request to what was then called the Benjamin Foundation.[35] To my everlasting surprise, a few weeks later they offered us $20,000 a year for five years: a $100,000 total commitment. Suddenly we had a bridge program, and the college was able to leverage that pledge to secure additional funding from the Sorenson Legacy Foundation. We now had money to pay my SLCC co-instructor, an in-class transfer mentor, and summer CE tuition for up to twenty students. We could also provide a $2,000 "transition" scholarship to every bridge student who transferred to the U and majored in WRS. Full-time in-state tuition and fees at the U total just under $9,000 a year, so $2,000 is nowhere close to a full ride, but that scholarship reduces the initial price hike transfer students face at the U, and it can be the difference between transferring or not for students unable to apply for federal financial aid. We decided to call the program Writing Studies Scholars (WSS), a name signaling students' membership in an intellectual community. We also awarded scholarships to ten still-enrolled "senior" Writing Studies Scholars who'd helped lay the foundation for the program (see Interstitial I).

We titled the bridge course WRTG 3030: Writing across Locations, foregrounding connections between writing, place, social locations, and mobility. We wanted to frame transfer between SLCC and the U as a lateral move. Andrea Malouf volunteered to co-teach the pilot section of WRTG 3030 in summer 2017, with Nate as transfer mentor and Kelly as in-class co-researcher. Cassie Goff volunteered to assist in the course, as well. Throughout the spring, I visited SLCC colleagues' classrooms, posted flyers around campus, and sent recruitment messages through faculty and advisors. We tabled at the U's spring transfer orientations to connect with SLCC students who would be arriving in the fall, and we sent a survey to interested students for input on what day, time, and location would work best with their schedules. The most popular choice was Monday and Wednesday evenings at SLCC's South City campus. A total of twelve SLCC students enrolled, all of whom completed the course. Half were students of color, two-thirds were first-generation college students, and 58 percent were women. As of summer 2021, eleven students in the 2017 cohort had transferred to universities, ten of them to the U. Nine declared a major in WRS, becoming our first transfer cohort of Writing Studies Scholars.

In summer 2018, SWRC director Clint Gardner and I co-taught WRTG 3030 with Joanne Castillo. This time, nineteen students enrolled and eighteen completed the class; one student withdrew but returned the following summer. Seventy-two percent of those who completed were students of color, two-thirds were first-generation college students, and 83 percent identified as women. This large and racially diverse cohort was the result of Claudia's recruitment efforts, particularly her work tabling and connecting with students in ODMA. On interest surveys, students once again expressed a preference for evening classes, this time at SLCC's Redwood campus. As of summer 2021, fourteen students in the summer 2018 cohort had transferred to the U, thirteen declaring a major or minor in WRS.

In summer 2019, I co-taught WRTG 3030 with SLCC colleague Bernice Olivas and transfer mentor Cristina Guerrero Perez, who had taken the class in 2018. Enrollment was lower: thirteen students signed up and ten completed. Forty percent were students of color, 60 percent were first-generation college students, and 60 percent were women. We attributed the dip in enrollment to three factors. First, we offered the class midday based on preferences expressed in an early-spring interest survey, but that schedule ended up precluding some students from participating. The second factor was spring 2019 staffing challenges. I was trying to complete this book manuscript while serving as the department's director of undergraduate studies, and Claudia was completing her final U semester while piloting the WRS Dream Center Fellowship. Neither of us had as much time for tabling or classroom visits as the previous spring. Guided Pathways restructuring of SLCC advising also meant some of our most reliable advocates with students had retired or moved to other roles.

However, the 2019 enrollments did suggest that WSS was becoming a recognizable "path" for SLCC students interested in writing. More than half the cohort had been involved in writing-related programs at SLCC, including working at the SWRC and/or CWC, participating in Publication Center programs, and/or pursuing the writing certificate. The students finding this path included many first-generation college students and women. As of summer 2021, five students from the 2019 cohort had transferred to the U, and all majored or minored in WRS. However, the 2019 group was not as racially, ethnically, and linguistically diverse as they could and should have been. I began to worry that our interinstitutional disciplinary ecology was at risk of reproducing rather than countering local racial transfer gaps.

We tried to mitigate this possibility by sustaining multiple entry points for WSS. Requiring completion of WRTG 3030 would create a barrier to accessing support for students who were, for a variety of reasons, unable to take the summer course. With the help of Lisa Shaw and Paul Fisk, we sought to connect with SLCC students interested in WRS degrees who had already arrived at the U or were transferring without taking WRTG 3030. Between fall 2017 and fall 2019, we added seventeen students to WSS through alternative entry. Two-thirds were students of color, 82 percent were first-generation college students, and three-quarters identified as women or gender nonbinary. Nearly half were immigrants or the children of immigrants.

Between spring 2017 and fall 2019, fifty-seven students became Writing Studies Scholars. Comparison with demographics of Salt Lake County, SLCC, and the U suggests that WSS has been countering local racial transfer gaps (see Table 5 in this chapter and Table 2 in Chapter 3).

Table 5. Writing Studies Scholars racial/ethnic identities

	% Population of Salt Lake County (2017)	**% SLCC Enrollment (Fall 2017)**	**% U Enrollment (Fall 2017)**	**% Writing Studies Scholars (Spring 2017-Fall 2019)**
White	71	67	67	42
Latinx	18	18	12	33
Asian and Asian American	4	4	6	7
Two or more races	3	3	5	11
Black	2	2	1	4
Native Hawaiian or other Pacific Islander	2	1	0	2
Native American or Alaska Native	1	1	0	2

Source: Data for SLCC and U enrollments from the National Center for Education Statistics College Navigator (nces.ed.gov/collegenavigator/).

Note: The table excludes NCES figures for students who were classified as "non-resident alien" or did not report their race or ethnicity.

WSS students also held additional identities often subject to transfer gaps. Fifty-four percent were immigrants or the children of immigrants, and 46 percent were multilingual. Seventy-four percent were first-generation college students, and 53 percent were older than twenty-four when they joined. Sixty-eight percent identified as women or gender nonbinary, and 19 percent had children. During the first years we did not systematically survey students about sexual or disability-related identities. However, 18 percent voluntarily disclosed LGBTQIA+ identities, and 28 percent disclosed disabilities.

WRTG 3030 was not just about engaging with writing studies on an academic level. It also created an opportunity to form a cohort so transfer students would arrive at the U with a peer network in place. Between fall 2017 and spring 2019, we hosted once-a-semester get-togethers so pre- and post-transfer students and alumni could catch up with one another and learn about opportunities and resources. Aware that many transfer students find social connection at the university primarily through their academic interests and professional goals, we continuously sought ways to make WSS a community.

Over time, WSS students helped us identify multiple means of addressing material inequities transfer students face. Most live outside the close-in metro area well-serviced by public transportation, and many could not afford the $260 up-front fee for an annual U parking pass. Paying for parking by the hour meant students were less likely to stay after class to talk with faculty or peers, attend campus events, or use the library and other on-campus resources. We started providing parking pass subsidies. We also helped WSS students apply for scholarships, on and off campus. By fall 2019, nearly half of WSS students had received additional U and/or community scholarship funding beyond the $2,000 we guarantee.

We also sought to create access to writing-related professional-development opportunities. Some were within the WRS department. By fall 2019, I had worked with sixteen Writing Studies Scholars on co-teaching, co-researching, and coauthoring

Writing Studies Scholars Andrea Valverde, Joanne Castillo, Katherine Allred, and Claudia Sauz Mendoza graduating in 2019. Photo credit: Jay Jordan.

projects, usually paid and/or offering undergraduate research credits that count toward the major. I presented with students at academic conferences around the country. My department colleagues Jay Jordan, Maureen Mathison, Romeo García, Natalie Stillman-Webb, and José Cortez also hired Writing Studies Scholars to work on research and teaching projects. Several WSS students helped edit the undergraduate *Journal of Contemporary Issues and Media.* Others were paid interns in LuMing Mao's Teaching across Borders program, which provided online English tutoring for children in China. Meanwhile, SLCC continued to provide professional development opportunities for our mutual students. Thirteen WSS students worked in the SWRC and/or CWC *after* transferring to the U.

Based on the first three years of WSS, we concluded that the following practices helped make the program successful and more equitable:

- Offer the WRTG 3030 summer course in the evening.
- Recruit prospective Writing Studies Scholars through writing-related courses and programs associated with ELWS.
- Do not rely on ELWS alone. Build and sustain relationships with SLCC advisors and programs that serve first-generation college students, students of color, immigrants, LGBTQIA+ students, and students with disabilities.
- Provide a transition scholarship to incentivize transfer and find or create additional scholarships for SLCC transfer students throughout their time in WRS degree programs, particularly students who are not eligible for federal financial aid.
- Create a variety of opportunities for WSS students with diverse interests, schedules, and family/community responsibilities to sustain a sense of community at the U *after* they have transferred.
- Create a variety of flexible professional-development opportunities for WSS students that support their transitions to postgraduate education and/or employment aligning with their personal and community goals.

Evolving Curriculum. From the beginning, WRTG 3030 had a local theme informed by the ecological framework we develop in Chapter 1. During the 2017 pilot year, this focus was enriched by the knowledge Andrea brought from her years directing the

CWC, as well as input from Claudia, Nate, Nic, Wes, Kelly, Cassie, Sandra, Shauna, and Justin, all of whom helped develop the initial curriculum during a paid full-day workshop that spring. In 2018, we revised the curriculum based on student feedback from the previous summer and the expertise and perspectives of Clint, Joanne, and rhetoric and composition PhD candidate Charissa Che. In 2019, we revised again with input from the previous summer's students and co-teachers Bernice and Cristina. Although the readings, assignments, and classroom dynamics built on one another year to year, one core idea was consistent: We spend the summer figuring out what writing and rhetoric studies *is* by considering what writing and rhetoric studies *does* in the Salt Lake Valley.

Throughout the summer, students read texts by writing faculty and students at SLCC and the U. Most readings incorporate some element of personal narrative, discussion of the writer's teaching, and/or insights into place and community. Week by week, the authors come to class as guest speakers, and students ask questions about their scholarship, their personal and educational trajectories, and what motivates them to participate in writing and rhetoric studies. The goals of this curriculum are threefold: (1) to introduce students to some of WRS's major concerns, methodologies, and disciplinary discourses; (2) to humanize scholarly writing so students can see how personal experiences, embodied identities, and political commitments fuel academic work; and (3) to help students expand their social networks by connecting with faculty who will be their teachers and prospective mentors.

This program of readings and classroom visits had some unanticipated benefits. It brought nearly all my tenure-line departmental colleagues to the SLCC campus—some of them for the first time—to talk about their scholarship and teaching. That made SLCC and its students more "real" to WRS faculty and increased their investment in interinstitutional collaborations. The curriculum also created opportunities for my SLCC co-teachers to learn about intellectual work in our department. I, in turn, learned a great deal about my SLCC colleagues' wide-ranging projects. The curriculum for WRTG 3030 thus helps us co-constitute a local disciplinary ecology in which we have a deeper mutual understanding of one another's scholarship, teaching, art, and activism.

The other guiding principle of WRTG 3030 is that those of us who are faculty are inviting SLCC transfer students to co-construct writing and rhetoric studies *with* us. They have knowledges the discipline does not, and we all stand to learn from one another about the writing ecology we co-constitute with the lands on which we live. The course becomes an extended conversation about the complex relationships between individuals, communities, languages, rhetorics, literacies, power, place, and land, and how scholars in our discipline negotiate the tensions those relations produce in and through writing. While the role of personal narrative in composition scholarship might be contested, writing in this discipline does not have to mean checking one's embodied identities, experiences, and community-based rhetorical capacities at the door. Rather, it can be an opportunity to gain critical awareness of how one's languaging and literacies are situated within system inequities and structures of oppression, and such awareness can foster solidarity, healing, and growth.

We ask students to complete a series of three interrelated projects. Each project goes through multiple rounds of revision based on peer and instructor feedback. The first is a literacy narrative students compose out of their experiences as language users. The second project, often a substantive reworking of the first, is an autoethnography in which students put their community-based language and/or literacy experiences in conversation with scholarly research: at least two sources located through the U library and two pieces that we've read for the course. They are also invited to put themselves in conversation with nonacademic theorists, including people in their alongside-school communities, and to draw on whatever languaging enables them to achieve their goals for the piece. WRTG 3030 students have written about a vast array of topics, from rhetorics surrounding bisexuality among Latter-day Saints to the racism experienced by children of Mexican immigrants in Salt Lake public schools; from local DACA literacies to hip-hop and Black identity formation in Salt Lake; from the Valley's rave scene to the emplaced rhetorics of mothers who have lost an infant. Every one of these projects has deepened my appreciation for the complex, contested writing ecology we are co-constituting.

The final project invites students to remediate their autoethnography into a multimodal project they have the option of publishing in an online archive, "Composing Salt Lake's Writing Ecology."[36] This project invites students to draw on their wide-ranging rhetorical capacities to share their scholarship with wider audiences. Students have composed podcasts, videos, and webtexts. They have made children's books, zines, scrapbooks, explosion boxes, flags, prison tattoo guns, and graffiti. They have produced projects incorporating Spanish, Japanese, African American English, and Arabic. Joanne's remediation, a cover of Luis Fonsi's "Despacito" she recorded with her brother, was entirely in Tagalog. Year by year, these projects add to our complex, constellating understandings of emerging languaging and literacy practices in the Salt Lake Valley.

This assignment sequence has three important benefits for incoming transfer students. First, it values their experiences and community knowledges as making important contributions to the discipline, an antideficit orientation aligning with principles of transfer-receptive culture. Second, students get to know one another while peer-workshopping these pieces, which can provide opportunities to build supportive networks across differences in age, racial and cultural identities, language backgrounds, gender and sexual identities, abilities, sensory processing, faiths, and life experiences. Third, I connect with students through conversations around their writing projects, which provides a basis for developing long-term supportive relationships with each of them. Andrea, Clint, and Bernice shared my excitement about students' WRTG 3030 projects. The curriculum allowed us all to get to know our students and the Salt Lake Valley in new ways.

WRTG 3030 students come into WRS with a clearer understanding than most nontransfer majors have about what writing and rhetoric studies can encompass, what faculty in our department research, and how their interests might fit into the discipline. Throughout the summer, we also introduce students to resources and support services at the U. In this sense, the course functions like an extended orientation. In the first three years, students made valuable suggestions for course improvements, including adjustments to assignments, classroom seating arrangements, and the role of transfer mentors. Course evaluations were strong, completion rates high, and levels of student interest in pursuing WRS gratifying. Most affirming was how first-generation college students, older/returning students, multilingual students, students of color, LGBTQIA+ students, and students with disabilities responded to the course.[37] Every year, we got closer to co-constructing a composition studies in which *all* students can engage the discipline on something closer to their own terms.

Critical Reflections. WSS became much bigger than I could have imagined when we first started talking about a bridge course, and that growth happened fast. If it hadn't been for faculty and staff at SLCC and the U and the transfer students who helped bring it all together, there is no way we would have pulled it off. Given the timelines we were working under, I think we accomplished something valuable. However, there were many things I would have done differently with more time to plan, process, and reflect. Every aspect of WSS would have been done better post-tenure. Producing a book about a program as we were trying to create it was stressful, especially with my job on the line, and our arguments would be stronger with more years of data and time to work through emergent challenges.

A case in point is team-teaching. I am glad my SLCC faculty colleagues insisted on co-teaching WRTG 3030. As Joanne suggests in her TYCA-West keynote, our different positionalities shape how students perceive our approachability and whom they might initially trust. It is also important that students recognize WRTG 3030 as an interinstitutional effort. The transfer mentors are also indispensable contributors to the course: they can connect with fellow students in ways faculty cannot. While co-teaching is an experience I treasure each summer, I did not initially know how to do it very well. Teaching together across complex power differentials is a process that requires careful planning, explicit negotiation of responsibilities, and open and continuous communication. I am grateful for the patience my SLCC colleagues extended as I unlearned university-centric professor habits and relearned how to teach collaboratively.

Program recruitment is another time-intensive dimension of WSS. Our first three years showed me the importance of being present in person to connect with SLCC students in as many spaces as possible—classrooms, lobbies, major fairs, transfer orientations, readings, award ceremonies, and events associated with a wide range of student programs. My presence in these spaces *as a U faculty member* mattered—many students told me I was the only U professor they ever met at SLCC. The presence of WSS student co-coordinators like Claudia also mattered. The differences in our embodied identities and languaging enabled co-coordinators to connect with prospective students in ways I could not. There was no shortcut for being physically present in this way—not through web content, email blasts, social media, flyers, sharing information with advisors and SLCC faculty, or campus visits by U advising staff (although all those strategies were also valuable). To the extent the university's labor structures prevented me from being present at SLCC and transfer orientations as much as I could and should have been, they worked against the institution's commitment to creating and sustaining equitable "transfer pathways."

A third area demanding more time and attention than I was able to spend was sustaining community for *all* WSS students throughout their time at the U. With the input of students, we got good at fostering a supportive community in WRTG 3030. However, in 2019, I coauthored a collaborative autoethnographic essay with six first-generation college students from the 2018 cohort: Cristina, Jose, Adi, Joseph, Kate Henderson, and Jacque Thetsombandith. Through that writing, they taught me that a strong sense of community in WRTG 3030 does not automatically carry over to students' post-transfer experiences. Some WSS students found community on the transfer team, projects with other department faculty, and through positions in SLCC's writing centers. However, once-a-semester WSS gatherings were not enough to sustain community for all students in the program. We needed to find more ways to foster a sense of connection and belonging post-transfer, particularly for first-generation college students and students of color, who often find the U alienating (Toth et al., "Bridging"). As we entered the 2019–20 academic year, one of our goals was to create a more robust set of post-transfer mechanisms for WSS students to stay connected by having monthly get-togethers and creating a stronger social media presence among program participants. Cristina had a brilliant idea that we launched in fall 2019: inviting students to form one-credit peer study groups each semester paid for with an additional WSS scholarship.

A fourth concern was WSS students' achievement of their post-graduation goals. I resist the idea that WRS curricula should prioritize the expectations of employers, but prospective students and some SLCC faculty had legitimate concerns about whether a bachelor's degree in WRS would lead to secure, meaningful employment. As one SLCC colleague put it, "Are we building a bridge to nowhere?" When the first WSS students started graduating, we realized we needed to build in more advising about graduate school options, more engagement with the Career and Professional Development Center, and more co-curricular opportunities that could lead to post-graduation employment. In fall 2019, I began collaborating with Ned Khatrichettri, the College of Humanities internship coordinator, and Megan Randall, the college's designated career coach in the Career and Professional Development Center, to develop a plan ensuring all WSS students would engage with career advising from their first months in the program.

One failure haunting me is how few Indigenous students joined WSS in its first three years. This failure is particularly shameful given my history as a teacher and scholar, this book's indebtedness to Indigenous theorists, and the U's espoused commitments to "partnership with Native Nations and our Urban Indian communities through research, education, and community outreach activities" (*Indigenous*). Native students are underrepresented at SLCC relative to their population in Salt Lake and the state, but they are even more underrepresented at the U, which uses the Ute name with an explicit promise to support Native students (*Memorandum*). We cannot be a transfer-conducive writing ecology until we are co-constituting educational spaces where students indigenous to the lands on which we live and learn can thrive. WSS could and should have played a role in co-constituting those spaces from the outset.

Despite my shortcomings and the limitations of our successes, the first three years of WSS taught us several lessons about what it took to foster a more transfer-conducive writing ecology in the Salt Lake Valley. It took awareness of relevant scholarship: critical higher education research, composition scholarship, and studies of our local context. It took U faculty's willingness to get "off the hill" and spend time on SLCC campuses. It took rejection of deficit discourses about transfer students, appreciation for their experiences as whole people pursuing education amid myriad constraints, and willingness to value the wide range of languaging and literacy practices they brought. It took partnership between SLCC and U faculty, advisors, and administrators. It took collaboration with transfer students as co-researchers, co-designers, and co-teachers. It took willingness to put student interests ahead of professional priorities. It took strategically repurposing institutional structures and policy discourses. It took a commitment to providing students with social as well as academic support. And it took money to fund scholarships and pay student and faculty colleagues for their labor.

I'll close, then, with critical reflection on the funding mechanisms for this program. Since 2015, I have worked day in and day out with students who are pursuing degrees at a flagship research university amid serious material constraints. Watching the toll those constraints take on their bodyminds (Price), seeing how those pressures undercut the joy they might otherwise take in learning, has made me pragmatic. Money *can* make certain problems go away, or at least hold those problems at bay for a semester, and some students need that money *now* if they are going to stay in school. It would be obscene privilege for me to decide I'm too "critical" to take money that could go toward their tuition bills, their rent, or their medications. But I am under no illusions about the cost of funding this program through individual donations and private foundation grants.

Some of that cost is personal. Money attracts institutional attention. It requires me to put on a suit and talk about our work in ways that are palatable to powerful people. It requires me to allow the college to use my name and my image to raise funds, attention I find distasteful and anxiety-inducing. I have insisted that students who choose to get involved in fundraising for WSS maintain control over their images, voices, and stories, and I am adamant that *no* WSS student should ever feel pressure to interact with development staff or donors. Whenever possible, I do that work so students can focus on learning. I enjoyed these transfer projects most when no one was paying attention to what we were doing, but I'm willing to shoulder these personal costs to try to address the immediate material challenges transfer students face.

I am more troubled by the political price. I will always be grateful for what I have seen money from private donors do for individual SLCC transfer students, particularly students who do not qualify for federal financial aid and who, for a variety of reasons beyond their control, do not have the near-perfect GPAs required for many U scholarships. But the challenges these students face are the result of decades of failed policy: failures to provide federal financial aid that covers the actual cost of college attendance; failures to regulate for-profit institutions that prey on low-income students and use up their lifetime financial aid eligibility; failures to allocate enough resources to community colleges to support adequate advising and fairly compensated faculty; failures to provide the kind of social services and access to comprehensive healthcare that would enable students to focus more time and energy on their studies; failures to ensure affordable housing and transportation; failures to accommodate cultural expectations in students' families and communities; failures to pass comprehensive immigration reform that would give undocumented people full access to postsecondary education. We have *failed* generations of college students on a massive scale, and I glimpse the consequences daily.

The generosity of donors should not determine which students, transfer or otherwise, deserve access to a public university education. We should be developing institutional, state, and federal policies that address these inequities systemically. The struggle for a truly public postsecondary education system is ongoing. In the meantime, I am going to use every short-term option I can find to help get these students through, not least because we need *them* in positions of power. However, I hope the future of WSS will be collective action toward public policy that expands access to lifelong literacy learning for every member of the community, not continuous capital campaigns.

UNANTICIPATED ECOLOGICAL CHANGE

The story of WRTG 3020 and WRTG 3030 was shaped by emerging local conditions, including the sudden availability of funding to develop WSS. Our efforts to establish these courses also contributed to ecological changes beyond our classrooms and the bridge program. Here, I discuss changes I have been positioned to observe at multiple levels: within the WRS department, within the U's College of Humanities, across the wider university, and at SLCC.

Working to create a more transfer-conducive writing ecology helped shape WRS's major program. In 2014, WRS had twenty-five majors. In fall 2019, we had over a hundred, more than half of whom were transfer students. As a point of reference, transfer students make up around 35 percent of U undergraduates and 40 percent of humanities majors. While many factors contributed to the major's rapid growth, our efforts to connect with transfer students played a significant role. Likewise, those efforts shaped *who* was in WRS degree programs. By 2019, most students of color in our major—particularly Latinx and Black students, as well as students of Southeast Asian heritage—had transferred from SLCC, as did most of the major's first-generation and older/returning students. Our transfer initiatives helped create a more diverse undergraduate community in WRS.

Those initiatives also shaped our department's emerging reputation within the university. When the U turned its attention to "transfer pathways" in 2018, WRS was held up as a leader. That year, WRTG 3020 received an Innovation in General Education award. The following year, WRS and ELWS were invited to speak at first-ever SLCC-U Transfer Pathways Summit, and our articulation agreements and Principles for Partnership statement (see Part III) were featured on the new Transfer Pathways website. This external recognition informed the department's sense of itself. One pivotal moment for me came in summer 2018, when LuMing visited WRTG 3030 and told the students WSS was "part of our identity" in WRS. While I was aware of how quickly that sense of identity could fade, I felt we were beginning to discipline differently.

Disciplining differently changed the professionalization of our graduate students. The university-centrism of composition studies is reproduced in graduate education, where two-year college contexts are often absent from the curriculum and two-year college careers tend to be ignored, misrepresented, or outright discouraged. I tried to counter that stigma in my own graduate teaching and mentorship, but our transfer partnerships *enacted* a local composition studies far more inclusive of two-year colleges than is common in most research universities. Four master's students between 2015 and 2019—Shauna, Nate, Cassie, and Alice Lopez—experienced sustained interaction with SLCC colleagues as an integral part of their graduate education.

Likewise, PhD students Justin, Charissa, Nina, and Kenna had opportunities to teach in WRTG 3020 or 3030. Justin worked on the transfer research team in 2015–16, and, with guidance and logistical support from several SLCC colleagues, conducted his dissertation research with South Korean international students at SLCC (see Whitney "Avoiding" and "Perpetual"). Justin, Charissa, and Kenna presented on our transfer collaborations at TYCA and CCCC. Justin and Charissa benefited from two-year college colleagues' mentorship while on the job market. Both went on to accept tenure-track faculty positions at associates-granting institutions: Justin at SUNY-Delhi in 2018,[38] and Charissa at Queensborough Community College in 2019. In 2021, Charissa became the book review editor at *TETYC* and incoming chair of the TYCA National Conference.

Our transfer initiatives spurred unanticipated changes in the College of Humanities. Even as WRS grew rapidly, several other humanities departments experienced a decline in majors, and some looked to transfer to offset those losses. The Department of Communication decided to expand its longstanding one-credit Transfer Interest Group to a more substantive two-credit course. The Department of Philosophy created an SLCC transfer track in its major program and coauthored a department-to-department "Framework for Friendship" document that extended those partnerships to faculty professional development and mentorship opportunities for graduate students. The Department of Linguistics reached out to SLCC's ELWS Department to form articulation agreements that included the establishment of new 2000-level major courses. The U's Department of English also reached out, creating their own 3000-level bridge course offered at SLCC. This course, developed and taught by PhD candidate 'Ila Tua'one, focused on narratives of the Pacific Islands and was open to both prospective transfer students and community members. Although not all U colleagues embraced an antideficit orientation, these developments seemed positive. SLCC students deserve access to *all* areas of study that interest them, rather than defaulting to WRS because we are the only department reaching out. To me, these new opportunities signaled that we were using our disciplinary status to shake the university-centrism of other departments, pushing them to devote more attention and resources to SLCC students.

Another exciting ecological development was the inclusion of a bridge program for SLCC transfer students in the U's new Pacific Islands Studies Initiative. This interdisciplinary initiative, which encompasses scholarship, curriculum development, and new forms of engagement with the valley's large Pacific Islander community, is housed in the School for Cultural and Social Transformation (TRANSFORM). In 2018, the PI Studies Initiative received a one-million-dollar Mellon Foundation grant. The portion of the grant proposal focusing on a proposed transfer program borrowed from the model and budget materials we had developed for WSS. That funding has been used to create new academic, social, and material support for Pacific Islander students who enroll at SLCC and want to transfer to the U.[39] In this small way, the transfer work we did in

WRS helped generate resources to address one of our most pressing local transfer gaps.

The activities of the students in WSS spurred change elsewhere on campus. Joanne's efforts to push back against institutional barriers for transfer students led to the creation of the Spark Team, a group of transfer student consultants in UGS that also included WSS students Kelly, Adi, Joseph, Matt Nepute, and Lisa Donaldson. Together, they provided feedback on transfer students' experiences with the university website, admissions process, financial aid, transfer orientation, and accessibility of other resources and programs on campus. Joanne also pushed for mandatory trainings for faculty who perpetrate discriminatory behavior, and for departments—particularly in the STEM fields—to disaggregate outcomes data to identify systemic inequities. Claudia worked with staff at the U's Dream Center to create the WRS Dream Center Fellowship, which is funded through WSS and provides individualized writing support for undocumented students. Joseph and Cristina spoke about transfer student experiences to an audience of hundreds at the inaugural Transfer Pathways Summit in 2019. Transfer students were having more of a say in program development across and beyond campus than ever before.

Our efforts to foster a more transfer-conducive local writing ecology also led to changes at SLCC. I won't speak for my SLCC colleagues: they are a big department, and I only get glimpses of these changes through conversations with the folks I know best. However, I can say that by fall 2019 WRS had a much deeper relationship with SLCC's English department. We regularly invited one another to guest speaker events on both campuses. U faculty participated in SLCC reading circles on topics related to literacy, pedagogy, and social justice. Romeo García and Clint Gardner began collaborating on a multi-institutional study of transfer student experiences in writing centers, and we began planning a regional symposium on transfer students and writing centers cosponsored by SLCC, the U, and Westminster College. Stephen Ruffus and I started discussing a community college apprenticeship program for graduate students.

The most significant development to emerge through our collaborations was SLCC's AS degree in writing studies. By design, this degree articulated into the WRS major at the U. The AS is SLCC's to write about, so I will not dive into details here, except to say it became an occasion to co-develop a new 2000-level course—ENGL/WRTG 2040: Intro to Writing Studies—which is now offered at both SLCC and the U. We also articulated an existing SLCC course, ENGL 2310: Digital Writing, into the WRS major. Courses in the AS in Writing Studies became key recruitment sites for WSS. Based on these transfer partnerships, SLCC's Department of English changed its name to the Department of English, Linguistics, and Writing Studies (ELWS) in 2019.

In my view, the AS degree and department name change mark key moments in the "disciplinary turn" in writing studies—a moment not visible from a university-centric perspective. A transfer degree signals that writing studies is sufficiently established to warrant a lower-division in-major curriculum. It also signals that a critical mass of two-year college faculty have the disciplinary expertise in writing studies to teach specialized major courses—expertise recognized by university colleagues in the discipline. And this disciplinarity is expanding educational opportunities for students disadvantaged by systemic inequities. By 2019, the AS degree in writing studies plus a major in WRS added up to a critical writing, rhetorics, and literacies education rivaling any university degree in the country.

PATHWAYS AND ECOLOGIES

In fall 2020, as I was revising this manuscript, I reread *Redesigning America's Community Colleges* with three members of that semester's transfer team—Heather Graham, Jem Ashton, and Keyon Hejazi-Far, all of whom attended SLCC before Guided Pathways reforms. Their reaction to the book was also ambivalent. They agreed with many of the critiques of the "cafeteria model" as they had experienced it, especially the lack of effective advising, the ambiguities of the transfer process, and the implications of poor guidance for students' long-term financial aid eligibility and accumulated educational debt. They were, however, uncomfortable with the book's conceptualization of education as career preparation and the inequities of constrained choice. As Heather asked, *who* is deciding what pathways are available to which students, and why are those entities the ones to decide?

Between 2016 and 2019, the push for pathways created legible-to-administrators exigence for work we as writing faculty were already undertaking. In our 2018 vision statement, we acknowledged this strategic association:

> The idea of an AS in Writing Studies aligned with several principles driving the guided pathways movement: that students would be more motivated to persist to degree completion and transfer if they were able to take courses in their areas of interest sooner; that such engagement would enable them to better integrate their learning and prepare for upper-division courses in their discipline; and that more clearly defined pathways would help maximize the number of credits that transferred to four-year degree programs and majors (see Bailey et al). However, the AS in Writing Studies enabled SLCC English faculty to leverage their partnership with the U to retain disciplinary authority over the writing studies curriculum. (*Articulating* 12)

From my perspective, this authority was important not as an exercise in turf protection, but because our field's best critical perspectives on languaging, literacies, rhetorics, and pedagogies are essential to understanding and countering inequities in community college transfer. In our interinstitutional disciplinary partnerships, transfer students—particularly those from groups subject to transfer gaps—were crucial collaborators in researching, designing, implementing, and revising the "paths" we were creating.

We are not the only community college-university partnership to use Guided Pathways strategically. Steven Accardi and Jillian Grauman of the College of DuPage describe taking up their administration's call for pathways to expand an existing professional writing certificate into a writing studies program articulating with

DePaul University's writing, rhetoric, and discourse BA. They suggest that, if community college faculty are to become teacher-scholar-activists,

> [t]here needs to be structural reform. We need four-year colleges and universities partnering with us, forming 2 + 2 transfer agreements, and building a comprehensive and cohesive structure that directly connects our programs together. . . . It's time two-year writing programs are recognized for what they are, the starting point of a four-year writing program. (84)

While not all community college students intend to transfer to a four-year institution, I see powerful potential to engage strategically with Guided Pathways to enact collaborative, critical reform in pursuit of a more equitable postsecondary education system.

However, even as we engage strategically with "pathways" I maintain a preference for the framework of ecologies. The metaphor of the "pathway" is often represented as a road, with the implication that we're paving something over, putting up (and policing) enforceable traffic markers, and prescribing one standardized, unidirectional travel route to a predetermined destination. An ecology, on the other hand, is a complex system, a network. The actual "pathways" in networks are *relationships*: they are the connections between people, places, and various forms of support. The more connections we form, the more possible paths we co-constitute across and beyond our institutions. The stronger and denser our relationships, the more transfer-conducive we become. That conductivity creates more opportunities for students—and *with* students—to make agentive choices in a system that values who they already are as well as what they aspire to become.

The End of the World as We Know It

Cassie Goff, Nic Contreras, and Nate Lacy at my "End of the World as We Know It" party. Photo credit: Dave Hyams.

THE YEAR 2020 STARTED OUT SO WELL. We had just received positive reviews on the full manuscript of this book. The revisions seemed like a few months' work, which I thought I could finish in time to submit my tenure materials in June. I was six months pregnant and scheduled for family leave that spring, with plans to return to work in mid-May to co-teach WRTG 3030. I waddled around SLCC's Redwood campus for the first few months of the year, tabling in the Student Center and visiting classes to recruit for the summer bridge courses. Those classes were filling fast, thanks to the AS in writing studies and improvements to advising through Guided Pathways. We had a generative initial planning meeting to form a WSS Advisory Board: a group of pretransfer students, current students, and alumni of the program who would meet every semester to provide guidance and make decisions about the future of the program. We were also piloting the Community College Professional Apprenticeship program, with Writing-Studies-Scholars-turned-MA-students Nate Lacy and Cassie Goff as co-developers and participants.

On February 8, my longtime friend Chris Baczek hosted a baby party for us at Luminaria, her photography studio in Salt Lake's Granary District. We shared the evening with people across my Salt Lake ecology: friends from book club and our Dungeons and Dragons campaign, faculty colleagues at SLCC and the U, and current and former transfer students in WSS, including my fellow travelers on the research team. Baczek and her partner, Dave Hyams, set up props and a backdrop so I could make the baby a photo book of our Salt Lake family. Insistent that the gathering was *not* a baby shower, we gave it a tongue-in-cheek theme: "The End of the World as We Know It."

A month later, the COVID-19 lockdowns started. My partner Ben and I attended our last birthing class on March 12, the same day the U announced it would be moving all classes online. The students and I worked quickly to get the WSS study groups into virtual meeting formats. Four days later, I fell in my back yard and spent the evening on a fetal monitor while being treated for a broken right wrist. Two days after that, my water broke. At 7:09 a.m. on March 18, I was high up on the hill in a University of Utah hospital room, breathing through early waves of pain, when the building gave a long shudder and the power flickered. It was an earthquake, magnitude 5.7, with aftershocks that followed later in the day and rippled through the next month. Between contractions, I responded to a flurry of texts from U and SLCC faculty colleagues as well as several students on the transfer research team checking in to make sure everyone was okay. By 7:00 p.m., I was holding Maris, who at five and a half pounds was tiny but healthy. And the world as we knew it ended.[40]

THE COVID STRESS TEST

Ben and I spent the first months of the pandemic figuring out how to operate a newborn in social isolation with three normatively functioning arms between us. Friends and colleagues from SLCC and the U left food on our doorstep. Within a few weeks of Maris's birth, two things were clear. First, my co-teachers and I were going to have to move the summer bridge courses online. We had a month to figure out how many of the students who had signed up would stick with us, how to support them amid the upheavals of the summer, and how to build community when the class could no longer meet in person. Second, there was no way I was going to finish revisions to this book by June, not with a newborn, a broken wrist, a summer program to redesign, and the current Writing Studies Scholars to support as best we could. I took an extension on the tenure clock.

I have an anxiety disorder that sometimes derails my writing under far less stressful circumstances than these. In summer 2020, I was sleep-deprived, unable to access childcare, and attempting to teach two classes remotely with no room of my own. The racial justice uprisings catalyzed by the police murder of George Floyd unfolded—the world as we know it *must* end—but the election loomed. I was sloshing with dread, and writing seemed impossible. Teaching, too, would have been impossible without the summer 2020 instructional team: SLCC faculty colleague Jennifer Courtney and transfer mentor Jose Loeri co-teaching WRTG 3030 with me; Kenna Onwuzuruoha and transfer mentor Jem Ashton teaching Write4U@SLCC; and Cristina Guerrero Perez coordinating the Summer Writing Studio with Heather Graham as an additional peer writing consultant. Together, we Zoomed through the uncertain summer.

We worried that many students who had signed up for face-to-face courses would drop, but we actually saw increases in enrollment when we moved online and announced that Write4U@SLCC would be tuition-free for all students (a call I made without being sure how we'd pay for it). Twelve students signed up, eight of whom were BIPOC and seven of whom were women. Four were considering a double major in WRS along with their primary areas of study. The composition of WRTG 3030 also shifted. Twenty students enrolled, eight of whom were BIPOC and thirteen of whom were women. We had far fewer Latinx students than in previous summers, probably a reflection of which communities were hardest hit by the pandemic. However, this WRTG 3030 cohort also included a greater percentage of older students and students with children, as well as a greater percentage of students disclosing disabilities and/or LGBTQIA+ identities—an indication the online format might be providing greater access to the program for these groups than our usual face-to-face format. Half the WRTG 3030 students came to us through the AS in writing studies.

In early April, we surveyed enrolled students about what online format they would prefer for the course. Based on their responses, Kenna and Jem converted Write4U@SLCC to an asynchronous format. Given the demands of the online conversion, we held off on making major changes to the curriculum. Jennifer, Jose, and I reconfigured WRTG 3030 to a hybrid remote format, with a one-hour Zoom meeting each Wednesday evening featuring a Q&A session with our faculty guest speakers. These meetings were recorded and posted in our online course management system for those who could not attend, and we also posted weekly videos from members of the instructional team providing context for the week's readings and activities. In both courses, we sought to foster peer interaction, including collaborative annotations of the readings and group discussion posts. We built in opportunities for students to hold video conferences with instructors, transfer mentors, and writing studio consultants. We maintained flexible due dates and were proactive about reaching out to students who were falling behind. We also formalized a no-penalty drop policy so students could leave the course at any point in the semester without receiving

Ws on their permanent records at the U. We provided all students in our transfer programs with information about the U's emergency laptop and wi-fi hotspot loan program, and we continued to run the online study groups for already-transferred Writing Studies Scholars to support those taking summer courses.

Completion rates in the bridge courses reflected the inequitable burdens the pandemic placed on students and their communities throughout summer 2020. The Write4U@SLCC course took the hardest hit. Only five of the twelve students completed the course, three of whom were BIPOC. Everyone else had to take the no-penalty drop option. We know several of these students were struggling with housing insecurity, family caretaking responsibilities, unpredictable work hours, and/or health issues during the pandemic. The WRTG 3030 students fared somewhat better. Fifteen completed the course, six of whom were BIPOC—a lower completion rate than in previous summers, but not as low as I'd feared it might be. The five who had to drop the course were all experiencing economic challenges and/or health difficulties related to the pandemic.

As of summer 2021, WSS seems to have survived COVID. Major donors have sustained their support. We have maintained the study groups online and opened them to pretransfer WSS students, as well. We helped several already-transferred students secure emergency scholarships. In June 2020, we received an unexpected $15,000 federal CARES grant from the Utah Humanities Foundation. Those funds could not be used for scholarships, but they could be put toward other program operations, so we hired ten Writing Studies Scholars who had experienced pandemic-related loss of income into $15-an-hour research, teaching, and program development positions throughout the 2020–21 academic year. Those positions—a tiny Works Progress Administration in our department—provided students with social connections, academic learning, and professional development while supporting them with safe, flexible employment.

Christie Toth and Writing Studies Scholars Jose Loeri, Kelly Corbray, Natalia Anderson, and Joanne Castillo at the College of Humanities Convocation in May 2021. Photo Credit: Unknown University of Utah employee staffing graduation.

Most WSS students are doing okay. Seven of the eight who planned to graduate in 2020 did so. By summer 2021, eight more had persisted through a year of all-online coursework to complete their bachelor's degrees. During the 2020–21 year, we added four more already-transferred SLCC students to the program, and eleven Writing Studies Scholars transferred from SLCC to the U. Seven more who are still at SLCC plan to transfer during the 2021–22 academic year. Despite our inability to do any face-to-face recruiting, the summer 2021 WRTG 3030 course filled by early March. This time, more than 60 percent were BIPOC, and, in a sign that conditions were improving in Salt Lake's hardest-hit communities, Latinx students were back.

That said, there has been damage. Several WSS students got COVID, and some experienced multiple rounds of quarantine. A few had family members become very ill. One lost her mother. Four Writing Studies Scholars who had transferred to the U stopped out for pandemic-related reasons, including difficulties with childcare, mental health, and struggles with online learning. Three of the four who stopped out were BIPOC. We are working to raise funds for pandemic reentry scholarships to help these students get back into classes when their circumstances allow. As Nate Lacy and Joanne Castillo's 2021 comments in the interstitials demonstrate, some recent WSS alumni found their post-graduation employment opportunities constrained in ways that left them discouraged and in financial peril. The program has taken some hits, too. In summer 2021, we put Write4U@SLCC on hiatus. We hope to bring it back in summer 2022, when we have developed a new curriculum and secured sustainable funding to make the course free to all.

The stress test of COVID has shown us what a more transfer-conducive writing ecology makes possible. As Claudia Sauz Mendoza remarked in a research team meeting in spring 2018, what we've been doing is a kind of community organizing. That community enabled us to share the labor of supporting transfer students during a time of duress. It became a network through which we could channel resources to students who might otherwise be disconnected. It became a net, catching at least some students who, in a large-scale crisis like the pandemic, might slip through the U's gaping cracks. As I struggled to complete this book from my privileged but precarious professional position, the net caught me, too.

THE ECOLOGY CATCHES ME

By mid-August, I was back to full-time teaching plus an overload course and my administrative duties as director of undergraduate studies. I soon realized I would not be able to revise this manuscript in time for my deferred tenure review unless we had more help with Maris. Utah's COVID numbers were rising, and in a city with a crisis-level childcare shortage *before* the pandemic, we had few options. We moved in with Ben's parents in Washington State. Ben worked part-time as a carpenter, and he and our parents tag-teamed childcare while I held down my job via Zoom. In the waning months of 2020, I found myself revising this book on Nisqually lands—an old sandstone quarry where my in-laws raise sheep. Every time I reopened the manuscript, I had to summon my Salt Lake relations back into immediacy.

As always, students were my most vital connections. Every week, I met with the latest instantiation of the transfer research team—Heather, Jem, and Keyon, all funded by CARES. Week after week, they watched me flail: setting revision goals, failing to meet those goals, trying again, and clawing my way through each chapter. They were patient and supportive, even as they struggled to balance their own work, relationships, and stresses. Other students helped keep our transfer programs going: Kimberly Gamarra maintained our online presence, and Heather, Cristina, and Jose all provided students with writing support. Cassie, Natalia Anderson, Russ Fugal, Gabby Garibay, Yazmín Zarate Sandoval, Lindsay Simons, and Henry Tanaka served on the inaugural WSS advisory board. Natalia, Kimberly, Heather, Cassie, Bella Ang, Fatima Badran, Angie Gamarra, Rachel Mills, and Rebecca Trusty all helped represent the program to donors. Nate took care of my house and cat.

Despite a tumultuous year in their own department, my SLCC colleagues buoyed me when I was ready to quit this book and the academy. They were willing to go forward with a second year of our Community College Professional Apprenticeship program. We worked together to apply for the Diana Hacker TYCA Outstanding Programs in English Award, which we received in the category of "Reaching across Borders." In spring 2021, an ELWS faculty reading group led by Clint Gardner provided invaluable feedback on this manuscript as I was revising. Except for the students, no one's assessment of my scholarship matters more.

THE END OF THE BEGINNING

In Chapter 1, we suggest that understanding ourselves as part of a local writing ecology enables us to see how the lands on which we live, our own mobilities, and our languaging and literacy practices are always co-constituting our relations with one another across and beyond institutions. Those relations entail responsibilities that we must endeavor to recognize and meet. In Chapter 2, I assert that if composition studies is to become a discipline worth being, a discipline that does right by *all* student and faculty colleagues, we must reimagine community college–university relations in our knowledge making, our professional organizations, and our local interinstitutional contexts. In Chapter 3, I develop the concept of transfer-conducive writing ecologies as a discipline-specific contribution to creating transfer-receptive institutional cultures that counter inequitable transfer gaps. Chapter 4 narrates the first three years of our efforts to foster such an ecology in Salt Lake. While those efforts are always emergent, working to change our local disciplinary relations has had unanticipated effects on our (inter)institutional ecologies. These changes offer hope that reimagining community college–university relations in composition studies can play some role, however incomplete, in countering the inequities of our postsecondary system.

Reviewers of an earlier version of this manuscript asked about implications for writing programs at other community colleges and universities. From the inception of this project, I have resisted pressures to produce a "model" for supporting transfer student writers. I am not offering the rhet/comp version of Guided Pathways. Instead, I am sharing a story of specific people during a specific historical moment on specific land—Shoshone, Goshute, and Ute land, land where mountain waters on the edge of a basin desert have long brought different peoples into contact, sometimes, to borrow Mary Louise Pratt's phrase, under highly asymmetrical relations of power (Blackhawk; Farmer). This land co-constitutes our relations and the writing through which we enact those relations. I mean that quite literally. The land shook as I was bringing my child into the world, and loving words composed by people in this book—people who were, at that moment, scattered across the Salt Lake Valley—appeared on my phone.

I won't tell other people at other institutions on other lands, entangled in complex histories that keeps unfolding, what they should do. All I can say is that community college faculty, university faculty, students, and their communities are already interrelated. It is a question of identifying those relationships, as well as the met and unmet responsibilities they entail. It is a matter of working to understand the consequences of our actions and inactions for everyone in the ecology, especially the students and communities whose opportunities are constrained by our failures to relate equitably across institution types. This Salt Lake story shows it is possible to reimagine community college–university relations in composition studies, at least at the local level. Readers can take, remake, or leave the idea of transfer-conducive writing ecologies. It is, perhaps, an unhelpful reiteration of Dimpal Jain and colleagues' concept of *transfer receptive culture*, or an unnecessarily academic way of trying to articulate insights Indigenous theorists have long known. Constructing a notion of transfer-conducive writing ecologies has done imperfect but useful work here in Salt Lake, and that is enough for me.

As Part III of this book demonstrates, our work is far from done. I suspect we will always be *countering* university elitism—"doing," as Romeo García writes, rather than arriving at some socially just destination where elitism has been dismantled. But there is much that can be done in the doing. In the doing, we can support transfer students materially and socially. We can co-constitute spaces where they engage academic literacies on something closer to their own terms, extend their communities, and create paths into futures they might not otherwise have imagined. In the doing, we can co-constitute a different composition studies with graduate students, one in which two-year colleges are recognized as essential sites of teaching, scholarship, and activism. In the doing, we can transform one another and the complex, contested writing ecologies we are all co-constituting with and on these colonized lands.

PART III:
EMERGENT PRINCIPLES FOR PARTNERSHIP

Part III:

Emergent Principles for Partnership

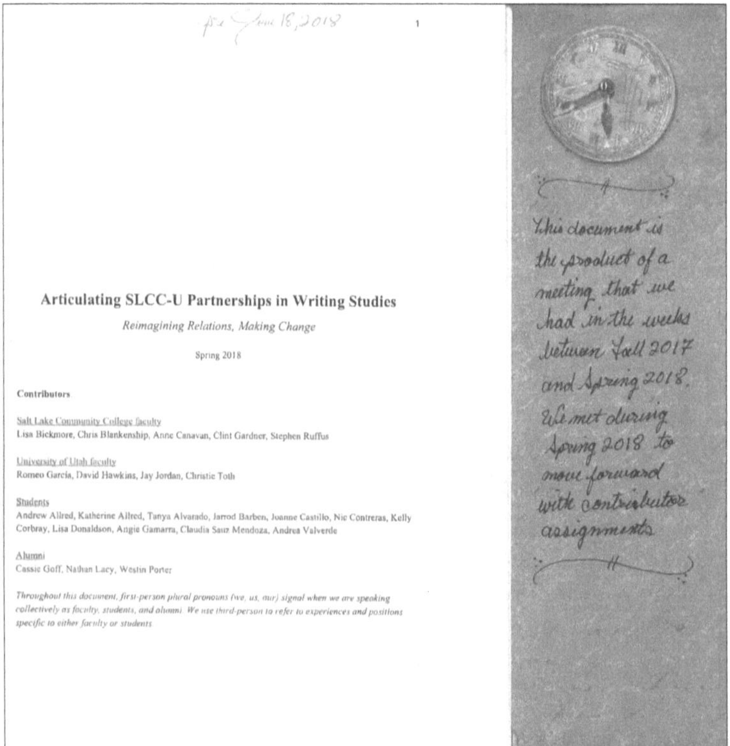
1

Articulating SLCC-U Partnerships in Writing Studies

Reimagining Relations, Making Change

Spring 2018

Contributors

Salt Lake Community College faculty
Lisa Bickmore, Chris Blankenship, Anne Canavan, Clint Gardner, Stephen Ruffus

University of Utah faculty
Romeo García, David Hawkins, Jay Jordan, Christie Toth

Students
Andrew Allred, Katherine Allred, Tanya Alvarado, Jarrod Barben, Joanne Castillo, Nic Contreras, Kelly Corbray, Lisa Donaldson, Angie Gamarra, Claudia Sauz Mendoza, Andrea Valverde

Alumni
Cassie Goff, Nathan Lacy, Westin Porter

Throughout this document, first-person plural pronouns (we, us, our) signal when we are speaking collectively as faculty, students, and alumni. We use third-person to refer to experiences and positions specific to either faculty or students.

This document is the product of a meeting that we had in the weeks between Fall 2017 and Spring 2018. We met during Spring 2018 to move forward with contributor assignments.

Joanne Castillo's scrapbooked copy of Articulating SLCC-U Partnerships in Writing Studies

IN FALL 2017, COLLABORATIONS BETWEEN SLCC and WRS were well underway. We had articulated SLCC's writing certificate into the WRS major, SLCC faculty were shepherding the AS degree in writing studies through the state's approval process, we had piloted both WRTG 3020 and WRTG 3030 at SLCC, and WSS was attracting external funding to provide scholarships and other forms of support for SLCC transfer students. We had co-presented at CCCC, TYCA-West, and CCW conferences, and we had begun writing together for publication. Our local interinstitutional disciplinary relations seemed stronger than any I knew about elsewhere. At this juncture, SLCC's then-Associate Dean of English Stephen Ruffus suggested we compose a formal statement of partnership. Part of the exigence was concern about whether our collaborations hinged on me. If I was denied tenure, moved away, lost interest, or was otherwise incapacitated—or when the leadership of WRS changed—how strong was the department's commitment to sustaining these relationships? How might we formalize our efforts at change so they were less dependent on one overextended assistant professor? And could we do it in ways that strategically engaged "pathways" discourse without capitulating to neoliberalism?

Articulating SLCC-U Partnerships in Writing Studies was our best effort. In December 2017, a group of SLCC and U writing faculty, transfer students, and WSS alumni met at SLCC's Redwood campus to brainstorm what the document should include. Based on our meeting, I assembled a draft with three parts: (1) a statement of "Principles for Partnership"; (2) an overview of our collaborations to date; and (3) possibilities for future collaborations. I revised that document several times with students on the spring 2018 transfer team: Nate Lacy, Cassie Goff, Nic Contreras, Claudia Sauz Mendoza, Joanne Castillo, Angie Gamarra, and Tanya Alvarado. I then sent the draft to the SLCC and U faculty who had participated in the brainstorming session and made additional revisions based on their feedback. Finally, in June 2018, we circulated a close-to-final draft to all participants. Those who were available met at the U to finalize the document.

The heart of *Articulating SLCC-U Partnerships in Writing Studies* is the Principles for Partnership statement, which opens with the following declaration:

> Over four years of iterative collaboration, program development, and community building, writing faculty and transfer students at SLCC and the U have arrived at seven core principles from which we agree our partnerships should proceed: (1) recognize inequities; (2) be colleagues; (3) value difference; (4) center students; (5) address material conditions; (6) educate for social justice; and (7) engage with communities.[41]

The statement, which unpacks each of these principles, became an agent of change in our writing ecology. I used the document to introduce our partnerships to LuMing Mao when he became the externally hired WRS department chair in 2018. When other U departments asked me for advice about improving transfer "pathways," I gave them this document as a way to move the conversation beyond deficit-oriented concerns about student "preparedness." Leaders in the Office of Undergraduate Studies posted the statement as a model on their Transfer Pathways resource page. And, as Anne Canavan discusses below, SLCC colleagues used it to articulate the relations they expect with other U departments seeking to establish partnerships.

In early 2018, when the transfer team and I developed the first drafts, this document felt like a manifesto. It was an articulation of the academy and the discipline I wanted, rather than the one I saw enacted in research universities, graduate education, and the professional organizations. I thought we were doing something risky, that we'd get pushback, but it never came. I don't know if that means we weren't all that daring, or that folks didn't understand the critique of academic elitism we were trying to make, or that I should have given U colleagues more credit for being persuadable. It wouldn't be the first time I've built a bunker only to realize there wouldn't be a battle. Or maybe the battle is yet to come.

We sought to put this document into circulation across the broader disciplinary ecology. In 2019, we presented the principles at the first-ever National TYCA conference in Pittsburgh. They appear in the *CCC* article "Two-Year College Teacher-Scholar-Activism: Reconstructing the Disciplinary Matrix of Writing Studies" (Toth et al.). Darin Jensen describes them as an "exemplar" of "equity-centered" partnership that "demonstrates [writing studies'] political turn in a way that addresses inequity, provides students with opportunities, and serves a democratic notion of education" ("Political Turn" 169–70). His words are daunting praise for an effort I've lived as messy and constrained by my many limitations as a professional and a person. But maybe his endorsement is a sign that, as Nate says, our writing "will be doing . . . work for us when we're busy spinning plates elsewhere" (see Chapter 1).

Articulating SLCC-U Partnerships in Writing Studies is a snapshot of our relations in 2018, but our ecology is always changing. The Principles for Partnership belong in this book, but I couldn't just close with them as though we have, in Romeo García's words, "'achieved'" social justice. I wanted to crack the statement back open and invite colleagues who have been involved in these partnerships—U and SLCC faculty, graduate students, and transfer students who've been on our research team—to extend and complicate the principles. I'm relying on these colleagues to help me head off "the distortions of a singular account" (Fleckenstein et al. 389). I present the text of each principle as it appeared in the 2018 document, followed by short commentaries on that principle written between 2019 and 2021. This open ending enacts my reluctance to conclude when our collaborations are very much ongoing. It also reflects my conviction that I shouldn't have the last word. It takes many people thinking and acting from many positions to reimagine community college–university relations in composition studies. We don't have all the answers in Salt Lake, but we might have possibilities for new, better questions. We also have a stronger basis for laboring together to answer those questions, and for enacting the kind of solidarity systemic change requires.

We are continuously adding essays and other multimodal compositions to this collection as our collaborations emerge. You can access them at transferwritingecology.lib.utah.edu/principles-of-partnership/.

RECOGNIZE INEQUITIES

Our hierarchical postsecondary system—nationally and within USHE—accords higher status and devotes more per-pupil resources to selective-admissions research universities than to open-admissions community colleges. Those differentials have implications for the relative professional status of faculty, for the material conditions and labor structures in which we teach and learn, for the backgrounds and identities of the students at our respective institutions, and, most troublingly, for those students' access to educational, professional, and civic opportunities. Our interinstitutional partnerships must proceed from an open recognition of the power differentials and difficult histories these inequities have wrought and a commitment to establishing more equitable relations as educators and students. Ultimately, our work together is motivated by a shared commitment to challenging the social injustices reproduced by the hierarchical educational system in which we labor and learn.

Chris Blankenship (he/him), Professor of English, Salt Lake Community College

When I came to SLCC, I had virtually no experience with community colleges. In my previous university job, I knew we had students transferring from the local community colleges, and I knew many of their faculty were our former master's students, but I never sat down with them to discuss the relationship between our institutions. Considering that I spent two years as a writing program administrator for my university, this was a very bad thing.

As a new SLCC faculty member, I soon heard about the traditionally antagonistic relationship between us and our biggest transfer institution, the U. I learned of the "great credit grab"[42] that had occurred some years before. The justification was simple: U faculty were looking out for themselves; it was just economics, right? But then I learned of some of the specifics. We had a pair of literature courses that could transfer directly to the English department, but only on the condition that the curriculum and textbook were determined by the university faculty. A linguistics course wouldn't transfer because the faculty member teaching it at that time had "only" a master's degree.

My initial feeling of offense on behalf of the SLCC faculty (What about *our* expertise on these topics? Who are *they* to tell *us* what is acceptable or not in *our* courses?) turned to outrage when I thought of our students. They would end up paying much more for a four-year degree because they would need to transfer to the university earlier to take all the necessary credits. And that's a best-case scenario. What about the students who didn't know whether they wanted a bachelor's degree, so they pursued an associate's first? Or those who, like many of our first-generation college students, didn't know about these transfer issues, thinking, completely reasonably, that a college course at one institution should be equivalent to an identically named course at another? Those students would see many of their credits wasted, dumped into the "general elective" bucket, of which they needed very few, if any, to complete their bachelor's.

As I fumed over this injustice to our students, I realized that, in my university days, I myself had been complicit in this very problem. I had never refused a meeting with two-year college faculty, but neither had I reached out to them. I had never argued that we shouldn't accept certain courses from two-year colleges, but neither had I had any idea what our policies or practices had been. As part of the institution that received the transfers rather than sending them, I had the privilege to be completely ignorant because we held the power. And I never thought to ask these questions because in all my graduate training and professional development, two-year schools, transfer, and articulation simply didn't come up, despite the wide array of scholarship I now know exists on these topics.

For this reason, I appreciate the consciousness-raising work in this book. I entreat graduate programs in writing studies to educate their students about two-year colleges. Only by working at both types of institutions did I learn how fraught these relationships can be and how much they can harm our most vulnerable students when approached competitively rather than collaboratively.

Anne Canavan (she/her), Professor of English, Salt Lake Community College

From the perspective of a two-year-college faculty member, articulation agreements with a four-year partner can, at their worst, feel like a one-sided affair; our job is to recruit students for the upper-level courses that professors at universities prefer to teach, and to teach one or two basic courses that lead into that major.

There is often little respect for the content expertise of two-year college faculty. This sentiment has, in the past, led to onerous expectations, such as requiring that faculty with PhDs teach certain courses at the two-year college, courses that might be taught by graduate students at the university. However, our Principles for Partnership statement, which privileges the need for collegiality where both partners view each other as equals with different expertise, provides a better way to navigate this discussion. Given the success of the partnership between the WRS department and ELWS, other university partners are more willing to accept the framework that our partnership operates under. In this way, the living document of our responsibilities to each other will frame future relationships as well.

Because the current method of creating articulation agreements is based on individual relationships between departments, every new discussion can feel like starting over. This is especially true at SLCC, where our English courses correspond to the U's departments of WRS, English, and linguistics. While we have excellent rapport with our WRS colleagues, we do not have the same systematized articulations with the English and linguistics departments. However, in 2018, the U's linguistics department reached out to our department to create a 2+2 path for our English students to transfer in their major program. While this process (which is still ongoing) has necessitated the typical logistical questions of course numbering and substitutions, the faculty at SLCC are basing our goals for our professional relationship with these partners on the values set out in our vision statement with WRS. The mutual respect we have with our WRS colleagues has given us a stronger position to advocate for teaching more classes at our campus with our faculty as we develop a course outline that both ELWS and the U's Department of Linguistics are excited about putting into effect.

Jay Jordan (he/him), Associate Professor of Writing and Rhetoric Studies, University of Utah

"Articulation" typically labels the formal relationships that selective-admissions universities and open-admissions community colleges have. Articulation most often means, in my own institutional context, making sure the university is accessible in a basic sense—that is, making sure we've worked enough with transfer-sending institutions at a state level to create a reliable, efficient, one-way process so students can enroll, complete majors, and graduate within a six-year window. It would be best, so "articulation" goes, if transfer students had been fully prepared through lower-division and/or general education coursework to meet our expectations on arrival. It would be strange and difficult to conceive of transfer students' engaging in give-and-take or to imagine they might have critical responses to what we consider responsive pedagogies. After all, *they* came to *us* to get access to literacies of power. Just ask them. It's what they're paying for, right?

What Christie and Stephen and Clint and Andie and Tif and Lisa and Justin and Nate and Nic and Cassie and Claudia and Joanne and Katherine and Kelly and others have done and are doing is setting new criteria at the U for what "articulation" means. There's a history they're helping us all challenge. In that history, limited definitions of articulation fed not only university goals to speed up time to graduation, but also fed departmental goals to put butts in seats. During my time as WRS chair, the institutional budget model shifted to reduce the premium on pure enrollment and increase the incentive to attract majors. To be honest, if that shift hadn't occurred, it would have been financially difficult to encourage the creation of the shared and closely articulated courses Christie describes in Chapter 4.

In principle, there has been every reason to create them—to push and pull by meeting students in SLCC classrooms, to reinforce the fantastic work our colleagues there are already doing, to teach students why the young and brash field of writing studies might help them make sense of the literacies in which we are all embedded, and in which they daily negotiate agency. In more pragmatic terms, our department has attracted some of the most eager, most experienced, most diversely talented majors we've ever seen—some of whom have already transitioned into graduate programs where they are even more motivated to thicken our interinstitutional ecology. While we need to remain vigilant against the harms of past efforts simply to grab student enrollments, I am optimistic about other departments' recent efforts to join us in articulating more equitably and with broader impacts. 'Ila Tua'one's course, for instance (described below), promises not only to attract students to an underrepresented area of literary studies but also to enhance connections within local Pacific Islander communities. I look forward to our collaborations with 'Ila and with other colleagues across departments as our ecology becomes thicker and richer.

BE COLLEAGUES

Forging more equitable relationships requires viewing and treating one another as colleagues. While faculty at both institutions have different ranks and roles, and a range of transdisciplinary interests, they are connected through the ever-evolving discipline of writing studies. As co-constructors of knowledge and pedagogy, transfer students are also colleagues. Together, we are working to strengthen writing relationships across and beyond our institutions. Through such local reimagining, we seek to model and ultimately effect change in community college–university relations across the national writing studies community.

Andrea Malouf (she/her), Professor of English, Salt Lake Community College

The years 2013 through 2016 had been some of the most interesting during my tenure as a faculty member of SLCC and the director of its Community Writing Center, but also an informative junction in my now twelve years at SLCC. Not only had the CWC moved in interesting directions with the lead of our writing assistants (most of them also students at SLCC), but many of those same students/writing assistants were also embarking on a research project that would change the relationship between the U and SLCC's writing studies efforts, and, for some, change the trajectories of their lives.

In 2009, with the knowledge that the CWC might lose its funding, a VIP asked me and the current director what community ripple-effect would happen if the CWC went away. From that time forward, and throughout my tenure as director, I encouraged my young staff writing assistants to reimagine the ways our center could exist without four walls or a ceiling should they go away (luckily they did not). And with that charge, these writing assistants researched, instigated, and achieved some highly significant community collaborations, which put our programming in various community spaces such as the county jails, homeless shelters, youth programs, and senior centers. Many of the sustainable program changes at the CWC, as they exist now, were due to a group of writing assistants during 2011–15.

I'm not sure whether these students knew at the time what an impact on the CWC and community-based education as a whole they had made possible. When I've looked back and wondered whether it was just an exceptional group of people that came together at the right place, right time, I'm convinced it was more about stepping back and letting bright people conceive of a better way of education and community work. It was more than just "treating" these young adults as colleagues, but instead it was acknowledging and honoring that as students and community members, they knew more than I did and had better ideas than I did.

In 2015, Christie asked if I knew of students in the SLCC writing certificate program who would be interested in her research on transfer. I did, but I also thought of these bright CWC colleagues who had already proven that, given space, they could change the paradigm of how we think about education. This book represents the work and accomplishment of these student colleagues, and their voices are represented here.

Too often in our academic work, there exists the conspicuous absence of experiences and voices of others, particularly our students. Sure, they show up in research as "products of our teaching" or as younger, less-knowing scholars. My experience with this group of students at the CWC and then later with this transfer project has shown how incorrect assumptions in academia may be about the contributions our students can make to the field of education if we just back up and let them reimagine and recalibrate research and practices.

Clint Gardner (he/him), Director of SLCC's Student Writing and Reading Center

At the start of fall semester 2017, I was excited to learn that WRS at the U had hired Dr. Romeo García as a member of its faculty. I knew Romeo primarily from his *Writing Center Journal* article "Unmaking Gringo-Centers," in which he asks the writing center community "to listen, well and deeply, to how members have discussed and pursued anti-racist agendas" and how those agendas may be excluding Latinx student writers (29). Given that 23.4 percent of students who visit the SLCC Student Writing and Reading Center (SWRC) are Latinx, and given my own interest in antiracist work, I was excited by the prospect of inviting Romeo to come speak with the staff of the SWRC. The close relationship developed between our two institutions enabled me to easily contact Romeo and invite him to come share his insight with us. Romeo's presentation and article gave the SWRC staff the opportunity to critically reflect on how to avoid commonly accepted writing center practices that are detrimental to students.

I didn't know it at that time, but this was just the start of an exciting collaborative research project that focuses on institutional transfer, writing centers, and antiracist activist pedagogies. The research project examines how students who transfer from two-year institutions are received into writing centers at their transfer institution, and what steps the originating and receiving writing centers can take to help ease that transfer. Since many transfer students are of color, the study will necessarily focus on writing center practices that represent inculcated racism and present covert or overt obstacles to students of color. A key outcome of the study is to develop writing center pedagogy that allows students to succeed in their transfer. We also plan to hold a joint symposium for two- and four-year (plus) institutions in the Rocky Mountain region to explore writing center pedagogies and policies that will be both transfer-supporting and antiracist. During the symposium, attendees will develop policy and best practices statements on assisting students in their interinstitutional transfer.

It is clear to me that this new research project could not have happened if our two institutions had not developed such a close, mutually beneficial, and respectful working relationship. It is the first attempt to co-design a research project between SLCC and WRS faculty, and we believe it will have lasting impact on not only our institutions, but on interinstitutional transfer in general. Although we are only in the preliminary stages, we've already learned a lot about the attitudes of transfer students toward writing centers at both their originating and receiving institutions, and whom students trust to give them feedback on their writing. I, for one, believe this research will have lasting impact on writing center practice nationally.

Joanne Castillo (she/her), Writing Studies Scholar, BS in Writing and Rhetoric Studies (2019)

"I am excited to learn from you." As I mentioned in the speech in Interstitial IV, this phrase reframed the way I perceived myself in a variety of academic spaces. One of the many ways this latest academic experience differed from the ones I had a decade or two earlier was in the way I believed my professors seemed to perceive me and what I brought into the academy. Whether it was Andie being confident enough in my new rhet/comp literacies to suggest reading Homi Bhabha, Jay asking what I observed about a classroom in South Korea, working with Claudia and Romeo to change the way we were presenting at a national conference, Clint supporting me in moving chairs and tables around to facilitate the work that was going to be happening in a classroom on a given day, or Christie asking for my perspective on a piece she had written, my opinions were valuable. This idea that, as a student, I could be considered a colleague in the eyes of my professors was one of the biggest shocks of my academic career. This way of seeing me and the knowledges I brought with me into spaces that were designed to keep me out gave me access to resources I never would have had otherwise. The payment I received for some of my intellectual work went toward food and gas, and it allowed me to take advantage of the resources found only on campus. If monetary payment could not be given, my work counted as academic credit toward my degree. In many ways, these opportunities to work with my professors induced me to *stay*.

But what made many of these working relationships unique was how my professors worked with their colleagues across institutions. Having bounced between SLCC and the U a few times over the last two decades, I was well aware that they didn't necessarily communicate well. But from my first introduction to the Writing Studies Scholars program, I noticed the beginnings of potentially powerful relationships. It's not that mistakes weren't made while these collegial relationships were being established. But the work that went into acknowledging mistakes and learning from them—being teachable—made it easier for me to trust the work that was happening *and* the folks who were committed to doing the work. This ethos shaped me as an individual, and it influenced how I interacted with staff and administration outside the classroom. As a result, some U administrators have learned the value of creating paid positions for students in the design, building, testing, and implementation of programs intended for transfer students. The success I experienced in these co-curricular collaborations helped me feel empowered to take advantage of the opportunities presented to me and, more importantly, to challenge elements in the classroom and the institution that did not align with the stated ethos of each.

VALUE DIFFERENCE

Faculty professional differences are partly a function of the distinctive institutional missions they have inherited. . . . Our inter-institutional partnerships must proceed from open recognition of these differences in institutional mission and in our student demographics. We must value those differences, even as we seek to challenge the inequities that sometimes result. We must appreciate the wide-ranging pedagogical, professional, and disciplinary engagement demanded of writing faculty in our respective settings. Further, we must work together to honor differences among students and support their efforts to achieve their varied personal, professional, and community goals. We must strive to build writing faculties and programs at both institutions that reflect and respond to such diversity.

Charissa Che (she/her), Writing and Rhetoric Studies PhD (2019), Assistant Professor of English, Queensborough Community College

Being an "in-betweener" is a phenomenon I've explored in my own scholarship as a first-generation college graduate, second-generation Asian American, and speaker of Cantonese as a first language. These lengthy descriptors, aside from being a mouthful to say, posed challenges as I sought to self-identify agentively, all while knowing that my heritage culture, race, and linguistic background marked me as an "other" to my teachers and peers. To write about being "in-between" cultures can be a lonely task. I wondered just how many of my experiences were simply due to the eccentricities of my family, and how many were shared by those with similar backgrounds as mine. How can I contribute my knowledge to a greater public if I can't tell the difference?

I was grappling with these questions in summer 2017 when Christie invited me to speak to her WRTG 3030: Writing across Locations class about autoethnography in preparation for their assignment. I was nervous: Would the concept of autoethnography be overwhelming to digest in one fifteen-to-twenty-minute talk? However, when I was done speaking, students raised their hands one by one. An Asian American student told me how much she related to my background. Another student asked if it was too much to write about his and his friends' musicianship, *No*, I told him, *you're doing the work that explores the place of your experiences within larger cultural phenomena!* I sensed an excitement growing in the air about their assignment: autoethnography was both an academic methodology *and* a mode through which writers can agentively tell their stories.

The next summer, I had the privilege of co-instructing WRTG 3030 with Christie, Clint Gardner, and Joanne Castillo as the class's autoethnography and writing consultant. Like the previous summer's class, the students ranged from being "traditionally" college-aged individuals to returning students who wanted to finish their degrees after having spent years juggling families, careers, and personal challenges. From hearing their self-introductions and literacy narratives, I knew we were in for projects that revealed a multitude of life experiences, niche interests, and investments in social change.

This time, I was able to observe the development of students' projects over the course of a semester. They challenged monolithic views of "the college dropout," prison tattoo culture, nationalism, and the gaming community, to name just a few subjects. Their autoethnographies and multimodal remediations demonstrated how this research approach can be an act of subversion that takes place in the classroom, whether because or in spite of the knowledge that classrooms are nested within larger institutional structures. Christie and her colleagues placed student-centered learning at the heart of writing across locations. As a result, the resources of a very diverse student population that spanned linguistic, class, ethnic, and age backgrounds reaffirmed how I, as an instructor, conceptualized writing as a social practice.

Now, as an assistant professor of English at Queensborough College (CUNY), I actively strive to abide by this principle. Located in Queens, New York, the college is one of the most diverse two-year campuses in CUNY and in the nation. Queensborough

Joanne Castillo, Nic Contreras, and Charissa Che after their autoethnographic performances at CCCC 2019 in Pittsburgh. Photo credit: Cassie Goff.

entering students come from sixty-two different countries, and 84.7 percent of them are ethnic minorities (*2019–2020 Factbook*). The top five non-English native languages for all undergraduates are Spanish, Chinese, Bengali, Korean, and Creole (CUNY Task Force on Developmental Education). In my teaching, flexibility and openness are key: whenever the opportunity arises, I detour from the lesson at hand and have an impromptu conversation about code-switching, or translanguaging, or language brokering: Why do we do it? When have they made these moves? What was the outcome? I'd throw into the ring my own embarrassing and successful attempts at languaging, and together, my students and I would ride the waves of seriousness, awkwardness, and silliness that our stories produced. In bits and pieces, we were answering the question of where our singular experiences end, and our cultural commonalities begin.

It's one thing to write an autoethnography of your own. It's quite another when you see an autoethnography unfold through others. It is in the latter that I learned the full *humanity* behind this "research method." The potential for collaborative teaching and learning is there in our classrooms, and sometimes, learning how to tap into it lies in the stories of those we teach.

Justin Whitney (he/him), Writing and Rhetoric Studies PhD (2018), Assistant Professor of English, Tennessee State University

Transfer student is a not an easy term to define. Though widely relied upon in higher education, *transfer student* hides a lot under its umbrella. Requiring no more than having moved from one institution of higher education to another, transfer students can be just about anyone. And the magnitude of that diversity is not always obvious. I've come to regard the term *transfer student* with some skepticism. I just don't know what folks mean when they use it, nor do I know what results from that ambiguity.

What I do know is that universities cannot adequately support their transfer students without some specificity, if only on a local level. Further, my experience tells me that receiving institutions cannot get the specificity they need working alone. Developing a sense of what students learned before transfer, for example, is vital for facilitating their success after transfer, and that information is not available at universities. There's just too much going on under the umbrella. A peek will not suffice. We are going to have to work together to see what's under it.

SLCC was the site for my dissertation research, and I learned a lot about transfer students there. My time there helped me appreciate how internationalized community colleges are becoming. I learned that, in addition to significant numbers of immigrant and refugee students, almost a hundred thousand international students enroll in community colleges across the United States each year, and many want to transfer. But I also gained a sense for how folks outside community colleges were thinking about transfer students. I learned that not everyone knows international students are transferring into universities. And, if universities don't know, how can they be prepared?

But it's not enough to say that international students are transferring into universities. *International student* is another umbrella term concealing significant diversity, and international *transfer* students are special in their own right. The students participating in my dissertation study chose SLCC because they couldn't enter a top-tier university otherwise. Unable to afford much English education back in South Korea, they came to the United States also unable to pass university English proficiency exams and having studied almost no college writing in English. However, students at SLCC can begin taking classes with very little English fluency and almost no familiarity with college writing and still transfer to the university. In this case, SLCC becomes their primary source for college-level English fluency and almost the only source for college writing education before transferring. Such experiences have profound effects on what students bring with them to universities. Such experiences should have profound effects on how universities prepare for their transfer students, as well.

Community colleges have long made higher education available to diverse students, but today they increasingly do so on an international scale. I hope the stories told in this book illustrate the breadth of the *transfer student* umbrella and the need for collaboration across transfer institutions to support those who pursue their education under it.

Sabita Baskakoti (she/her), BA in Writing and Rhetoric Studies (2021) and MA Student in Rhetoric and Composition, University of Utah

I immigrated to the United States at fifteen, after almost a decade of my father (who had moved here when I was just six) visiting immigration lawyers, filling out paperwork, and pouring money into the immigration system. The biggest question I get as an immigrant tends to be, "Did you experience a big culture shock when you moved here from Nepal?" The answer to that question is complicated. American/Western imperialism in the forms of the English schools that I attended, the Hollywood movies I watched, and the literature I consumed had prepared me for the culture, albeit through the perspective of white cis men. I romanticized and longed for the image this country projects as a safe haven for the oppressed, as a land of freedom. However, imperialist education had failed to prepare me for the racism, sexism, and other forms of oppression I would face every day. It had not prepared me for this constant state of displacement, of what it means to live in cultural borderlands.

Because of my model minority status as an Asian immigrant, I keep finding myself in predominantly wealthy white spaces where I am tokenized and fetishized, but never accepted. This fact manifested itself more than ever during my first year at the University of Utah. As a first-generation college student, I was desperately trying to fit in. I would be walking down the hallway of one of our campus buildings with wealthy donors' names plastered on the walls, hallways full of wealthy white LDS students whose experiences I could never relate to, and those feelings of displacement and unbelonging would weigh down my shoulders and I would ask myself, "Do I belong here?" The names on the walls, the pale faces of most of my peers and professors seemed to always scream at me, through polite smiles: there is no place for you here.

During the end of my first year, I stumbled upon WRS and decided to take Introduction to Rhetoric and Theory from Dr. José Cortez. The majority of my classmates were transfer students, and almost half of us were students of color. Being a part of that class gave me a sense of community. From the very beginning, José encouraged us to theorize upon our own experiences. This notion that my experiences as a woman of color, as an immigrant, as a first-generation student, were valuable and important in academia—in knowledge building—was new to me. Being among this group of diverse students made me feel less alone. We shared our knowledge and our experiences and theorized together about the meaning of rhetoric and writing. As I took more classes and became involved in the transfer research team, it became clear to me that all our experiences and knowledge mattered to our professors. I was shocked to learn that more than a third of the U's student body is transfer students, the majority of whom are from SLCC, and yet I had never been made aware of this statistic. If I had known this and had been able to connect earlier with transfer students, I would have felt less alone and tokenized. It felt to me that while trying to assert its position as a global university, the U has been alienating its local students. From my experience, this doesn't just impact transfer students, but also students like me who start at the U. It also takes away from the valuable knowledge and experiences that we all bring to classrooms.

Whatever time and place you happen to come across this book, I encourage you to commit to real diversity, not just tokenized, two-brown-people-in-the-brochure, need-that-funding "diversity." I mean REAL diversity. Create a space where minority students feel safe and valued, where mutual learning—on the side of both the faculty and the student—can occur. Listen to us and our needs, acknowledge our material conditions and our experiences, and work to assure that we are in fact welcomed and valued in academic settings.

CENTER STUDENTS

Writing faculty at both SLCC and the U have legitimate investments in sustaining their distinctive professional, disciplinary, and institutional identities. Despite these investments, our interinstitutional partnerships must proceed from a shared recognition that the educational experiences and opportunities of students—particularly the often structurally disadvantaged students at SLCC—are more important than institutional, professional, or disciplinary "turf." Students enroll at SLCC trusting that our institutions are working together to offer an accessible, affordable pathway to a bachelor's degree, and we have a moral obligation to center their interests and well-being. Fulfilling this obligation requires involving students, both before and after transfer, in collaborative program development and decision making. Such involvement requires intentionally creating spaces for their voices and listening with intent to their experiences and ideas, even—especially—when what they say challenges faculty and departmental self-perceptions.

Cassie Goff (she/her), Writing Studies Scholar, BS in Writing and Rhetoric Studies (2017) and MA in Rhetoric and Composition (2020), University of Utah

As my descriptors above may suggest, as I'm writing this, I'm taking up space in a weird nether region of academia. I'm a graduate student, which means I am both a student and an instructor teaching writing at the U. But, because those identities can be viewed as paradoxical, I never feel as if I can fully claim either. Before this, I completed my bachelor's degree at the U, but only after transferring between three different institutions, including SLCC, multiple times. Looking back on those uncertain and messy years, I realize how the idea of centering students played an important role in my own career.

The idea of centering students can influence and motivate a slew of different behaviors from professors, instructors, advisers, administrators, etc. I'd like to use a student-centric behavior Christie exhibited toward me as an example. During my first semester at the U, I signed up for full-time credit hours while working as a manager at a local café, meaning I always worked forty hours a week on paper but continually worked more hours off the clock.

As you might imagine, that meant by midterms I was drowning. I continually missed class because of work and embarrassment over being absent and not having my homework done; maybe being a first-generation college student factored into that embarrassment. Somewhere in between midterms and finals, I received an email from Christie. Without reciting it word for word, the message went something like, "I noticed you've been absent. I want to make sure you're okay. If you are okay, let's figure out how you can pass this class," which we ended up doing.

As another example, and as testament to many of my colleagues and friends mentioned within this book, as an undergrad I don't remember being exposed to many "turf" battles. The identity of "transfer student" that was thrust upon me never influenced how I was treated in the writing classroom. It was only after I graduated that I learned about the Great Credit Grab and other complicated situations leading to specific lingering tensions.

I try to keep these experiences in mind as I'm teaching my own students now. I remind myself, and my fellow teachers (many of whom are graduate students in the Department of English), that we can never fully know what a student's background is and what's happening in their life. And that many students in our FYC classrooms are unaware, and probably don't care, about some of the disciplinary turf battles we might be fighting. Lastly, I am reminded frequently by my own struggles between identities that "student" is only one identity the humans in my classroom take on. Those humans also struggle with identities such as family member, partner, friend, employee, etc.

With all that in mind, I encourage the humans in my classroom to draw on their backgrounds and identities. I allow them to turn things in late. I allow absences when necessary. I make it a personal goal to know all students' names by the end of the second week of class so I can communicate with them on a personal level throughout the rest of the semester. In addition, while I am increasingly more aware of and have more at stake in some of the turf battles continuously occurring, I make sure that doesn't enter my classroom. I leave that shit at the door.

Some of my fellow teachers think I'm too lenient with my students. They might be right. But I think it's worth it. If I can help ensure that the humans I've shared a classroom with are going to stick around to obtain that bachelor's degree, it's worth it. And that's what centering students is all about. It's about them. Assisting and encouraging them not only to degree completion, but beyond.

Bernice Olivas (she/her), Assistant Professor of English, Salt Lake Community College

Dr. Ann Penrose uses the term "thin network" to describe the "intermittent connections to the academic community" from which first-gen students must derive "support, confidence, and inspiration for learning" (455). Any student with a "thin network" will face a host of challenges at the four-year university. This shouldn't be a surprise—we already know that a healthy network of support is a critical part of student success—yet we shy away from talking explicitly about how our students can craft those networks. We seldom, if ever, talk about creating constellating networks of folks who are part of the larger academic community. This coyness frustrates me since networking is a reality of academic life. We network at conferences, talks, gatherings and online, but we don't *teach* networking.

It's time to say it, loudly and without hesitation—yes, academic success is about *whom* we *know*. If we want our students to succeed, especially first-gen two-year students transferring to the university, then two-year faculty need to find ways to bring a wide variety of academics and scholars into their own networks and connect them to their student's networks. Any bridge program designed to help students shift from the two-year college to the university must *teach* networking and help students build networks with other scholars.

The most successful leadership programs, and programs that center on preparing students for higher and postgraduate education, like the McNair Scholars Program, actively teach networking. It's where I learned it. Later, as a professor in the program, I was part of a robust network maintained by our staff. From the director of the program to the administrative assistant, we worked together to create a vast humming wheel of professors, scholars, and university staff we could connect to our students.

Now, as a professor at a two-year college, I don't see that hub. During the summer of 2019, I co-taught WRTG 3030 with Christie. The class is a bridge class intended to help students transition from the two-year college to the university. All the students reported the same thing. Our class was the first class that introduced them to faculty from the university. These students began class with a woefully "thin" network.

It's a real issue we need to address. And it seems to me that we need to begin by acknowledging that our constellating networks are critical to success. We need to acknowledge that our students—two-year college students—will certainly lack the privilege to build those networks without help. We need to acknowledge that our students will begin at the university with the disadvantage of a "thin" network. We need to recognize that if we want our students to succeed after transfer, they will need a thriving network of peers and other academics to support them across both institutions. We need to ask ourselves: how do we make this happen?

Lisa Bickmore (she/her), Associate Dean of English, Salt Lake Community College

As others have discussed, we have recently entered a grand New Era of Prosperity and Diplomacy, collaboration-wise, between our two nations, and it is most welcome, because it has created better, more productive conversations among us and with our students about their opportunities, and about how they can most effectively spend their time at our respective institutions. One good evidence of this is how many students, having done some of their undergraduate work at the community college, have transferred and completed the WRS program at the university, engaging in research projects around transfer as they've done so, and thereby gaining a remarkable viewpoint on academic life and future work. This, to me, is the great leap forward for both programs: we've collaborated directly and intentionally, and thereby built a more effective bridge, well-lit and signposted, by which students can leave the community college and enter a university program, with fewer pitfalls, more familiar faces and points of access, and ongoing opportunities well underway.

Speaking for myself, I feel lucky to be a part, in whatever contributing way, of building this new transfer infrastructure. I feel lucky, full stop. Still, I believe we have questions to ask ourselves about what, for instance, it means to note that "our interinstitutional partnerships must proceed from an open recognition of the power differentials and difficult histories these inequities have wrought and a commitment to establishing more equitable relations as educators and students." Would it be possible, for instance, to interrogate the position the transfer institution—the university—occupies, and continues to occupy, by virtue of its institutional mission? To address the program development that has always already been happening within the community college department not as a site of rescue or remediation—for students, but also for the faculty who work there—but as authentic intellectual work?

A graduate student in the WRS program asked to speak with me recently. She was constructing a research project around preparing for community college teaching. In our conversation, it emerged that, for her, preparation for community college work meant preparation for a teaching life. She's not alone in this construction of community college work, and it's hard to argue that it *isn't* a teaching life—but I found myself rather strenuously asserting that the key to finding community college work rewarding is to understand it as intellectual work, as participating in the knowledge making of a field, and as program-building work. I've been at this—community college work—for a long time. One thing that keeps me going is a sense of the larger scope of our work—of its place in the bigger picture—but also its far-reaching consequences, and the importance of the frame in which we place it, to understand ourselves as participating in larger conversations. It will always be true that keeping students centered—of engaging their voices and desires, of hearing what they need and want from our programs, and of prioritizing this as we proceed—must be our highest aim. But it means something different when university faculty say "center students"—at the community college, this easily becomes a trope for limiting faculty participation in governance, for instance, or arbitrarily cutting short innovative program development. To the extent that we can truly "re-imagin[e] . . . how we can and should relate to one another," which means, among other things, interrogating *even our ideals* and how we enact them, I think we might have a pretty good shot at "effect[ing] change in community college–university relations across the national writing studies community."

ADDRESS MATERIAL CONDITIONS

Recognizing inequities, being colleagues, valuing difference, and centering students will require us to work within, across, and beyond our institutions to address the material conditions that inhibit students' access to learning and constrain faculty teaching and professional engagement. This work includes finding resources within our departments and institutions and collaborating to attract additional resources to support students and faculty. It will also require us to engage politically—within USHE, with state and federal policymakers, and with regional and national professional organizations—to address the broader structures that subvert fair labor conditions for faculty and equitable access to the learning experiences we aim to provide for all interested students across our institutions.

Katherine Allred (she/they), Writing Studies Scholar, BS in Writing and Rhetoric Studies (2019)

When I reenrolled in college as an older, "nontraditional" student, I was a married mother of four in my late thirties. I'd dropped out of high school at the beginning of my senior year because of mental health issues and a chaotic home life. I got my GED, lived out of my pickup truck, and worked at a bagel shop for a year to earn money for college tuition. I enrolled at Utah Valley State College (now UVU) but failed all my classes that first semester. I married when I was twenty, partly in an effort to force stability into my life, and reenrolled at UVSC. I found myself pregnant soon after the wedding, but I completed one semester. When caring for an infant consumed all my energy, I put my dream of earning a college degree on hold. Nearly a decade and a half later, I was able to reenroll in college when my youngest child entered elementary school full-time.

When considering going back to school, I worried about my ability to handle the courseload and how to pay for everything. I wasn't sure if I'd even be admitted to the U, but expense was the biggest factor I considered. The community college offered a path forward, with tuition costing half as much as at the U. I started as an English major and sought scholarships, work-study jobs, and tuition waivers, but I continued to worry about transitioning to the U.

Near the end of my time at SLCC, one of my professors, Justin Jory, told me to go meet with a Professor Toth in the nascent WRS department. I had first learned about the department from my academic advisor. She told me if I earned a Writing Certificate of Completion while at SLCC, it could count for two electives in the WRS major. Because of my tuition waiver at SLCC, I could get those six U credits essentially for free. Then I met with Christie and she told me about WRTG 3020 and the Writing Studies Scholars program, which included scholarships, and I was decided. I was switching from English to WRS.

On my first day at the U in fall 2018, there was a solar eclipse. Campus came to a halt while hundreds of us looked skyward. Though it got pretty dark, we weren't quite in the line of totality, so even at the height of the eclipse you could still see a tiny sliver of sun. It's become an apt metaphor for how I seemed to be expected to view my educational experiences. Casual remarks dropped by personnel in a variety of departments revealed that my U experience was expected to eclipse whatever had happened at SLCC.

I switched majors because WRS offered me funding, but, more than that, it was because many in the department made it clear they valued what all students brought to our learning community, and they wanted to understand our challenges and what each of us needed to succeed. Many professors made a point to acknowledge our experiences, including knowledge gained at previous educational institutions, and encouraged us to draw on this as we theorized new knowledge. I also took several courses in the English department, but I felt invisible there, like one more cog in an academic machine.

This chapter demonstrates a remarkable community effort. Professors and staff at both institutions made conscious choices to work together, which had a concrete effect on the lives of my classmates and me. I now have a bachelor's degree because, while I'm an active agent in my own education and not a passive receiver, many people showed me how to take advantage of resources I didn't even know existed, making my goals possible. I couldn't have done it otherwise.

Nina Feng (she/they), Writing and Rhetoric Studies PhD Candidate, University of Utah

In the fall of 2018, I had the privilege of teaching WRTG 3020: Write4U, an upper-division writing class for transfer students at the U. I've worked with an array of students at four-year and two-year institutions previous to joining WRS, though I'd never participated in a class that was specifically structured for transfer students. The transfer team designed the course as a support system for students to explore writing in their majors, weaving in speakers from campus resources, such as transfer advisors, financial aid experts, and student advocates.

Many students face transitional challenges when entering new learning environments, but as my WRTG 3020 students emphasized, four-year institutions are particularly daunting, since they may not value the knowledge and unconventional experiences of transfer students. Many of my students simultaneously juggled a full academic workload, jobs, family, childcare, legal disputes, and different disabilities. Some were first-generation college students, some were students of color; all of them encountered faculty at the U who believed their academic work should be unaffected by the other factors in their lives, a stark contrast to the supportive experiences they had had with faculty at previous institutions like SLCC.

If we could continue learning from these students' material conditions, and the institutions where they've thrived, instead of highlighting student differences and responsibilities as deficiencies, perhaps we could change our approaches to be more holistic, encouraging student progress toward learning goals. The challenges transfer students confront lead to sophisticated and nuanced understandings of navigating a large institution—several of my students won scholarships through the resources they encountered in class. They took the initiative to create relationships and apply for funding, information they then taught to other students in the course. Many of the transfer students I encountered became stronger leaders inside and outside our classroom because we worked toward empowering one another to share alternative ways of learning and our varied knowledges in classes and communities.

WRTG 3020's contract grading system, opportunities for revision, and availability of individual paths for student interests and writing led students to become more confident and committed—when the learning environment is geared toward understanding through difference, not punishing difference, students strive to learn. As Christie, Patrick Sullivan, and Carolyn Calhoon-Dillahunt discuss in their article on two-year–four-year relations, we should engage in "mutual transformation," a critical, interinstitutional dialogue that aims to create radical change by diminishing boundaries, drawing from the rich experiences of faculty and students across institutions ("Two-Year College Teacher-Scholar-Activism" 107). As a graduate student invested in addressing inequity and supporting diverse language practices, I learned from WRTG 3020 that we have the potential to disrupt systems of injustice at the university by inviting collaboration with students and faculty from SLCC. The transfer students I worked with helped me recognize the multiple ways resilience, success, and intelligence are defined. As instructors, faculty, and administrators, we have the opportunity to work with these insightful students to learn their needs, goals, successes, and failures, transforming the way we approach inequity within our communities of learning.

EDUCATE FOR SOCIAL JUSTICE

Both community colleges and universities have long been under pressures to deliver instruction that prioritizes the interests of employers, and such instrumentalism is particularly prevalent at community colleges. The desire for fairly compensated and personally meaningful employment is often the primary goal motivating students to pursue postsecondary education, and two- and four-year institutions have a shared obligation to provide students with well-designed education for rewarding careers in a rapidly changing economy. However, as writing teachers and students, we also have a common commitment to literacy education that [equips] students to compose fulfillingly, read critically, and engage socially. In the face of neoliberal policy movements that would reduce postsecondary education to a narrow economic good, we must work together across institutions to defend our pedagogical commitments to writing education for personal growth, community responsibility, democratic participation, and social justice.

Nkenna Onwuzuruoha (she/her), Adjunct Instructor of English, Salt Lake Community College (2012-2018), Writing and Rhetoric Studies PhD Candidate, University of Utah

As a pedagogue invested in critical cultural studies methods, I believe asking students to read and discuss a range of texts from academic literature to personal testimonies that offer a real-world perspective is instrumental in an FYC course. This is a space designed for students to continue to strengthen their writing skills and their ability to contribute to discourse communities. I painstakingly craft my class reading lists, asking for advice along the way. While I always intend to find literature that compels students to speak up or even push back, I sometimes struggle to avoid reverting to a nonreciprocal relationship with students where I bestow knowledge, and they are the receptacles for what I know.

Of course, there have been several students, and colleagues for that matter, who resist a social justice slant for any FYC course that does not have a diversity designation. Or they object to introducing anything outside the department readers teachers have the option of tacking onto the course as a required text. What is most important to remember is that students do not necessarily start anew when it comes to classroom conversations on inequality that may arise—they reach deep into their memory banks to build on their thoughts and ideologies.

No matter what readings I choose to shape the classroom experience, the goal is to see writers grow. I have been an advocate for validating students' experiences instead of buying into how the educator, in a savior-like fashion often depicted in pop-culture films, saves or transforms a student's life. Many students have learned how to use language in spaces outside of academe to articulate the injustices they witness long before they arrived in my classroom.

I taught WRTG 3020 two summers at SLCC and one fall at the U. In 2020, COVID-19 meant moving the summer f2f class to an online platform. I've learned that a fundamental principle for educating for social justice is a respect for student experiences, an ear for active listening, and the critical reading skills I often preach to my students but rarely get to practice as the professional skimmer that an FYC instructor needs to be. I try to use my time wisely and focus on what's present in student writing. In a class like WRTG 3020, I often recognized the unswerving truths about social disparities being expressed. I saw this even in the unassigned reading and writing students had to do to succeed in the course: email exchanges between them and me. For example, one Spanish-speaking student almost always initiated an exchange with "sorry to bother you," though her request for clarification was so easy to respond to that I once composed a reply over my phone while waiting in line at the grocery store. The email exchange helped us both. Her questions highlighted places where I needed to revise my wording in assignments, inadvertently providing feedback to make my writing and communication with students better.

As someone who is easily identifiable as a Black woman in appearance and name, teaching a class like WRTG 3020, a composite of learners who are ethnically diverse and often left-leaning, offers a refuge from the air of contempt that bubbles up in other classes I've taught in Utah. It's not always easy to read the essays from students raised with conservative beliefs that deny that structures keep marginalized people oppressed. It's not a solution, and words can trigger an array of emotions that will make getting through even a few sentences difficult, but reading is a place to start.

Romeo García (he/him), Assistant Professor of Writing and Rhetoric Studies, University of Utah

Social justice is a complicated term. What does it mean and what does it look like? Any possible response already risks defining, establishing, and marking the boundaries of what is and what is not social justice. That in turn risks determining who can and cannot do social justice. I for one am a firm believer that whatever is formalizable must remain in an irresolvable and paralogical limit of knowing. This is not to say that in the demand for something else we ignore the cry for social justice as a vision of well-being for all. Rather, it is to say that in the tension between what can be hoped for and what can be, we must commit social justice to an understanding as knowing and understanding as a practice of unknowing. We know social justice is needed. But we cannot know for certain or guarantee what that work might yield.

Social justice, like antiracism, cannot be treated as a toolkit. There is no one easy solution or generic definition. One is not inherently a social-justice and/or antiracist worker. To create ecological change, for oppression continues to have an ecological impact, there must be a rethinking of social justice, one that detaches social justice, perhaps, from capital-K Knowledge. Social justice inevitably fails by design if it is centered on "rights" and "duties." Instead of the question, "What is social justice?" how about we focus on the question, "What do people do in and with conceptualizations of social justice"? Rather than focus on binaries—us and them—how about we work toward reconciling relationships? Stepping-stones to a social justice agenda include reflection, redress, dialogue, and action. Each one of these aspects contain elements of "doing" that are central for transformative changes capable of having ecological impacts. "Doing" is stressed over "achieving" because it describes a discursive process that is uncertain in design. That is what makes social justice work potentially dangerous and possibly radical.

Social justice situates us squarely on an-other set of choices, options, and responsibilities. You see, what makes it potentially dangerous is that all walks of life can partake in this human project regardless of how one initially came to see and walk the world and interact and exchange meaning with others. I tend to invoke the term *stories-so-far* here to speak to how we are but in stages and junctures of multiple returns, careful reckonings, and becomings. What makes social justice possibly radical is that neither assumptions nor automatic equations can take refuge in it. This is because it reflects a sense of ethos and an epistemic obligation and responsibility to a praxis of confronting, unveiling, and unsettling the unfolding of oppressions across the domains of human experience. Social justice, in other words, requires both *a return* to the place where one's "I am," always already one's "where I do and think," is constituted, and a *careful reckoning* with how we continue to be settled into our local and global histories of hauntings, as the starting point for (re)imagining and weaving together possibilities of new stories.

I would like now to mention another concept, antiracism. By definition, to be antiracist involves an action—to oppose racism. This suggests that antiracism can be described as a noun and a verb. Yet so often it is possible to discover a disparity between the being and the doing. The former fails by design while the latter remains fragile yet promising toward the idea of sustainable action. Fragile in the sense that its condition of possibility within the academy is also its condition of impossibility. The success of antiracist and social-justice work is met by three predicaments: (1) the absorption of political resistance by the institution, (2), the grafting upon political resistance by departments, and (3) uncertainty. And yet, in that state of uncertainty, where idealism and egalitarianism potentially collapse because a dissenting rhetoric realizes that neoliberal principles are being cloaked, it is the component of "doing" that proves to be a hopeful catalyst for transformative change. Limited however much by institutional and personal constraints, "doing" remains an active process that is predicated upon both discourse and praxis and that acknowledges, rather that assumes, that the prefix of "anti" comprises various components of "doings." One such doing is a commitment by SLCC and the U to engage in literacy and rhetorical work that is premised upon inquiry into, critique of, and opposition to any form of oppression.

Social justice and antiracism are, it is important to recognize, inward and outward projects. Now, we all have this vision of what social justice and antiracism are and what they look like, until we encounter others. Rather than proceed to think of this as an interruption, though, interinstitutional work exemplifies the productive metaphor of friction: two or more visions having the opportunity to get to work. The outcome is a vision of social justice and antiracism that is no longer an individual burden, but an injunction on all: teachers, students, administrators.

ENGAGE WITH COMMUNITIES

As faculty and students, we belong to a range of national and international communities, as well as multiple communities rooted in and around the Salt Lake Valley. These place-based relations connect us to one another, and how we tend to our relations with one another and our communities is always making and remaking the places where we live, labor, and learn. Our interinstitutional partnerships must proceed from a shared commitment to listening and responding to our communities as we develop initiatives, programs, and resources. We must continuously ask ourselves, "Who isn't here?" And then we must act to address that absence, which will often require us to change. Such responsiveness demands humility and reflexivity, and, in some cases, a willingness to think outside the conventional values and reward structures of our institutions. It requires the community-based expertise of faculty at SLCC and the U, and, perhaps most important, the investments and insights of students at both institutions. Through these engagements, we can build a stronger and more diverse network of relationships that advance social justice for students, faculty, and our communities.

Shauna Edson (she/her), MA in Rhetoric and Composition (2018), University of Utah

I made the decision to enroll at SLCC the summer just before my youngest son started first grade. He had been attending a summer reading program for kindergarteners at the U that had been recommended to boost his reading skills for first grade. I sat in the grass by the student union and imagined what it would be like to go inside the buildings, sit in a classroom, and learn. I also wanted a job with benefits to cover bills when my then-husband's work slowed down at the small electrical contracting company we owned and ran. I didn't know a lot about higher education and the opportunities it could provide, but I hoped college could lead to a new, yet to be determined, stable career. However, it wasn't long before I came to realize that higher education knew about me.

I struggled to identify with the texts I was interacting with until my junior year at the U, when I read Katherine Kelleher Sohn's "Whistlin' and Crowin' Women of Appalachia: Literacy Practices since College," in a course on writing as social practice. The article talked about nontraditional women students from working-class families. The participants were mothers and service workers, and like me went to college with the hope to supplement their husband's income. My stomach dropped when I read about two women who directly connected their divorces to increased education. Why didn't anyone tell me about this risk before I started school? Was my divorce during my sophomore year somehow due to my choice to return to school? My anxieties were slightly eased as I read more about the women in the study: "[W]omen are making their voices heard by using literacy in their jobs, community, and homes. Knowing the power of literacy, they are invested in the concept of lifelong learning" (443).

Since that first summer imagining myself as a student nearly ten years ago, I have been a student at SLCC and then an intern and a writing coach at the CWC, a transfer student at the U studying writing and rhetoric, a graduate student and teaching fellow, a research assistant, a digital-inclusion fellow, a mom, a bike taxi driver, a digital-inclusion librarian and digital-inclusion coordinator at the Salt Lake City Public Library, chair of Utah Communities Connect (Utah's digital alliance), a fellow for the National Digital Inclusion Alliance, and a mentor to other students exploring their educational pathways.

At times I received mentorship and recommendations from faculty and bounced between these community spaces and roles seamlessly. Other times I bounced up against institutional barriers and seemingly tense relationships among the faculty and staff at different institutions. I did find a job with benefits, but it was through engaging with the communities in all these spaces along the Wasatch Front that I learned to make my voice heard, discovered the power of literacy, and have made a career of lifelong learning.

N.S. ʻIlaheva Tuaʻone (she/her), English PhD (2020), Assistant Professor of Women's and Ethnic Studies, University of Colorado–Colorado Springs

As a PhD candidate in English, I focus on travel narratives about the Pacific Ocean. I love my research, and I'm also very serious about teaching. What I love about teaching, broadly, is bringing old ideas to new minds, asking students to question these old ideas, and guiding them along to their own new, thoughtful conclusions.

At the U, roughly half of the English Department's majors are transfer students from SLCC. The WRS department's work has been invaluable in providing a model of how to create a successful transfer course, built as a bridge between the university and the community college. The English Department wanted to better serve transfer students, including giving them a "bridge experience" that would prepare them to be successful English majors. This course could help the U's English Department establish a visible presence at SLCC and push the idea of English as a viable major. I wished for this course to show the depth and breadth, the variety and diversity of topics we cover in our English courses. Scott Black, the chair of the U's English Department, and I designed this class to be as meaningful to the student as possible while fulfilling undergraduate and English major requirements. So ENGL 3780: Global and Transnational Literature simultaneously fulfills upper-division requirement hours that all undergraduates need, the upper-division international requirement (IR) that, again, all undergraduates are required to complete, and the "post-1800s" course requirement for English majors and minors.

But for me and my interests, this class does double work: I not only want to find English majors, and help transfer students, I also want to make my studies available to the larger community that I'm deeply involved in, the Pacific Islander community here in the

Salt Lake Valley. Two years ago, the U started the Pacific Islands Studies Initiative, which aims to provide more Pacific Islander scholars and scholarship, actively engage with the Pacific Islander community, attract more Pacific Islander students, and show how Pacific Islands Studies is not only important, but extremely relevant to a major population of people here in Utah: the largest population of Tongans in the continental United States. The need for Pacific Islander scholarship is obvious to me and the U, which is why this specific course, taught at this specific community college to transfer students who will eventually be studying at a PAC-12 R1 university, is so exciting. And it is also a great example of what a person who loves books, and who loves to read, write, and teach, can do with an English degree.

The class is subtitled Transpacific Literature: South Sea Tales, and I love it, not just because it's my baby, but because of all the things that I can do with it. We watch movies like *Mutiny on the Bounty*; we read captains' logs from the 1770s, Herman Melville's Pacific novels, Pacific Island mythology and folklore, and the autobiography of Queen Liliuokalani; and we closely study her famous Song, "Aloha Oe." And all along the way, secondary sources make us think about difficult things, like colonialism, imperialism, racism, sexuality, and class systems. We think hard and critically question who is represented, who is not, who gets to represent, and whose representations matter.

I want this class to do that double work: to show how I transformed my passion of reading into an English degree, and then how I was able to use that English degree and attend to my other passion, the Pacific Ocean. The course proves that transfer-related work helps English and WRS come together across disciplinary divides to provide lifelong literacy for students and communities while creating opportunities to think critically about social-justice issues.

NOTES

1. In this book, I use the term *two-year college* to refer to the broad category of postsecondary institutions—usually with open or nearly open admissions—that award associates' degrees, including transfer degrees intended to fulfill lower-division requirements for a bachelor's degree. Already we have a problem with labels: many students enroll at these colleges for longer than two years, others take only a class or two before moving on, and some "swirl" between institutions concurrently. Similarly, the term *four-year institution*, meant to encompass liberal arts colleges as well as universities, also elides the reality that many students take more than four years to complete a bachelor's degree (Jain et al., *Power*). As I note in Interstitial II, I have chosen to use the term "two-year college" to align with the terminology used by the Two-Year College English Association (TYCA) and to account for associate's-degree-granting institutions that are not comprehensive community colleges.
2. When I read Jacqueline Jones Royster's description of the afrafeminist approach to mentoring Black women undergraduates that she developed in the SAGE Writers/Scholars Internship Program at Spelman College, I was reassured by its resonance with the ethic that emerged in our transfer research team. Among my many limitations as a white scholar was not being well-read enough in afrafeminist theory to have started with Royster's ideological framework in 2015.
3. Throughout this book, I use *Latinx* because it is the term used by NCTE/CCCC's Latinx caucus and because, unlike *Hispanic*, it avoids assumptions about students' languaging and ancestry. However, I will note that relatively few WSS students who might be recognized in this category have identified themselves using this term. All student coauthors in the book identify themselves

in their own terms, and I use their preferred identifications when referring to them elsewhere in the text.

4. To view a map of the Salt Lake Valley that locates many of the places and layers of social geography discussed in this chapter, visit transferwritingecology.lib.utah.edu/wrtg3030.
5. Subsequent iterations of the transfer team included several students with other LGBTQIA+ identities. These co-researchers brought additional, much-needed perspectives on the localized experiences of transfer students with minoritized gender and sexual identities.
6. We have adapted this alternating typeface strategy from Lauren Rosenberg's *The Desire for Literacy: Writing in the Lives of Adult Learners.*
7. As one SLCC colleague observed while discussing an earlier version of this manuscript, an overriding focus on the transfer function is also a form of university-centrism: two-year colleges offer many nontransfer career and technical programs that can provide a means of earning a middle-class income.
8. In many ways, the purportedly meritocratic postsecondary education system is an example of the "Matthew effect": Higher-status institutions that already have more get more, thereby bestowing greater rewards on their already privileged students and faculty. Initial advantages thus compound over time, increasing social stratification and inequality (Rigney; Bahr).
9. These national studies do not provide data on transfer gaps for Native American/American Indian, Alaska Native, and Pacific Islander students, but there are transfer gaps for these groups in Salt Lake (see Chapter 3).
10. Students unable to apply for federal financial aid include undocumented students, students whose parents claim them as dependents for tax purposes but are unwilling to complete the Free Application for Federal Student Aid (FAFSA), and many students who are unable to enroll in courses full-time because of work and/or family caretaking responsibilities.
11. See Norbert Elliot's discussion of fairness and opportunity structures in writing assessment. Elliot began his faculty career at a community college.
12. In his chapter "Rhetoric and Composition Studies and Latinxs' Largest Group: Mexican Americans," Jaime Armin Mejía outlines ways the discipline has failed Mexican American students and faculty, an inequity with implications for two-year colleges, which

make up 41 percent of the nation's Hispanic-serving institutions (*List*).

13. Those sessions responded to demands of the 1970 "Seattle Resolution," written by Black leaders in CCCC (Gilyard 636; Mitchell).
14. For discussions of the impact of Connors's review, see Sommers, "Instructional," and Hassel et al., "Editorial Perspectives." Likewise, Shelley (Rochelle) Rodrigo and Susan Miller-Cochran discuss Maureen Daly Goggin's failure to include *TETYC* in her review of composition journals in "Composing"; also see Goggin's *Authoring* as another example of how the intellectual work of two-year college faculty has been overlooked by university-based scholars.
15. The Alabama community college where Mark Reynolds taught is named after a Confederate political leader. I am unwilling to participate in honoring that figure and have chosen not to repeat the name of the college in print.
16. University-based composition scholars who began their careers at community colleges—including Trimbur, Shor, Miller-Cochran, and Rodrigo, as well as Victor Villanueva and David Russell—have also described how those experiences informed their intellectual work (e.g., Villanueva; Tinberg, "An Interview with Ira Shor—Part I"; Trimbur, *Solidarity*; Rodrigo and Miller-Cochran).
17. With full recognition of the critical limitations identified by Jain and colleagues, I would observe that Strempel's use of the term "ecosystem" signals that higher education researchers are finding ecological frameworks useful for theorizing transfer. More recently, Lauren Schudde and colleagues have explored "How Political and Ecological Contexts Shape Community College Transfer" and Chris DuVal and Wayne Artis have called for moving beyond transfer agreements to foster "a web of connections." These metaphors resonate with our concept of transfer-conducive writing *ecologies.*
18. Outcomes for Native American/American Indian, Alaska Native, and Pacific Islander students were not reported in this study.
19. Maureen Mathison has told me that her background with transfer student writing contributed to her interest in my candidacy for a faculty position at the U.
20. This curriculum anticipates aspects of the Writing about Writing (WAW) pedagogies later advanced by Doug Downs and Elizabeth Wardle (Downs and Wardle; Wardle and Downs, "Reflecting").
21. Local readers might guess that "traditional" means "Latter-day Saint," an interpretation Mathison confirms.

22. As a teacher and mentor to many Writing Studies Scholars, Mathison has made essential contributions to WRS's transfer conductivity.
23. OBIA provided these data on the understanding that we would not publish them. Here, we report the general nature of the findings to explain how they shaped our understanding of local transfer gaps and informed our subsequent program development.
24. When we conducted this survey in 2015, we were still sometimes using the discourse of "preparation." As our work unfolded, I became increasingly concerned about the deficit-minded implications of this term, and I no longer use it as a framing concept.
25. Dana Driscoll and Jennifer Wells observe that dispositions toward value-expectancy—how useful someone thinks what they are learning will be in the future—can affect writing knowledge transfer from first-year writing courses. This finding suggests that internalized transfer stigma, particularly if it manifests itself as devaluing community college instruction, could prevent students from transferring writing knowledge encountered at their community college.
26. Syllabi, assignment handouts, and other course materials from each year's iterations of WRTG 3020 and 3030 are available online at transferwritingecology.lib.utah.edu.
27. I met Claudia Sauz Mendoza while tabling at transfer orientation. See Chapter 1 for Claudia's description of this meeting and Interstitial III for more of my reflections on how significant that encounter turned out to be for the development of our transfer programs.
28. Such a policy shift would end the U's monopoly on public upper-division instruction in the Salt Lake Valley.
29. One downside of the TIG model is that CE courses do not count toward U faculty members' regular teaching loads. At least initially, we thought we needed the course to bring in enough revenue to compensate the instructor. We reasoned that if twelve students enrolled at $450 each, that would bring in enough to pay the instructor WRS's standard "overload" rate of $4,800 per course, and any surplus revenue would go to scholarships for future Write4U@SLCC students. In spring 2017, I taught the pilot course without additional compensation because I had a one-course release from UGS to develop our transfer initiatives, with the hope that we would bring in enough revenue to "prime the pump" for funding future iterations of the course. Unfortunately,

the low enrollments that semester worked against that plan, and we were left scrambling to fund the course summer-by-summer from 2018 to 2020. As I describe in "The End of the World as We Know It," at the outset of the pandemic we decided to offer the course online and tuition-free for all students and cobbled together funds from multiple sources to pay the instructor. We had no funds to offer the course in summer 2021. In summer 2022, we used American Rescue Plan funds disbursed through the Utah Humanities Foundation to pay the instructor, which enabled us to offer the course for free to all students. We have yet to secure a permanent funding source but have entered into conversations with the U's new Office of Transfer Student Success about embedding the course in a larger bridge program supported by the Office of Undergraduate Studies.

30. Another benefit of CE is that we can pay students' full tuition for the courses directly without involving the federal financial aid system. We do not need any documentation of financial need or evidence of eligibility for federal aid, including citizenship or residency status.
31. SLCC's Office of Diversity and Multicultural Affairs (ODMA) includes services and student-led organizations for students of color, refugees and immigrants (including DACA and undocumented students), LGBTQIA+ students, and students with disabilities.
32. WRTG 3020 counts toward the WRS major or minor and fulfills the major's Writing in the Disciplines and Professions requirement. Thus, taking both courses enables students to earn six upper-division major credits prior to transfer.
33. Post-2019 iterations of the course have incorporated additional critical concepts from *(Re)Considering What We Know: Learning Thresholds in Writing, Composition, Rhetoric, and Literacy* (Adler-Kassner and Wardle).
34. Due to the disruptions of the pandemic, we were unable to undertake this course redesign until spring 2022. That semester, I worked with Nkenna Onwuzuruoha and Jem Ashton to reimagine a curriculum that kept the critical orientation of the original WRTG 3020 but began with career exploration and a critical workplace genre analysis before turning to major exploration and a second critical genre analysis of journal articles in students' prospective majors. As we complete copyedits to this manuscript in summer 2022, Jem and I are piloting the new Write4U@SLCC curriculum at the Redwood campus.

35. In 2020, this organization changed its name to the Garbett Family Foundation but continued to support WSS.
36. This archive can be viewed at transferwritingecology.lib.utah.edu/wrtg3030/.
37. The only overt resistance to the 3030 curriculum came from four white students across three cohorts who were uncomfortable with the extent to which the course focused on issues of identity, particularly race. One of those students left the course, and two completed the course but opted not to major in WRS.
38. Justin has since moved on to Tennessee State University, an HBCU.
39. In 2021, WRS colleague Hua Zhu and I had the opportunity to participate in a course development workshop for the new Pacific Islands Studies Certificate. I hope contributing to this certificate will help WRS connect with more Pacific Islander transfer students.
40. This conclusion is inspired by ELWS professor Marlena Stanford's *Utah Birth Stories Project*, a digital archive hosted by the SLCC Library at slccdigiarchives.org/project/utah-birth-stories.
41. The full *Articulating SLCC-U Partnerships in Writing Studies* document is archived at transferwritingecology.lib.utah.edu.
42. See Ruffus and Toth for an extended discussion of the "great credit grab" and academic freedom in two-year colleges.

WORKS CITED

2019–2020 Factbook. Queensborough Community College, Office of Institutional Research and Assessment, 2020.

"About SLCC." *Salt Lake Community College*, www.slcc.edu/about/index.aspx. Accessed 5 May 2022.

Accardi, Steven, and Jillian Grauman. "Structural Barriers and Knowledge Production at the Two-Year College." *Writing Program Administration*, vol. 43, no. 3, 2020, pp. 73–87.

Ackermann, Susan P. "The Benefits of Summer Bridge Programs for Underrepresented and Low-Income Transfer Students." *Community/Junior College Quarterly of Research and Practice*, vol. 15, no. 2, 1991, pp. 211–24.

Adams, Peter, et al. "The Accelerated Learning Program: Throwing Open the Gates." *Journal of Basic Writing*, vol. 28, no. 2, 2009, pp. 50–69.

Adler-Kassner, Linda. "2017 CCCC Chair's Address: Because Writing Is Never Just Writing." College *Composition and Communication*, vol. 69, no. 2, 2017, pp. 317–40.

Adler-Kassner, Linda, and Elizabeth Wardle, editors. *Naming What We Know: Threshold Concepts of Writing Studies*. UP of Colorado, 2015.

———, editors. *(Re)Considering What We Know: Learning Thresholds in Writing, Composition, Rhetoric, and Literacy*. UP of Colorado, 2019.

Agnew, Lois, et al. "Octalog III: The Politics of Historiography in 2010." *Rhetoric Review*, vol. 30, no. 2, 2011, pp. 109–34.

Agnew, Lois, et al. "Rhetorical Historiography and the Octalogs." *Rhetoric Review*, vol. 30, no. 3, 2011, pp. 237–57.

Alexander, Jonathan. "Queered Writing Assessment." *College English*, vol. 79, no. 2, 2016, pp. 202–05.

Alexander, Sereeta, et al. *Transfer Student Experiences and Success at Berkeley*. Center for Studies in Higher Education, U of California Berkeley, 2009.

Alford, Barry, and Keith Kroll, editors. *The Politics of Writing in the Two-Year College*. Boynton/Cook, 2001.

American Association of Community Colleges. *2017 Fact Sheet*. www.aacc.nche.edu/AboutCC/Pages/fastfactsfactsheet.aspx.

Andelora, Jeffrey. "Forging a National Identity: TYCA and the Two-Year College Teacher-Scholar." *Teaching English in the Two-Year College*, vol. 35, no. 4, 2008, pp. 350–62.

———. Greeting from the TYCA Chair. Opening General Session. Conference on College Composition and Communication, 16 Mar. 2017, Portland, Oregon.

———. "The Professionalization of Two-Year College English Faculty: 1950–1990." *Teaching English in the Two-Year College*, vol. 35, no. 1, 2007, pp. 6–19.

———. "The Teacher/Scholar: Reconstructing Our Professional Identity in Two-Year Colleges." *Teaching English in the Two-Year College*, vol. 32, no. 3, 2005, pp. 307–22.

———. "Teacher/Scholar/Activist: A Response to Keith Kroll's 'The End of the Community College English Profession.'" *Teaching English in the Two-Year College*, vol. 40, no. 3, 2013, pp. 302–07.

———. "TYCA and the Struggle for a National Voice: 1991–1993." *Teaching English in the Two-Year College*, vol. 35, no. 2, 2007, pp. 133–48.

———. "TYCA and the Struggle for a National Voice: 1994–1997." *Teaching English in the Two-Year College*, vol. 35, no. 3, 2008, pp. 252–65.

Andrus, Sonja, et al. "Teaching for Writing Transfer: A Practical Guide for Teachers." *Teaching English in the Two-Year College*, vol. 47, no. 1, 2019, pp. 76–89.

Anson, Chris M., and Jessie L. Moore, editors. *Critical Transitions: Writing and the Question of Transfer*. WAC Clearinghouse / UP of Colorado, 2016.

"Appendix A: The Elon Statement on Writing Transfer." Anson and Moore, pp. 347–58.

Archer, Jerome W., and Wilfred A. Ferrell, editors. *Research and the Development of English Programs in the Junior College: Proceedings of the Tempe Conference*. NCTE, 1965.

Articulating SLCC-U Partnerships in Writing Studies: Reimagining Relations, Making Change. Spring 2018, ugs.utah.edu/faculty-resources/transfer-pathways/mou-folder/humanities/SLCC-U%20Writing%20Studies%20Vision%20Statement%202018.pdf.

Bahr, Peter Riley. "Double Jeopardy: Testing the Effects of Multiple Basic Skill Deficiencies on Successful Remediation." *Research in Higher Education*, vol. 48, no. 6, 2007, pp. 695–725.

Bahr, Peter Riley, et al. "A Review and Critique of the Literature on Community College Students' Transition Processes and Outcomes in Four-Year Institutions." *Higher Education: Handbook of Theory and Research*, vol. 28, edited by Michael B. Paulsen, Springer, 2013, pp. 459–511.

Bahr, Peter Riley, et al. *Transition Processes of Transfer Students in the School of Education at the University of Michigan*. Center for the Study of Higher and Postsecondary Education, U of Michigan, 15 Apr. 2012.

Bailey, Thomas R., et al. *Redesigning America's Community Colleges: A Clearer Path to Student Success*. Harvard UP, 2015.

Baird, Neil, and Bradley Dilger. "How Students Perceive Transitions: Dispositions and Transfer in Internships." *College Composition and Communication*, vol. 68, no. 4, 2017, pp. 684–712.

Barton, David. *Literacy: An Introduction to the Ecology of Written Language*. 2nd ed., Blackwell Publishing, 2007.

Barton, Thomas L., and Anna M. Beachner. *Teaching English in the Two-Year College*. Cummings Publishing, 1970.

Bauer, Paul F., and Karen W. Bauer. "The Community College as an Academic Bridge: Academic and Personal Concerns of Community College Students before and after Transferring to a Four-Year Institution." *College and University*, vol. 69, no. 2, 1994, pp. 116–22.

Bawarshi, Anis. "The Ecology of Genre." Weisser and Dobrin, pp. 69–80.

———. *Genre and the Invention of the Writer: Reconsidering the Place of Invention in Composition*. UP of Colorado, 2003.

Bawarshi, Anis S., and Mary Jo Reiff. *Genre: An Introduction to History, Theory, Research, and Pedagogy*. Parlor Press, 2010.

Beach, J[osh] M. *Gateway to Opportunity? A History of the Community College in the United States*. Stylus Publishing, 2012.

Beaufort, Anne. *College Writing and Beyond: A New Framework for University Writing Instruction*. Utah State UP, 2007.

Belfield, Clive R., and Thomas Bailey. "The Benefits of Attending Community College: A Review of the Evidence." *Community College Review*, vol. 39, no. 1, 2011, pp. 46–68.

Berlin, James A. *Rhetoric and Reality: Writing Instruction in American Colleges, 1900–1985*. Southern Illinois UP, 1987.

Bird, Nancy Kenney. *The Conference on College Composition and Communication: A Historical Study of Its Continuing Education and*

Professionalization Activities, 1949–1975. 1977. Virginia Polytechnic Institute and State U, PhD dissertation.

Blaauw-Hara, Mark. "Transfer Theory, Threshold Concepts, and First-Year Composition: Connecting Writing Courses to the Rest of the College." *Teaching English in the Two-Year College*, vol. 41, no. 4, 2014, pp. 354–65.

Blackhawk, Ned. *Violence over the Land: Indians and Empires in the Early American West*. Harvard UP, 2006.

Blackmon, Samantha, et al., editors. *Listening to Our Elders: Working and Writing for Change*. Utah State UP, 2011.

Blankenship, Chris, et al. "Re-Assessing Composition at Open Access Institutions: Using a Threshold Framework to Reshape Practice." *Journal of Writing Assessment*, vol. 10, no. 1, 2017.

Blythe, Stuart. "Attending to the Subject in Writing Transfer and Adaptation." Anson and Moore, pp. 49–68.

Bobrow, Robert, et al. *Focus: Photographs for Composition*. Dickenson Publishing, 1970.

Bonilla-Silva, Eduardo. *Racism without Racists: Color-Blind Racism and the Persistence of Racial Inequality in the United States*. 2nd ed., Rowman and Littlefield Publishers, 2006.

Bourdieu, Pierre. "The Forms of Capital." *Handbook of Theory and Research for the Sociology of Education*, edited by John G. Richardson, Greenwood, 1986, pp. 241–58.

Brandt, Deborah. *Literacy in American Lives*. Cambridge UP, 2001.

Brereton, John C. *The Origins of Composition Studies in the American College, 1875–1925: A Documentary History*. U of Pittsburgh P, 1996.

Brint, Steven, and Jerome Karabel. *The Diverted Dream: Community Colleges and the Promise of Educational Opportunity in America, 1900–1985*. Oxford UP, 1989.

Brittenham, Rebecca. "The Interference Narrative and the Real Value of Student Work." *College Composition and Communication*, vol. 68, no. 3, 2017, pp. 526–58.

Buck, Jo Ann, and MacGregor Frank. "Preparing Future Faculty: A Faculty-in-Training Pilot Program." *Teaching English in the Two-Year College*, vol. 28, no. 3, 2001, pp. 241–50.

Bureau of Labor Statistics. *Occupational Employment Statistics, May 2021: English Language and Literature Teachers, Postsecondary*. www.bls.gov/oes/current/oes251123.htm.

Calhoon-Dillahunt, Carolyn. "Finding Our Public Voice." *Structural Kindness: Essays on Literacy Education in Honor of Kent D. Williamson*, edited by Darren Cambridge and Patricia Lambert Stock, NCTE, 2015, pp. 163–69.

———. "'We've Come a Long Way, Baby': A Former TYCA Chair Looks Back." *Teaching English in the Two-Year College*, vol. 42, no. 4, 2015, pp. 352–58.

Calhoon-Dillahunt, Carolyn, et al. "TYCA Guidelines for Preparing Teachers of English in the Two-Year College." *College English*, vol. 79, no. 6, 2017, pp. 550–60.

Canagarajah, A. Suresh. *Translingual Practice: Global Englishes and Cosmopolitan Relations*. Routledge, 2012.

Carey, Kevin. "The Upshot: Revised Data Shows Community Colleges Have Been Underappreciated." *New York Times*, 31 Oct. 2017, www.nytimes.com/2017/10/31/upshot/revised-data-shows-community-colleges-have-been-underappreciated.html.

Carter, Shannon. *The Way Literacy Lives: Rhetorical Dexterity and Basic Writing Instruction*. SUNY P, 2008.

Casmier, Adam A. "Response to Counterstatement of Robert P. Saalbach." *College Composition and Communication*, vol. 24, no. 2, 1973, pp. 226–27.

Castillo, Joanne Rose Andres. "The Way of the Buffalo Puncher." 2018.

Castillo, Joanne Rose Andres, et al. "'Work' as Taking and Making Place." *Journal of College Literacy and Learning*, vol. 45, 2019, Forum: Views from the Field, pp. 104–06.

Castro, Erin L., and Edén Cortez. "Exploring the Lived Experiences and Intersectionalities of Mexican Community College Transfer Students: Qualitative Insights toward Expanding a Transfer Receptive Culture." *Community College Journal of Research and Practice*, vol. 41, no. 2, 2017, pp. 77–92.

Center for Community College Student Engagement. *Contingent Commitments: Bringing Part-Time Faculty into Focus*. U of Texas at Austin Program in Higher Education Leadership, 2014.

Clark, Burton R. "The 'Cooling-out' Function in Higher Education." *American Journal of Sociology*, vol. 65, no. 6, 1960, pp. 569–76.

Clark, Irene L., and Andrea Hernandez. "Genre Awareness, Academic Argument, and Transferability." *The WAC Journal*, vol. 22, 2011, pp. 65–78.

Claycomb, Ryan, and Rachel Riedner. "Cultural Studies, Rhetorical Studies, and Composition: Towards an Anti-Disciplinary Nexus." *Enculturation* vol. 5, no. 2, 2004, enculturation.gmu.edu/5_2/claycomb-riedner.html.

Cleary, Michelle Navarre. "Flowing and Freestyling: Learning from Adult Students about Process Knowledge Transfer." *College Composition and Communication*, vol. 64, no. 4, 2013, pp. 661–87.

Coe, Richard M. "Eco-Logic for the Composition Classroom." *College Composition and Communication*, vol. 26, no. 3, 1975, pp. 232–37.

Cohen, Arthur M., et al. *The American Community College*. 6th ed., John Wiley and Sons, 2014.

Coleman, Taiyon J., et al. "The Risky Business of Engaging Racial Equity in Writing Instruction: A Tragedy in Five Acts." *Teaching English in the Two-Year College*, vol. 43, no. 4, 2016, pp. 347–70.

"Community College FAQs." Columbia U, Teachers College, Community College Research Center, 2019, ccrc.tc.columbia.edu/Community-College-FAQs.html.

"The Composition/Communication Course in Junior Colleges." Panel and workshop reports from the CCCC Convention, 1959, *College Composition and Communication*, vol. 10, no. 3, 1959, pp. 179–81.

Connors, Robert J. *Composition-Rhetoric: Backgrounds, Theory, and Pedagogy*. U of Pittsburgh P, 1997.

———. "Review: Journals in Composition Studies." *College English*, vol. 46, no. 4, 1984, pp. 348–65.

Cook, Alice Rice. "English in the Junior College." *The Junior College Journal*, vol. 3, 1933, pp. 313–18.

Cooper, Alice Cecilia. "Completion Courses in the Junior College English Curriculum." *California Journal of Secondary Education*, vol. 11, 1936, pp. 409–12.

Cooper, Marilyn M. "The Ecology of Writing." *College English*, vol. 48, no. 4, 1986, pp. 364–75.

Cowan, Gregory. "1978 National Directory of Graduate Programs for Junior/Community College English Teachers." *Teaching English in the Two-Year College*, vol. 4, no. 3, 1978, pp. 179–212.

Cowan, Gregory, and Elisabeth McPherson. *Plain English Rhetoric and Reader*. 2nd ed., Random House, 1977.

Cowan, Gregory, et al. "Guidelines for Junior College English Teacher Training Programs." *College Composition and Communication*, vol. 22, no. 3, 1971, pp. 303–13.

Crisp, Gloria, and Anne-Marie Nuñez. "Understanding the Racial Transfer Gap: Modeling Underrepresented Minority and Nonminority Students' Pathways from Two- to Four-Year Institutions." *Review of Higher Education*, vol. 37, no. 3, 2014, pp. 291–320.

"Current Status of the Two-Year College." *College Composition and Communication*, vol. 12, no. 3, 1961, pp. 131–33.

Cushman, Ellen. "Decolonizing Validity." *Journal of Writing Assessment*, vol. 9, no. 1, 2016.

———. "The Rhetorician as an Agent of Social Change." *College Composition and Communication*, vol. 47, no. 1, 1996, pp. 7–28.

Davis, Marianna W. *History of the Black Caucus of the National Council of Teachers of English*. The Caucus, 1994.

Davis, Vivian I. "Our Excellence: Where Do We Grow from Here?" *College Composition and Communication*, vol. 30, no. 1, 1979, pp. 26–31.

———. "Paranoia in Language Politics." *Not Only English: Affirming America's Multilingual Heritage*, edited by Harvey A. Daniels, NCTE, 1990, pp. 71–76.

———. "Teachers as Editors: The Student Conference." *Tapping Potential: English and Language Arts for the Black Learner*, edited by Charlotte K. Brooks, NCTE, 1985, pp. 187–99.

———. "Working toward Language-Centered Writing and Literature Courses." *English Journal*, vol. 84, no. 1, 1995, pp. 35–40.

DeGenaro, William. "Class Consciousness and the Junior College Movement: Creating a Docile Workforce." *JAC*, vol. 21, no. 3, 2001, pp. 499–520.

———. "Social Utility and Needs-Based Education: Writing Instruction at the Early Junior College." *Teaching English in the Two-Year College*, vol. 28, no. 2, 2000, pp. 129–40.

———. "William Rainey Harper and the Ideology of Service at Junior Colleges." Donahue and Moon, pp. 181–98.

DeLong, Renee, et al. *Working toward Racial Equity in First-Year Composition: Six Perspectives*. Routledge, 2019.

Deloria, Vine, Jr. *For This Land: Writings on Religion in America*. Edited by James Treat, Routledge, 1999.

Devitt, Amy. "Transferability and Genres." *The Locations of Composition*, edited by Christopher J. Keller and Christian R. Weisser, SUNY P, 2007, pp. 215–27.

Devitt, Amy J., et al. "Materiality and Genre in the Study of Discourse Communities." *College English*, vol. 65, no. 5, 2003, pp. 541–58.

Dobrin, Sidney I.. "Introduction: Ecology and a Future of Writing Studies." *Ecology, Writing Theory, and New Media: Writing Ecology*, edited by Dobrin, Routledge, 2011, pp. 1–23.

Dobrin, Sidney I., and Christian R. Weisser. "Breaking Ground in Ecocomposition: Exploring Relationships between Discourse and Environment." *College English*, vol. 64, no. 5, 2002, pp. 566–89.

Donahue, Patricia. "Disciplinary Histories: A Meditation on Beginnings." Donahue and Moon, pp. 220–36.

Donahue, Patricia, and Gretchen Flesher Moon, editors. *Local Histories: Reading the Archives of Composition*. U of Pittsburgh P, 2007.

Dougherty, Kevin J. *The Contradictory College: The Conflicting Origins, Impacts, and Futures of the Community College*. SUNY P, 1994.

Downs, Douglas, and Elizabeth Wardle. "Teaching about Writing, Righting Misconceptions: (Re)Envisioning 'First-Year Composition' as 'Introduction to Writing Studies.'" *College Composition and Communication*, vol. 58, no. 4, 2007, pp. 552–84.

Driscoll, Dana Lynn, and Jennifer Wells. "Beyond Knowledge and Skills: Writing Transfer and the Role of Student Dispositions." *Composition Forum*, vol. 26, 2012, compositionforum.com/issue/26/beyond-knowledge-skills.php.

DuVal, Chris, and Wayne Artis. "Going beyond Transfer Agreements: The Best Choices Program and a Web of Connections." *New Directions for Community Colleges*, vol. 2020, no. 192, 2020, pp. 89–98.

Edbauer, Jenny. "Unframing Models of Public Distribution: From Rhetorical Situation to Rhetorical Ecologies." *Rhetoric Society Quarterly*, vol. 35, no. 4, 2005, pp. 5–24.

Eells, Walter Crosby. *The Junior College*. Houghton Mifflin, 1931.

Elliot, Norbert. "A Theory of Ethics for Writing Assessment." *Journal of Writing Assessment*, vol. 9, no. 1, 2016.

Enoch, Jessica. *Refiguring Rhetorical Education: Women Teaching African American, Native American, and Chicano/a Students, 1865–1911*. Southern Illinois UP, 2008.

Enos, Richard Leo, et al. "Octalog II: The (Continuing) Politics of Historiography (Dedicated to the Memory of James A. Berlin)." *Rhetoric Review*, vol. 16, no. 1, 1997, pp. 22–44.

Faigley, Lester. *Fragments of Rationality: Postmodernity and the Subject of Composition*. U of Pittsburgh P, 1992.

Fallon, Dianne, et al. "Taking the High Road to Transfer: Building Bridges between English and Psychology." *Teaching English in the Two-Year College*, vol. 37, no. 1, 2009, pp. 41–55.

Farmer, Jared. *On Zion's Mount: Mormons, Indians, and the American Landscape*. Harvard UP, 2008.

Fearing, Bertie B. "Renewed Vitality in the 21st Century: The Partnership between Two-Year College and University English Departments." Reynolds, pp. 185–95.

Fleckenstein, Kristie S., et al. "The Importance of Harmony: An Ecological Metaphor for Writing Research." *College Composition and Communication*, vol. 60, no. 2, 2008, pp. 388–419.

Ford, Nick Aaron. "The Negro Junior College." *Journal of Negro Education*, vol. 5, no. 4, 1936, pp. 591–94.

"The Founding of the Conference on College Composition and Communication." *University of Illinois Archives*, 2009, archives.library.illinois.edu/ncte/about/april.php.

Friedrich, Dick. "In Memoriam: Liz McPherson." *Teaching English in the Two-Year College*, vol. 24, no. 2, 1997, pp. 104–07.

Friedrich, Dick, and David Kuester. *It's Mine and I'll Write It That Way*. Random House, 1972.

Friedrich, Richard, and Elisabeth McPherson. "English at Forest Park Community College." *College English*, vol. 35, no. 8, 1974, pp. 879–916.

Frye, John H. *The Vision of the Public Junior College, 1900–1940: Professional Goals and Popular Aspirations*. Greenwood Press, 1992.

Fulkerson, Richard. "Composition Theory in the Eighties: Axiological Consensus and Paradigmatic Diversity." *College Composition and Communication*, vol. 41, no. 4, 1990, pp. 409–29.

Gabbin, Joanne, et al. "Black Rap." *Negro American Literature Forum*, vol. 5, no. 3, 1971, pp. 80–84, 110–14.

Gallagher, Chris W. *Radical Departures: Composition and Progressive Pedagogy*. NCTE, 2002.

García, Romeo. "Unmaking Gringo-Centers." *Writing Center Journal*, vol. 36, no. 1, 2017, pp. 29–60.

García, Romeo, et al., editors. *Viva Nuestro Caucus: Rewriting the Forgotten Pages of Our Caucus*. Parlor Press, 2019.

García, Romeo, and Damián Baca, editors. *Rhetorics Elsewhere and Otherwise: Contested Modernities, Decolonial Visions*. CCCC/NCTE, 2019.

Gardner, Clint. "Centering the Community College Writing Center." *The Writing Center Resource Manual*, edited by Bobbie Bayliss Silk, 2nd ed., NWCA Press, 2002, pp. 1–15.

———. "'Our Students Can Do That': Peer Writing Tutors at the Two-Year College." *Praxis: A Writing Center Journal*, vol. 15, no. 1, 2017.

Gardner, Clint, and Tiffany Rousculp. "Open Doors: The Community College Writing Center." *The Writing Center Director's Resource Book*, edited by Christina Murphy and Byron L. Stay, Lawrence Erlbaum Associates, 2006, pp. 135–45.

Garrison, Roger H. *Junior College Faculty: Issues and Problems, a Preliminary National Appraisal*. American Association of Junior Colleges, 1967.

———. *Teaching in a Junior College: A Brief Professional Orientation*. American Association of Junior Colleges, 1968.

Gere, Anne Ruggles, et al. "Mutual Adjustments: Learning from and Responding to Transfer Student Writers." *College English*, vol. 79, no. 4, 2017, pp. 333–57.

Gibson, W. Walker. *New Students in Two-Year Colleges: Twelve Essays.* NCTE, 1979.

Gilyard, Keith. "African American Contributions to Composition Studies." *College Composition and Communication*, vol. 50, no. 4, 1999, pp. 626–44.

Giordano, Joanne Baird, and Holly Hassel. "Intersections of Privilege and Access: Writing Programs, Disciplinary Knowledge, and the Shape of a Field." *Writing Program Administration*, vol. 43, no. 1, 2019, pp. 33–54.

Gleason, Barbara. "Connected Literacies of Adult Writers: Ethnographies of Work in College Composition." *Multiple Literacies for the 21st Century*, edited by Brian Huot et al., Hampton Press, 2004, pp. 39–56.

Goffman, Erving. *Stigma: Notes on the Management of Spoiled Identity.* 1963. Simon and Schuster, 2009.

Goggin, Maureen Daly. *Authoring a Discipline: Scholarly Journals and the Post–World War II Emergence of Rhetoric and Composition*. Routledge, 2000.

———. "Composing a Discipline: The Role of Scholarly Journals in the Disciplinary Emergence of Rhetoric and Composition since 1950." *Rhetoric Review*, vol. 15, no. 2, 1997, pp. 322–48.

Gold, David. "Remapping Revisionist Historiography." *College Composition and Communication*, vol. 64, no. 1, 2012, pp. 15–34.

———. *Rhetoric at the Margins: Revising the History of Writing Instruction in American Colleges, 1873–1947*. Southern Illinois UP, 2008.

Goldblatt, Eli. *Because We Live Here: Sponsoring Literacy beyond the College Curriculum*. Hampton Press, 2007.

Goldrick-Rab, Sara. *Paying the Price: College Costs, Financial Aid, and the Betrayal of the American Dream.* U of Chicago P, 2016.

Grant, David M. "Writing *Wakan*: The Lakota Pipe as Rhetorical Object." *College Composition and Communication*, vol. 69, no. 1, 2017, pp. 61–86.

Griffith, Marlene, and Ann Connor. *Democracy's Open Door: The Community College in America's Future.* Heinemann, 1994.

Griffiths, Brett. "Professional Autonomy and Teacher-Scholar-Activists in Two-Year Colleges: Preparing New Faculty to Think Institutionally." *Teaching English in the Two-Year College*, vol. 45, no. 1, 2017, pp. 47–68.

———. "Reinventing the Spiel: The Context and Case for Interinstitutional Collaboration in an Era of Education Austerity." *Writing Program Administration*, vol. 43, no. 3, 2020, pp. 88–105.

Griffiths, Brett, and Darin Jensen. "Conceptualizing English Department Resilience at Two-Year Colleges." *Pedagogy*, vol. 19, no. 2, 2019, pp. 301–21.

Handel, Stephen J. *Improving Student Transfer from Community Colleges to Four-Year Institutions: The Perspective of Leaders from Baccalaureate-Granting Institutions*. College Entrance Examination Board, 2011.

Harbour, Clifford P. *John Dewey and the Future of Community College Education*. Bloomsbury Academic, 2015.

Hassel, Holly. "Editor's Introduction: A Mirror or a Lamp?" *Teaching English in the Two-Year College*, vol. 44, no. 1, 2016, pp. 5–10.

Hassel, Holly, and Joanne Baird Giordano. "Occupy Writing Studies: Rethinking College Composition for the Needs of the Teaching Majority." *College Composition and Communication*, vol. 65, no. 1, 2013, pp. 117–39.

———. "Transfer Institutions, Transfer of Knowledge: The Development of Rhetorical Adaptability and Underprepared Writers." *Teaching English in the Two-Year College*, vol. 37, no. 1, 2009, pp. 24–40.

Hassel, Holly, et al. "Editorial Perspectives on *Teaching English in the Two-Year College*: The Shaping of a Profession." *College English*, vol. 81, no. 4, 2019, pp. 314–38.

Hassel, Holly, et al. "TYCA White Paper on Developmental Education Reforms." *Teaching English in the Two-Year College*, vol. 42, no. 3, 2015, pp. 227–43.

Herrera, Alfred, and Dimpal Jain. "Building a Transfer-Receptive Culture at Four-Year Institutions." *New Directions for Higher Education*, vol. 2013, no. 162, 2013, pp. 51–59.

Higgins, Kirsten, and Anthony Warnke. "Reform as Access, Reform as Exclusion: Making Space for Critical Approaches to the Neoliberal Moment." *Basic Writing E-Journal*, vol. 16, no. 1, 2020.

Himes, Catherine. "Composition in Chicago Junior Colleges." *Junior College Journal*, vol. 7, 1936, pp. 86–89.

Horner, Bruce. "Grounding Responsivity." *JAC*, vol. 34, nos. 1–2, 2014, pp. 49–61.

———. "Rewriting Composition: Moving beyond a Discourse of Need." *College English*, vol. 77, no. 5, 2015, pp. 450–79.

Horner, Bruce, et al. "Opinion: Language Difference in Writing: Toward a Translingual Approach." *College English*, vol. 73, no. 3, 2011, pp. 303–21.

Indigenous Land Acknowledgment Statement. U of Utah, 9 Oct. 2020, president.utah.edu/indigenous-land-acknowledgment/.

Inlow, Gail M. "English Composition Destined to Change." *Junior College Journal*, vol. 9, 1938, pp. 72–74.

Inoue, Asao B. *Antiracist Writing Assessment Ecologies: Teaching and Assessing Writing for a Socially Just Future*. WAC Clearinghouse, 2015.

———. "Racial Methodologies for Composition Studies: Reflecting on Theories of Race in Writing Assessment Research." *Writing Studies Research in Practice: Methods and Methodologies*, edited by Lee Nickoson and Mary P. Sheridan, Southern Illinois UP, 2012, pp. 125–39.

Inoue, Asao B., and Mya Poe. *Race and Writing Assessment*. Peter Lang, 2012.

Jackson, Rachel C. "Resisting Relocation: Placing Leadership on Decolonized Indigenous Landscapes." *College English*, vol. 79, no. 5, 2017, pp. 495–511.

Jain, Dimpal, et al. "Critical Race Theory and the Transfer Function: Introducing a Transfer Receptive Culture." *Community College Journal of Research and Practice*, vol. 35, no. 3, 2011, pp. 252–66.

Jain, Dimpal, et al. "Developing Transfer Pride: An Exploration of Critical Race Pedagogy and the Summer Transfer Enrichment Program." *Community College Review*, vol. 45, no. 3, 2017, pp. 171–89.

Jain, Dimpal, et al. *Power to the Transfer: Critical Race Theory and a Transfer Receptive Culture*. Michigan State UP, 2020.

Jarratt, Susan C., et al. "Pedagogical Memory: Writing, Mapping, Translating." *WPA: Writing Program Administration*, vol. 33, nos. 1–2, 2009, pp. 46–73.

Jenkins, Davis, and John Fink. *What We Know about Transfer: Research Overview*. Columbia U, Teachers College, Community College Research Center, Jan. 2015.

Jensen, Darin L. "The Political Turn and the Two-Year College: Equity-Centered Partnerships and the Opportunities of Democratic Reform." *Writing Democracy: The Political Turn in and beyond the Trump Era*, edited by Shannon Carter et al., Routledge, 2020, pp. 162–74.

———. *Tilting at Windmills: Refiguring Graduate Education in English to Prepare Future Two-Year College Professionals*. 2017. U of Nebraska, PhD dissertation.

Jensen, Darin L., and Joanne Baird Giordano. "Afterword: Placement, Equity, and the Promise of Democratic Open-Access Education." *Writing Placement in Two-Year Colleges: The Pursuit of Equity in Post-*

secondary Education, edited by Jessica Nastal et al. , WAC Clearinghouse, 2022, pp. 287–94.

Jensen, Darin L., and Christie Toth. "Unknown Knowns: The Past, Present, and Future of Graduate Preparation for Two-Year College English Faculty." *College English*, vol. 79, no. 6, 2017, pp. 561–92.

Jensen, Darin L., et al. "Embracing the Democratic Promise: Transforming Two-Year Colleges and Writing Studies through Professional Engagement." *New Directions for Community Colleges*, vol. 2021, no. 194, 2021, pp. 55–66.

Johnson, Sarah Z. "A Tale of Two Statements." *Teaching English in the Two-Year College*, vol. 45, no. 1, 2017, pp. 20–28.

Jory, Justin M. "Renewing the Promise at Open Access Institutions: Frameworks for Engaging Locally Responsive Writing Instruction." *Teaching English in the Two-Year College*, vol. 47, no. 4, 2020, pp. 365–91.

Karabel, Jerome. "Community Colleges and Social Stratification." *Harvard Educational Review*, vol. 42, no. 4, 1972, pp. 521–62.

Kates, Susan. *Activist Rhetorics and American Higher Education, 1885–1937*. Southern Illinois UP, 2001.

Kelly, Ernece B. "Murder of the American Dream." *College Composition and Communication*, vol. 19, no. 2, 1968, pp. 106–08.

———, editor. *Searching for America*. NCTE, 1972.

Kerschbaum, Stephanie L. "Avoiding the Difference Fixation: Identity Categories, Markers of Difference, and the Teaching of Writing." *College Composition and Communication*, vol. 63, no. 4, 2012, pp. 616–44.

———. *Toward a New Rhetoric of Difference*. CCCC / NCTE, 2014.

Kim, Dongbin, and John L. Rury. "The Changing Profile of College Access: The Truman Commission and Enrollment Patterns in the Postwar Era." *History of Education Quarterly*, vol. 47, no. 3, 2007, pp. 302–27.

King, Lisa, et al. "Introduction—Careful with the Stories We Tell: Naming *Survivance, Sovereignty, and Story*." *Survivance, Sovereignty, and Story: Teaching American Indian Rhetorics*, edited by King et al., UP of Colorado, 2015, pp. 3–16.

Kitzhaber, Albert R. *The Two-Year College and the Teaching of English: A Report of the Incoming President of the National Council of Teachers of English to the Executive Committee*. NCTE, 1963.

Klausman, Jeffrey. "Out of the Ivory Tower and into the Brand: How the New Two-Year College Mission Shapes the Faculty-Manager." *A Critical Look at Institutional Mission: A Guide for Writing Program*

Administrators, edited by Joseph Janangelo, Parlor Press, 2016, pp. 77–91.

———. "The Two-Year College Writing Program and Academic Freedom: Labor, Scholarship, and Compassion." *Teaching English in the Two-Year College*, vol. 45, no. 4, 2018, pp. 385–405.

Klausman, Jeffrey, et al. "TYCA White Paper on Placement Reform." *Teaching English in the Two-Year College*, vol. 44, no. 2, 2016, pp. 135–57.

Klempin, Serena, and Hana Lahr. *How Guided Pathways Reforms Can Improve Support for Adult Students: Lessons from Three Tennessee Community Colleges*. Columbia U, Teachers College, Community College Research Center, Jan. 2021.

Knodt, Ellen Andrews. "Graduate Programs for Two-Year-College Faculty: History and Future Directions." Reynolds and Holladay-Hicks, pp. 125–36.

Kristensen, Randi Gray, and Ryan M. Claycomb. *Writing against the Curriculum: Anti-Disciplinarity in the Writing and Cultural Studies Classroom*. Lexington Books, 2009.

Kroll, Keith. "Empowering Faculty as Teacher-Researchers." *Fostering a Climate for Faculty Scholarship at Community Colleges*, edited by James C. Palmer and George B. Vaughan, American Association of Community and Junior Colleges, 1992, pp. 30–44.

———. "The End of the Community College English Profession." *Teaching English in the Two-Year College*, vol. 40, no. 2, 2012, pp. 118–29.

———. "(Re)Viewing Faculty Preservice Training and Development." Reynolds, pp. 196–211.

Kynard, Carmen. *Vernacular Insurrections: Race, Black Protest, and the New Century in Composition-Literacies Studies*. SUNY P, 2013.

Kytle, Ray. "Slaves, Serfs, or Colleagues—Who Shall Teach College Composition?" *College Composition and Communication*, vol. 22, no. 5, 1971, pp. 339–41.

Laanan, Frankie Santos. "Making the Transition: Understanding the Adjustment Process of Community College Transfer Students." *Community College Review*, vol. 23, no. 4, 1996, pp. 69–84.

———. "Studying Transfer Students: Part I: Instrument Design and Implications." *Community College Journal of Research and Practice*, vol. 28, no. 4, 2004, pp. 331–51.

———. "Studying Transfer Students: Part II: Dimensions of Transfer Students' Adjustment." *Community College Journal of Research and Practice*, vol. 31, no. 1, 2007, pp. 37–59.

Laanan, Frankie Santos, and Dimpal Jain. "Advancing a New Critical Framework for Transfer Student Research: Implications for Institutional Research." *New Directions for Institutional Research*, vol. 2016, no. 170, 2016, pp. 9–21.

Laanan, Frankie Santos, et al. "Adjustment of Community College Students at a Four-Year University: Role and Relevance of Transfer Student Capital for Student Retention." *Journal of College Student Retention: Research, Theory and Practice*, vol. 12, no. 2, 2010, pp. 175–209.

Ladson-Billings, Gloria. "Toward a Theory of Culturally Relevant Pedagogy." *American Educational Research Journal*, vol. 32, no. 3, 1995, pp. 465–91.

Lane, David A., Jr. "The Junior College Movement among Negroes." *Journal of Negro Education*, vol. 2, no. 3, 1933, pp. 272–83.

Larson, Holly. "Epistemic Authority in Composition Studies: Tenuous Relationship between Two-Year English Faculty and Knowledge Production." *Teaching English in the Two-Year College*, vol. 46, no. 2, 2018, pp. 109–36.

Levin, John S. "The Business Culture of the Community College: Students as Consumers; Students as Commodities." *New Directions for Higher Education*, vol. 2005, no. 129, 2005, pp. 11–26.

Lewiecki-Wilson, Cynthia, and Jeff Sommers. "Professing at the Fault Lines: Composition at Open Admissions Institutions." *College Composition and Communication*, vol. 50, no. 3, 1999, pp. 438–62.

Lichtenberger, Eric, and Cecile Dietrich. "The Community College Penalty? Examining the Bachelor's Completion Rates of Community College Transfer Students as a Function of Time." *Community College Review*, vol. 45, no. 1, 2017, pp. 3–32.

List of Minority Serving Institutions. Rutgers U Graduate School of Education, Center for Minority Serving Institutions, 2020.

Lloyd-Jones, Richard. "Writing the Resolution: An Institutional History." CCCC Annual Convention, 31 Mar.–3 Apr. 1993, San Diego.

Lovas, John C. "All Good Writing Develops at the Edge of Risk." *College Composition and Communication*, vol. 54, no. 2, Dec. 2002, pp. 264–88.

Lyons, Scott Richard. "Rethinking Responsibility: A Response to Simon Ortiz." *Writing Environments*, edited by Sidney I. Dobrin and Christopher J. Keller, SUNY P, 2005, pp. 207–16.

Madden, Frank. "Crossing Borders: The Two-Year College." *College English*, vol. 61, no. 6, 1999, pp. 721–30.

Maher, Jennifer Helene. "Embracing the Virtue in Our Disciplinarity." Malenczyk et al., pp. 161–84.

Malenczyk, Rita, et al. "Editors' Conclusion: Where Are We Going and How Do We Get There?" Malenczyk et al., pp. 331–41.

Malenczyk, Rita, et al., editors. *Composition, Rhetoric, and Disciplinarity.* UP of Colorado, 2018.

Martinez, Magdalena, and Edith Fernández. "Latinos at Community Colleges." *New Directions for Student Services*, vol. 2004, no. 105, 2004, pp. 51–62.

Martinez-Wenzl, Mary, and Rigoberto Marquez. *Unrealized Promises: Unequal Access, Affordability, and Excellence at Community Colleges in Southern California.* U of California, Civil Rights Project, 14 Feb. 2012.

Mathison, Maureen. "Make Rhetoric Explicit: Demystifying Disciplinary Discourse for Transfer Students." *Teaching/Writing in the Late Age of Print*, edited by Jeffrey R. Galin et al., Hampton Press, 2003, pp. 53–63.

Mays, Chris. "Writing Complexity, One Stability at a Time: Teaching Writing as a Complex System." *College Composition and Communication*, vol. 68, no. 3, 2017, pp. 559–85.

McGrath, Dennis, and Martin B. Spear. *The Academic Crisis of the Community College.* SUNY P, 1991.

McPherson, Elisabeth. "All God's Children Don't Got Shoes . . . ." Conference on College Composition and Communication, 13–15 Mar. 1975, St. Louis. files.eric.ed.gov/ fulltext/ED117711.pdf

———. "Composition." *The Teaching of English: The Seventy-Sixth Yearbook of the National Society for the Study of Education*, edited by James R. Squire, National Society for the Study of Education, 1977, pp. 178–88.

———. "Language: Unites or Divides? The Students' Right in Retrospect." *Literacy as a Human Problem*, edited by James C. Raymond, U of Alabama P, 1982, pp. 73–95.

———. "Remembering, Regretting, and Rejoicing: The Twenty-Fifth Anniversary of the Two-Year College Regionals." *College Composition and Communication*, vol. 41, no. 2, 1990, pp. 137–50.

———. "Then, Now, and Maybe Then . . . ." *College English*, vol. 46, no. 7, 1984, pp. 697–701.

———. "Where Were We, Where Are We as Community College English Teachers?" *Teaching English in the Two-Year College*, vol. 17, no. 2, 1990, pp. 92–99.

———. "Will the Real Terminal Student Please Stand Up?" *College Composition and Communication*, vol. 18, no. 2, 1967, pp. 93–98.

McPherson, Elisabeth, et al. "Bait/Rebait: 'The Students' Right to Their Own Language' Was a Sensible Statement When It Was Adopted. We Need to Renew Our Efforts to Implement It Today." *English Journal*, vol. 69, no. 9, 1980, pp. 8–13.

Mejía, Jaime Armin. "Rhetoric and Composition Studies and Latinxs' Largest Group: Mexican Americans." Malenczyk et al., pp. 267–86.

Memorandum of Understanding between the Ute Indian Tribe and the University of Utah. 3 Mar. 2020, admin.utah.edu/ute-mou/.

Michaud, Michael J. "The 'Reverse Commute': Adult Students and the Transition from Professional to Academic Literacy." *Teaching English in the Two-Year College*, vol. 38, no. 3, 2011, pp. 244–60.

Miller, Carroll L. "The Negro Publicly-Supported Junior College." *Journal of Negro Education*, vol. 31, no. 3, 1962, pp. 386–95.

Miller, Thomas P. *The Evolution of College English: Literacy Studies from the Puritans to the Postmoderns*. U of Pittsburgh P, 2010.

Mitchell, Kendra. "Black Caucus: A Conversation with James Hill." Blackmon et al., pp. 45–55.

Moe, Peter Wayne. "What Works for Me, and for That Matter, for Us." *Teaching English in the Two-Year College*, vol. 40, no. 4, 2013, pp. 364–83.

Moore, Jessie L., and Chris M. Anson. Introduction. Anson and Moore, pp. 3–13.

Murphy, James J., et al. "The Politics of Historiography." *Rhetoric Review*, vol. 7, no. 1, 1988, pp. 5–49.

National Junior College Committee of the Conference on College Composition and Communication. "The Workload of the Two-Year College English Teacher: A Statement of Policy." *College Composition and Communication*, vol. 19, no. 3, 1968, p. 266.

Nilsen, Aileen Pace. "On the Twentieth Anniversary of the Founding of NCTE's Women's Committee." *Women in Literature and Life Assembly*, vol. 1, 1992, pp. 5–8.

Nist, Elizabeth A., and Helon H. Raines. "Two-Year Colleges: Explaining and Claiming Our Majority." *Resituating Writing: Constructing and Administering Writing Programs*, edited by Joseph Janangelo and Kristine Hansen, Boynton/Cook, 1995, pp. 59–70.

———. "Writing in the Margins: A Search for Community College Voices." *Writing Ourselves into the Story: Unheard Voices from Composition Studies*, edited by Sheryl I. Fontaine and Susan Hunter, Southern Illinois UP, 1993, pp. 293–321.

Nowacek, Rebecca S. *Agents of Integration: Understanding Transfer as a Rhetorical Act*. Southern Illinois UP, 2011.

Ornelas, Armida, and Daniel G. Solorzano. "Transfer Conditions of Latina/o Community College Students: A Single Institution Case Study." *Community College Journal of Research and Practice*, vol. 28, no. 3, 2004, pp. 233–48.

Ostman, Heather. *Writing Program Administration and the Community College*. Parlor Press, 2013.

Otte, George, and Rebecca Mlynarczyk. *Basic Writing*. Parlor Press, 2010.

Paris, Django. "Culturally Sustaining Pedagogy: A Needed Change in Stance, Terminology, and Practice." *Educational Researcher*, vol. 41, no. 3, 2012, pp. 93–97.

Paris, Django, and H. Samy Alim. "What Are We Seeking to Sustain through Culturally Sustaining Pedagogy? A Loving Critique Forward." *Harvard Educational Review*, vol. 84, no. 1, 2014, pp. 85–100.

Parks, Stephen. *Class Politics: The Movement for the Students' Right to Their Own Language*. 2nd ed., Parlor Press, 2013.

———. *Gravyland: Writing beyond the Curriculum in the City of Brotherly Love*. Syracuse UP, 2010.

———. "*Opportunity Lost*: Disciplinarity, Community Activism, and the Grand Compromise." *Trans-Scripts*, vol. 3, 2013, pp. 202–10.

Pease-Pretty On Top, Janine. "Events Leading to the Passage of the Tribally Controlled Community College Assistance Act of 1978." *Journal of American Indian Education*, vol. 42, no. 1, 2003, pp. 6–21.

Penrose, Ann M. "Academic Literacy Perceptions and Performance: Comparing First-Generation and Continuing-Generation College Students." *Research in the Teaching of English*, vol. 36, no. 4, 2002, pp. 437–61.

Pérez, Patricia A., and Miguel Ceja. "Building a Latina/o Student Transfer Culture: Best Practices and Outcomes in Transfer to Universities." *Journal of Hispanic Higher Education*, vol. 9, no. 1, 2010, pp. 6–21.

Pérez, William. *Americans by Heart: Undocumented Latino Students and the Promise of Higher Education*. Teachers College P, 2012.

Pickett, Nell Ann. "The Two-Year College as Democracy in Action." *College Composition and Communication*, vol. 49, no. 1, 1998, pp. 90–98.

Pickett, Nell Ann, and Ann A. Laster. *Writing and Reading in Technical English*. Canfield Press, 1970.

Pincus, Fred L. "The False Promises of Community Colleges: Class Conflict and Vocational Education." *Harvard Educational Review*, vol. 50, no. 3, 1980, pp. 332–61.

Poe, Mya, and John Aloysius Cogan Jr. "Civil Rights and Writing Assessment; Using the Disparate Impact Approach as a Fairness Methodology to Evaluate Social Impact." *Journal of Writing Assessment*, vol. 9, no. 1, 2016.

Poe, Mya, and Asao B. Inoue. "Toward Writing as Social Justice: An Idea Whose Time Has Come." *College English*, vol. 79, no. 2, 2016, pp. 119–26.

Poe, Mya, et al. "The Legal and the Local: Using Disparate Impact Analysis to Understand the Consequences of Writing Assessment." *College Composition and Communication*, vol. 65, no. 4, 2014, pp. 588–611.

Pough, Gwendolyn D. "2011 CCCC Chair's Address: It's Bigger than Comp/Rhet: Contested and *Un*disciplined." *College Composition and Communication*, vol. 63, no. 2, 2011, pp. 301–13.

Powell, Malea. "2012 CCCC Chair's Address: Stories Take Place–A Performance in One Act." *College Composition and Communication*, vol. 64, no. 2, 2012, pp. 383–406.

Powell, Malea, et al. "Our Story Begins Here: Constellating Cultural Rhetorics." *Enculturation*, vol. 18, 2014, www.enculturation.net/our-story-begins-here.

Pratt, Mary Louise. "Arts of the Contact Zone." *Profession*, 1991, pp. 33–40.

Price, Margaret. "The Bodymind Problem and the Possibilities of Pain." *Hypatia*, vol. 30, no. 1, 2015, pp. 268–84.

Raines, Helon Howell. "Reseeing the Past, Recounting the Present, Envisioning the Future: The Teaching of English in the Two-Year College." *Teaching English in the Two-Year College*, vol. 20, no. 2, 1993, pp. 100–08.

Reid, Gwendolynne, and Carolyn R. Miller. "Classification and Its Discontents: Making Peace with Blurred Boundaries, Open Categories, and Diffuse Disciplines." Malenczyk et al., pp. 87–110.

Reiff, Mary Jo, and Anis Bawarshi. "Tracing Discursive Resources: How Students Use Prior Genre Knowledge to Negotiate New Writing Contexts in First-Year Composition." *Written Communication*, vol. 28, no. 3, 2011, pp. 312–37.

Report of the CUNY Task Force on Developmental Education, 1 June 2016. City U of New York.

Reyes, Marie-Elena. "Unique Challenges for Women of Color in STEM Transferring from Community Colleges to Universities." *Harvard Educational Review*, vol. 81, no. 2, 2011, pp. 241–63.

Reynolds, Mark. "Checking the Rear View Mirror: The Preparation of Two-Year College Faculty." *MLA Commons*, 2016, hcommons.org/deposits/download/hc:11762/CONTENT/cmu_article.pdf/.

———. "The Intellectual Work of Two-Year-College Teaching." *ADE Bulletin*, no. 121, 1998, pp. 37–40.

———. "Response 1: The New 'Guidelines' Need New Implementation Efforts." *Teaching English in the Two-Year College*, vol. 45, no. 1, 2017, pp. 32–35.

———, editor. *Two-Year College English: Essays for a New Century.* NCTE, 1994.

———. "Two-Year-College Teachers as Knowledge Makers." Reynolds and Holladay-Hicks, pp. 1–15.

Reynolds, Mark, and Sylvia Holladay-Hicks. Introduction. Reynolds and Holladay-Hicks, pp. ix-x.

———, editors. *The Profession of English in the Two-Year College.* Boynton/Cook, 2005.

Reynolds, Nedra. *Geographies of Writing: Inhabiting Places and Encountering Difference*. Southern Illinois UP, 2004.

Richardson, O. D. "English for Semi-Professional Students." *Junior College Journal*, vol. 2, 1931, p. 30.

Rigg, Melvin. "The Course in Freshman English." *Journal of Higher Education*, vol. 3, no. 2, 1932, pp. 93–95.

Rigney, Daniel. *The Matthew Effect: How Advantage Begets Further Advantage*. Columbia UP, 2010.

Riley-Mukavetz, Andrea, and Malea D. Powell. "Making Native Space for Graduate Students: A Story of Indigenous Rhetorical Practice." *Survivance, Sovereignty, and Story: Teaching American Indian Rhetorics*, edited by Lisa King et al., UP of Colorado, 2015, pp. 138–59.

Ríos, Gabriela. "Cultivating Land-Based Literacies and Rhetorics." *Literacy in Composition Studies*, vol. 3, no. 1, 2015, pp. 60–70.

Rodrigo, Rochelle, and Susan Miller-Cochran. "Acknowledging Disciplinary Contributions: On the Importance of Community College Scholarship to Rhetoric and Composition." Malenczyk et al., pp. 53–69.

Rosaire, Pauline. "A New Technique in Teaching English Composition." *English Journal College Edition*, vol. 25, 1936, pp. 561–70.

Rose, Mike. *Back to School: Why Everyone Deserves a Second Chance at Education*. New Press, 2012.

———. "Reassessing a Redesign of Community Colleges." *Inside Higher Ed*, 23 June 2016, www.insidehighered.com/views/2016/06/23/essay-challenges-facing-guided-pathways-model-restructuring-two-year-colleges.

Rosenberg, Lauren. *The Desire for Literacy: Writing in the Lives of Adult Learners*. CCCC / NCTE, 2015.

Roth, Audrey J. "E-Z off, E-Z on, and the Super Highway." *College Composition and Communication*, vol. 23, no. 3, 1972, pp. 258–63.

Roth, Audrey J., and Thelma C. Altshuler. *Writing Step by Step: Exercises in Structured Creativity*. Houghton Mifflin, 1969.

Rousculp, Tiffany. "Connecting the Community and the Center: Service-Learning and Outreach." *Writing Lab Newsletter*, vol. 29, no. 8, 2005, pp. 1–6.

———. "Everyone Writes: Expanding Writing Across the Curriculum to Change a Culture of Writing." *Transformations: Change Work across Writing Programs, Pedagogies, and Practices*, edited by Holly Hassel and Kirsti Cole , UP of Colorado, 2021, pp. 105–22.

———. *Rhetoric of Respect: Recognizing Change at a Community Writing Center*. CCCC / NCTE, 2014.

———. "When the Community Writes: Re-Envisioning the SLCC DiverseCity Writing Series." *Reflections*, vol. 5, no. 1, 2006, pp. 67–88.

Royster, Jacqueline Jones. *Traces of a Stream: Literacy and Social Change among African American Women*. U of Pittsburgh P, 2000.

Ruffus, Stephen, and Christie Toth. "Inter-Institutional Partnerships for Academic Freedom: Reversing 'The Great Credit Grab.'" *Teaching English in the Two-Year College*, vol. 45, no. 4, 2018, pp. 338–42.

Ruffus, Stephen, et al. "It's Not Just the English Department: Reimagining Relations between Two-Year and Four-Year Institutions across English, Linguistics, and Writing Studies." *ADE Bulletin*, vol. 158, 2020, pp. 23–42.

Ruiz, Iris D. *Reclaiming Composition for Chicano/as and Other Ethnic Minorities: A Critical History and Pedagogy*. Palgrave Macmillan, 2016.

Ruiz, Iris D., and Raúl Sánchez. *Decolonizing Rhetoric and Composition Studies: New Latinx Keywords for Theory and Pedagogy*. Palgrave Macmillan, 2016.

Schudde, Lauren, et al. "How Political and Ecological Contexts Shape Community College Transfer." *Sociology of Education*, vol. 94, no. 1, 2021, pp. 65–83.

Shapiro, Doug, et al. *Completing College: A National View of Student Attainment Rates—Fall 2010 Cohort*. Signature Report 12, National Student Clearinghouse Research Center, Nov. 2016.

Shapiro, Doug, et al. *Completing College: A National View of Student Attainment Rates by Race and Ethnicity—Fall 2010 Cohort*. Signature

Report No. 12b, National Student Clearinghouse Research Center, Apr. 2017.

Shor, Ira. *Culture Wars: School and Society in the Conservative Restoration.* U of Chicago P, 1992.

Shugrue, Michael F. *The National Study of English in the Junior College.* ED037480, ERIC Clearinghouse on the Teaching of English in Higher Education, 1970.

Sirc, Geoffrey. *English Composition as a Happening.* Utah State UP, 2022.

Smitherman, Geneva. "CCCC's Role in the Struggle for Language Rights." *College Composition and Communication*, vol. 50, no. 3, 1999, pp. 349–76.

———. "The Historical Struggle for Language Rights in CCCC." *Language Diversity in the Classroom: From Intention to Practice*, edited by Geneva Smitherman and Victor Villanueva, Southern Illinois UP, 2003, pp. 7–39.

Sohn, Katherine Kelleher. "Whistlin' and Crowin' Women of Appalachia: Literacy Practices since College." *College Composition and Communication*, vol. 54, no. 3, 2003, pp. 423–52.

Sommers, Jeff. "The Instructional Note and the Professionalization of Two-Year College English Teaching." *Teaching English in the Two-Year College*, vol. 45, no. 1, 2017, pp. 69–88.

———. "Two-Year College English Faculty and the Scholarship of Teaching and Learning: The Journey Awaits." *Teaching English in the Two-Year College*, vol. 32, no. 1, 2004, pp. 14–25.

Sparrow, W. Keats. "The Genesis and Early Development of *TETYC*: A Silver Anniversary Reminiscence." *Teaching English in the Two-Year College*, vol. 27, no. 1, 1999, pp. 14–19.

Sparrow, W. Keats, and Bertie E. Fearing. "New Kid on the Block: Graduate Programs for Two-Year College English Teachers." *CEA Forum*, vol. 11, no. 1, Oct. 1980, pp. 7–12.

"Special Problems of the Composition/Communication Course in Junior Colleges." Panel and Workshop Reports, *College Composition and Communication*, vol. 9, no. 3, 1958, pp. 155–56.

Spiegel, Cheri Lemieux, et al. "Don't Call It a Comeback: Two-Year College WPA, Tactics, Collaboration, Flexibility, Sustainability." *Writing Program Administration*, vol. 43, no. 3, 2020, pp. 7–19.

Stein, Wayne J. *Tribally Controlled Colleges: Making Good Medicine.* Peter Lang, 1992.

Strempel, Eileen L. "Fostering a Transfer Student Receptive Ecosystem." *Planning for Higher Education*, vol. 41, no. 4, 2013, p. 12–18.

Suh, Emily, and Darin L. Jensen. "Examining Communities of Practice: Transdisciplinarity, Resilience, and Professional Identity." *Journal of Basic Writing*, vol. 39, no. 2, 2020, pp. 33–59.

Sullivan, Patrick, *Economic Inequality, Neoliberalism, and the American Community College*. Palgrave Macmillan, 2017.

———. "Meet My English 93 Class." *Basic Writing E-Journal*, vol. 16, no. 1, 2020.

———. *A New Writing Classroom: Listening, Motivation, and Habits of Mind*. UP of Colorado, 2014.

———. "Measuring 'Success' at Open Admissions Institutions: Thinking Carefully about This Complex Question." *College English*, vol. 70, no. 6, 2008, pp. 618–32.

———. editor. *Sixteen Teachers Teaching: Two-Year College Perspectives*. UP of Colorado, 2020.

———. "The Two-Year College Teacher-Scholar-Activist." *Teaching English in the Two-Year College*, vol. 42, no. 4, 2015, pp. 327–50.

Sullivan, Patrick, and Howard Tinberg. *What Is "College-Level" Writing?* NCTE, 2006.

Sullivan, Patrick, et al., editors. *What Is "College-Level" Writing? Volume 2: Assignments, Readings, and Student Writing Samples*. NCTE, 2010.

Sutherland, W.O.S. "Relation of Junior College English Programs to Four-Year Colleges and Universities." Archer and Ferrell, pp. 77–82.

Syverson, Margaret A. *The Wealth of Reality: An Ecology of Composition*. Southern Illinois UP, 1999.

Taylor, Jason L. "Call to Action: Embracing an Inclusive LGBTQ Culture on Community College Campuses." *New Directions for Community Colleges*, vol. 2015, no. 172, 2015, pp. 57–66.

Taylor, Quintard. *In Search of the Racial Frontier: African Americans in the American West, 1528–1990*. W. W. Norton, 1999.

"Teaching Composition/Communication in Junior College." *College Composition and Communication*, vol. 8, no. 3, 1957, pp. 153–54.

Thomson, Ruth H. "English in California Junior Colleges." *English Journal College Edition*, vol. 19, 1930, pp. 156–63.

Tinberg, Howard. *Border Talk: Writing and Knowing in the Two-Year College*. NCTE, 1997.

———. "The Idea of 'Shared Governance' at the Public Community College." *Teaching English in the Two-Year College*, vol. 45, no. 4, 2018, pp. 342–45.

———. "An Interview with Ira Shor--Part I." *Teaching English in the Two-Year College*, vol. 27, no. 1, 1999, p. 51.

———. "Reconsidering Transfer Knowledge at the Community College: Challenges and Opportunities." *Teaching English in the Two-Year College*, vol. 43, no. 1, 2015, pp. 7–31.

———. "We Do Theory, Too: Community Colleges and the New Century." *College English*, vol. 57, no. 8, 1995, pp. 945–49.

———. "Seeing Ourselves Differently: Remaking Research and Scholarship at the Community College." *Teaching English in the Two-Year College*, vol. 20, no. 1, 1993, pp. 12–17.

———. "Teaching English in Two-Year Colleges: A Review of Selected Studies." Reynolds and Holladay-Hicks, pp. 137–45.

———. "Teaching for Transfer: A Passport for Writing in New Contexts." *Peer Review*, vol. 19, no. 1, 2017, pp. 17–20.

Tinberg, Howard, and Jean-Paul Nadeau. *The Community College Writer: Exceeding Expectations*. Southern Illinois UP, 2010.

Tinberg, Howard, et al. "The Scholarship of Teaching and Learning at the Two-Year College: Promise and Peril." *Change: The Magazine of Higher Learning*, vol. 39, no. 4, 2007, pp. 26–33.

Toth, Christie. "Directed Self-Placement at Two-Year Colleges: A Kairotic Moment." *Journal of Writing Assessment*, vol. 12, no. 1, 2019.

———. "Getting Thorny: Elisabeth McPherson and the Activist Tradition of Two-Year College English." *Basic Writing E-Journal*, vol. 16, no. 1, 2020, pp. 1–54.

———. "Not Quite a Love-Letter-Manifesto." *Inventing the Discipline: Student Work in Composition Studies*, edited by Peter Wayne Moe and Stacey Waite, Parlor Press, 2022.

———. "Unmeasured Engagement: Two-Year College English Faculty and Disciplinary Professional Organizations." *Teaching English in the Two-Year College*, vol. 41, no. 4, 2014, pp. 335–53.

Toth, Christie, and Darin Jensen, editors. "Symposium: Responses to the TYCA Guidelines for Preparing Teachers of English in the Two-Year College." *Teaching English in the Two-Year College*, vol. 45, no. 2, 2017, pp. 29–46.

Toth, Christie, and Patrick Sullivan. "Toward Local Teacher-Scholar Communities of Practice: Findings from a National TYCA Survey." *Teaching English in the Two-Year College*, vol. 43, no. 3, 2016, pp. 247–73.

Toth, Christie, et al. "Bridging Literacies: First-Generation Transfer Students in a Writing Studies Major." *Beyond Fitting In: Rethinking First-Generation Writing and Literacy Education*, edited by Kelly Ritter, MLA, 2022, pp. 171–188.

Toth, Christie, et al. "'Distinct and Significant': Professional Identities of Two-Year College English Faculty." *College Composition and Communication*, vol. 65, no. 1, 2013, pp. 90–116.

Toth, Christie, et al. "A Dubious Method of Improving Educational Outcomes: Accountability and the Two-Year College." *Teaching English in the Two-Year College*, vol. 43, no. 4, 2016, pp. 391–410.

Toth, Christie, et al. "Traveling Together: Rewriting Transfer Student Literacy Sponsorship." https://us.utah.edu/student-resources/transfer-pathways/Toth%20et%20al%202016%20Traveling%20Together.pdf

Toth, Christie, et al. "Two-Year College Teacher-Scholar-Activism: Reconstructing the Disciplinary Matrix of Writing Studies." *College Composition and Communication*, vol. 71, no. 1, 2019, pp. 86–116.

Townsend, Barbara K. "Community College Transfer Students: A Case Study of Survival." *Review of Higher Education*, vol. 18, no. 2, 1995, pp. 175–93.

Townsend, Barbara K., and Kristin Wilson. "'A Hand Hold for a Little Bit': Factors Facilitating the Success of Community College Transfer Students to a Large Research University." *Journal of College Student Development*, vol. 47, no. 4, 2006, pp. 439–56.

———. "The Academic and Social Integration of Persisting Community College Transfer Students." *Journal of College Student Retention: Research, Theory and Practice*, vol. 10, no. 4, 2009, pp. 405–23.

Trimbur, John. *Solidarity or Service: Composition and the Problem of Expertise*. Boynton/Cook, 2011.

Two-Year College English Association. "Guidelines for the Academic Preparation of English Faculty in Two-Year Colleges." *Teaching English in the Two-Year College*, vol. 34, no. 1, 2006, pp. 7–19.

———. "Research and Scholarship in the Two-Year College." *Teaching English in the Two-Year College*, vol. 39, no. 1, 2011, pp. 7–28.

Urias, Marissa Vasquez, et al. "Narratives of Success: A Retrospective Trajectory Analysis of Men of Color Who Successfully Transferred from the Community College." *New Directions for Institutional Research*, vol. 2016, no. 170, 2016, pp. 23–33.

Vieira, Kate, et al. "Literacy Is a Sociohistoric Phenomenon with the Potential to Liberate and Oppress." Adler-Kassner and Wardle, *(Re) Considering*, pp. 36-55.

Villanueva, Victor, Jr. *Bootstraps: From an American Academic of Color.* NCTE, 1993.

Wardle, Elizabeth. "Understanding 'Transfer' from FYC: Preliminary Results of a Longitudinal Study." *Writing Program Administration*, vol. 31, nos. 1–2, 2007, pp. 65–85.

Wardle, Elizabeth, and Doug Downs. "Reflecting Back and Looking Forward: Revisiting 'Teaching about Writing, Righting Misconceptions' Five Years On." *Composition Forum*, vol. 27, 2013, compositionforum.com/issue/27/.

———. "Understanding the Nature of Disciplinarity in Terms of Composition's Values." Malenczyk et al., pp. 111–33.

Warnke, Anthony, and Kirsten Higgins. "A Critical Time for Reform: Empowering Interventions in a Precarious Landscape." *Teaching English in the Two-Year College*, vol. 45, no. 4, 2018, pp. 361–84.

Wassmer, Robert, et al. "Effect of Racial/Ethnic Composition on Transfer Rates in Community Colleges: Implications for Policy and Practice." *Research in Higher Education*, vol. 45, no. 6, 2004, pp. 651–72.

Weingarten, Samuel, and Frederick P. Kroeger. *English in the Two-Year College: Report of a Joint Committee of the National Council of Teachers of English and the Conference on College Composition and Communication*. NCTE, 1965.

Weisser, Christian R. "Ecology." *Keywords in Writing Studies*, edited by Paul Heilker and Peter Vandenberg, UP of Colorado, 2015, pp. 67–71.

Weisser, Christian R., and Sidney I. Dobrin, editors. *Ecocomposition: Theoretical and Pedagogical Approaches*. SUNY P, 2001.

Whitney, Justin G. "Avoiding the 'Cliffs': Korean International Community College Students and Rhetorical Flexibility." *Empowering the Community College First-Year Composition Teacher: Pegagogies and Policies*, edited by Meryl Siegal and Betsy Gilliland, U of Michigan P, 2021, pp. 182–96.

———. "Perpetual Convergence: Writing Knowledge Transfer and Figured Worlds." *Teaching English in the Two-Year College*, vol. 49, no. 2, 2021, pp. 107–23.

Wible, Scott. *Shaping Language Policy in the US: The Role of Composition Studies*. Southern Illinois UP, 2013.

Wilson, Gordon. "CCCC in Retrospect." *College Composition and Communication*, vol. 18, no. 3, 1967, pp. 127–34.

Wilson, Shawn. *Research Is Ceremony: Indigenous Research Methods*. Fernwood Publishing, 2008.

Womack, Anne-Marie. "Teaching Is Accommodation: Universally Designing Composition Classrooms and Syllabi." *College Composition and Communication*, vol. 68, no. 3, 2017, pp. 494–525.

Wood, Tara. "Cripping Time in the College Composition Classroom." *College Composition and Communication*, vol. 69, no. 2, 2017, pp. 260–86.

Worthen, Richard. "The Changing World of English." *ADE Bulletin*, vol. 32, 1972, pp. 38–44.

———. "Implications of the CCCC-NCTE Status Survey on English in the Two-Year College." Archer and Ferrell, pp. 21–27.

———. "Junior College English." *Bulletin of the Rocky Mountain Modern Language Association*, vol. 23, no. 1, 1969, pp. 40–47.

———. "Junior College English and the Discipline." MLA Workshop on Junior College English. NCTE Annual Convention, Milwaukee, 1 Dec. 1968. ERIC ED025540.

Worthen, Richard, and Florence Cohen. "Accountability English Style: Dialogue, a Two-Way Street, The Cards on the Table." *California English Journal*, vol. 8, no. 1, 1972, pp. 7–11.

"Yakima, WA, Census Data." *Infoplease*, www.infoplease.com/us/census/washington/yakima. Accessed 29 June 2022.

Yancey, Kathleen Blake. "Mapping the Turn to Disciplinarity: A Historical Analysis of Composition's Trajectory and Its Current Moment." Malenczyk et al., pp. 15–35.

Yancey, Kathleen Blake, et al. *Writing across Contexts: Transfer, Composition, and Sites of Writing*. UP of Colorado, 2014.

Yergeau, M. Remi, et al. "Multimodality in Motion: Disability and Kairotic Spaces." *Kairos*, vol. 18, no. 1, 2013, kairos.technorhetoric.net/18.1/coverweb/yergeau-et-al/.

Young, Vershawn Ashanti, and Aja Y. Martinez, editors. *Code-Meshing as World English: Pedagogy, Policy, Performance*. NCTE, 2011.

Zamani-Gallaher, Eboni M., and Devika Dibya Choudhuri. "Tracing LGBTQ Community College Students' Experiences." *New Directions for Community Colleges*, vol. 2016, no. 174, 2016, pp. 47–63.

INDEX

CONTRIBUTORS

Katherine Allred

Katherine Allred (she/they) graduated with an AS from Salt Lake Community College and a BS from the University of Utah. She currently lives in Salt Lake City and works professionally as a proposal manager. She is on the board of Lightscatter Press and spends her time occupied with activism, knitting, gardening, and writing personal nonfiction, memoir, and poetry.

Sabita Bastakoti

Sabita Bastakoti (she/her) is a graduate student in the Department of Writing and Rhetoric Studies at the University of Utah. She is invested in foregrounding underrepresented voice and is involved in research in decolonial and postcolonial rhetoric and multilingual writing. Sabita is also an activist and has worked with immigrant and refugee community members in the Greater Salt Lake area.

Lisa Bickmore

Lisa Bickmore (she/her) is recently retired from the English, Linguistics, and Writing Studies Department at Salt Lake Community College. A working poet, she has focused on multimodality, genre, poetics, and writing within public settings. She is the founder and publisher of the new nonprofit literary Lightscatter Press and the current Utah Poet Laureate.

Chris Blankenship

Chris Blankenship (he/him) is director of learning outcomes assessment at Salt Lake Community College and a faculty member in the English, Linguistics, and Writing Studies Department. He writes about assessment, academic labor, and writing program administration. An uprooted Tennessean, he constantly searches Utah for his next hit of BBQ, greens, and sweet tea.

Anne Canavan

Anne Canavan (she/her/hers) is an associate professor of English at Salt Lake Community College. A generalist in her scholarship, she focuses on second language learning, community college pedagogy, and narratology. As a displaced southerner, she is still looking for sweet tea here in Utah.

Joanne Castillo

Joanne Castillo (she/her/hers) hails from Honolulu and Los Angeles, but she remains in the Salt Lake Valley, where she actively participates in the local Filipino community. Currently a freelance editor, writing consultant, and now employee with the Utah Board of Education, she hopes to continue punching proverbial water buffalo wherever possible.

Charissa Che

Charissa Che (she/her/hers) is an assistant professor at Queensborough Community College (CUNY). Her scholarship centers on cultural rhetorics, translingualism, and second language writing. She thinks fondly of her time in SLC, and the smart, funny, and generous people she met at the University of Utah and SLCC. Also, the street cats in NYC just don't compare.

Nic Contreras

Nic Contreras (he/him/his) is a Latin American immigrant living in the United States. Hailing from Mar del Plata, Argentina, he and his family emigrated during the early 2000s, during the George W. Bush administration. He grew up in Anaheim, California, and Salt Lake City, Utah—plus many more places in between. In 2015, he graduated with an associate's degree from Salt Lake Community College before transferring to the University of Utah and completing a bachelor's degree in writing and rhetoric studies in 2018. A man who has already worn many hats in this lifetime, he currently daylights as a program manager for the nonprofit First Star Academy in their U of U chapter.

After twenty-one long years as undocumented citizens in the United States, he and his family stand at the precipice of documentation and future citizenship.

Kelly Corbray

Kelly Corbray (she/her) was raised in the Pacific Northwest and found her way to the University of Utah via multiple job, school, and career moves. After taking a meta-analytical approach to her movements, Corbray came to an understanding about education, equity, and inclusion that changed her trajectory in school and career. Corbray is currently a K–12 reading intervention teacher in New Orleans. She works to reach students early in their educational careers to help facilitate more inclusive and equitable educational practices, so that marginalized children recognize and seize every opportunity they are presented with in their lives . . . and become trailblazers who can create for themselves whatever paths they take in life toward future career or higher education.

Shauna Edson

Shauna Edson (she/her) is technology and digital equity manager at the Salt Lake City Public Library. She leads the library's digital-equity initiative and works with library staff and community partners to create long-term programming in the communities the library's eight locations serve.

Nina Feng

Nina Feng (she/they) is coordinator of equitable and inclusive pedagogy at the University of Utah's Center for Teaching Excellence. She received her doctorate in writing and rhetoric studies at the University of Utah, and she is a graduate of the Nonfiction Writing Program at the University of Iowa. Her research centers on antiracist language practices and pedagogy, along with game-based learning and queer methodologies.

Romeo García

Romeo García (he/him) is a faculty member in the Department of Writing and Rhetoric Studies at the University of Utah. His scholarship focuses on settler colonial histories in Texas and Utah. García's research appears in *College Composition and Communication*, *Rhetoric Society Quarterly*, *The Writing Center Journal*, and the *Studies in Writing and Rhetoric* series.

Clint Gardner

Clint Gardner (he/him/his) is director of student writing and reading centers at Salt Lake Community College (SLCC) in Salt Lake City, Utah. He has served in various leadership roles in the writing center and two-year college communities over the past thirty years.

Cassandra Goff

While being involved with this life-altering project, Cassandra Goff (she/her/hers) was working on her writing and rhetoric bachelor's degree as a first-generation transfer student. She has since earned her master's degree and spends her time continuing the ecology by teaching various writing classes at both the University of Utah and Salt Lake Community College.

Jay Jordan

Jay Jordan (he/him/his) is a faculty member in the Department of Writing and Rhetoric Studies at the University of Utah. His scholarship focuses on second language writing, international education, WAC/WID, and rhetorical theory. North Carolina born and raised, he still feels new to the Intermountain West after fifteen-plus years.

Nathan Lacy

Nathan Lacy (he/him/his) received his BS in writing and rhetoric studies and his MA in English in the time between when this project started and when the book came out. He continues to work as an adjunct instructor at Salt Lake Community College and the University of Utah and does instructional design.

Andrea Malouf

Andrea Malouf (she/her/hers) is a professor of English, linguistics, and writing studies at Salt Lake Community College, previous director of the SLCC Community Writing Center, and facilitator for the SLCC Center for Authentic Leadership and Mindfulness, as well as a trained college conflict resolution mediator. She has an MA in literature and a BA in English with a creative writing emphasis, both from the University of Utah. Prior to SLCC, Andrea worked as a professional writer and corporate executive.

Bernice Olivas

Bernice Olivas (she/her) teaches writing and rhetoric at Salt Lake City Community College. She is a first-generation Indigenous Mexican American scholar who began her academic career as a high-school dropout with a GED. In 2007, Bernice joined the McNair Scholars Program. In 2010, she completed her BA in English from Boise State University with a creative writing emphasis and continued on to complete her MA (2012) in the teaching of English and her PhD (2016) in composition and rhetoric at the University of Nebraska–Lincoln.

Nkenna Onwuzuruoha

Nkenna Onwuzuruoha (she/her/hers) moved to Salt Lake over ten years ago to serve as an AmeriCorps VISTA member for the SLCC Community Writing Center. She has taught first-year writing at Salt Lake Community College, Westminster College, and the University of Utah. Nkenna is currently a PhD candidate in the Department of Writing and Rhetoric Studies.

Westin Jay Porter

Westin Jay Porter (he/him/his) is a Salt Laker by way of Mormon settlers and Italian railroad workers. A first-generation college student, Porter fell in love with and continues to work with Salt Lake communities since he began at the SLCC Community Writing Center as an SLCC student. Westin enjoys beer, fishing, and complaining about academia.

Sandra Salazar-Hernandez

Born in California, Sandra Salazar-Hernandez (she/her/hers) is a first-generation college graduate from the University of Utah—in writing and rhetoric. The best department EVER. Sandra has welcomed the opportunity to work for Salt Lake County in the Office of Regional Development. This opportunity ties in with her youth advocacy with Volunteers of America and recent work with Head Start as a family advocate. She resides on the west side of Salt Lake City and lives with her favorite sister and four cockatiels, Luna & Soleil and Biggy & Ziggy.

Claudia Sauz Mendoza

Born in Mexico, Claudia Sauz Mendoza (she/her) is a first-generation college graduate who has enjoyed working with unhoused youth at a shelter and at-risk youth in a wilderness therapy setting. You'll often find her on trails with her dogs Piglet and Luna or buying random things she doesn't need at estate sales.

Christie Toth

Christie Toth (she/her) is an associate professor in the Department of Writing and Rhetoric Studies at the University of Utah. Her scholarship focuses on composition, two-year colleges, and the dream of postsecondary writing instruction that enacts the democratic potential of open admissions. For her, writing this book has been a transformative game of Words with Friends. She'd like to try it again when she's not on the tenure clock.

'Ilaheva Tua'one

N.S. 'Ilaheva Tua'one (she/her) received her PhD in British and American literature from the University of Utah in 2020. She is the new assistant professor of Indigenous/Native American studies in the Women's and Ethnic Studies Program at the University of Colorado at Colorado Springs.

Justin G. Whitney

Justin G. Whitney (he/him/his) is an assistant professor of languages, literature, and philosophy at Tennessee State University. His work focuses on writing pedagogy, the intersections of culture and writing knowledge transfer, and technical/professional writing.

BOOKS IN THE CCCC STUDIES IN WRITING & RHETORIC SERIES

Transfer in an Urban Writing Ecology: Reimagining Community College–University Relations in Composition Studies
Christie Toth with Joanne Castillo, Nic Contreras, Kelly Corbray, Nathan Lacy, Westin Porter, Sandra Salazar-Hernandez, and Colleagues

Teachers Talking Writing: Perspectives on Places, Pedagogies, and Programs
Shane A. Wood

Materiality and Writing Studies: Aligning Labor, Scholarship, and Teaching
Holly Hassel and Cassandra Phillips

Salt of the Earth: Rhetoric, Preservation, and White Supremacy
James Chase Sanchez

Rhetorics of Overcoming: Rewriting Narratives of Disability and Accessibility in Writing Studies
Allison Harper Hitt

Writing Accomplices with Student Immigrant Rights Organizers
Glenn Hutchinson

Counterstory: The Rhetoric and Writing of Critical Race Theory
Aja Y. Martinez

Writing Programs, Veterans Studies, and the Post-9/11 University: A Field Guide
D. Alexis Hart and Roger Thompson

Beyond Progress in the Prison Classroom: Options and Opportunities
Anna Plemons

Rhetorics Elsewhere and Otherwise: Contested Modernities, Decolonial Visions
Edited by Romeo García and Damián Baca

Black Perspectives in Writing Program Administration: From the Margins to the Center
Edited by Staci M. Perryman-Clark and Collin Lamont Craig

Translanguaging outside the Academy: Negotiating Rhetoric and Healthcare in the Spanish Caribbean
Rachel Bloom-Pojar

Collaborative Learning as Democratic Practice: A History
Mara Holt

Reframing the Relational: A Pedagogical Ethic for Cross-Curricular Literacy Work
Sandra L. Tarabochia

Inside the Subject: A Theory of Identity for the Study of Writing
Raúl Sánchez

Genre of Power: Police Report Writers and Readers in the Justice System
Leslie Seawright

Assembling Composition
Edited by Kathleen Blake Yancey and Stephen J. McElroy*Public Pedagogy in Composition Studies*
Ashley J. Holmes

From Boys to Men: Rhetorics of Emergent American Masculinity
Leigh Ann Jones

Freedom Writing: African American Civil Rights Literacy Activism, 1955–1967
Rhea Estelle Lathan

The Desire for Literacy: Writing in the Lives of Adult Learners
Lauren Rosenberg

On Multimodality: New Media in Composition Studies
Jonathan Alexander and Jacqueline Rhodes

Toward a New Rhetoric of Difference
Stephanie L. Kerschbaum

Rhetoric of Respect: Recognizing Change at a Community Writing Center
Tiffany Rousculp

After Pedagogy: The Experience of Teaching
Paul Lynch

Redesigning Composition for Multilingual Realities
Jay Jordan

Agency in the Age of Peer Production
Quentin D. Vieregge, Kyle D. Stedman, Taylor Joy Mitchell, and Joseph M. Moxley

Remixing Composition: A History of Multimodal Writing Pedagogy
Jason Palmeri

First Semester: Graduate Students, Teaching Writing, and the Challenge of Middle Ground
Jessica Restaino

Agents of Integration: Understanding Transfer as a Rhetorical Act
Rebecca S. Nowacek

Digital Griots: African American Rhetoric in a Multimedia Age
Adam J. Banks

The Managerial Unconscious in the History of Composition Studies
Donna Strickland

Everyday Genres: Writing Assignments across the Disciplines
Mary Soliday

The Community College Writer: Exceeding Expectations
Howard Tinberg and Jean-Paul Nadeau

A Taste for Language: Literacy, Class, and English Studies
James Ray Watkins

Before Shaughnessy: Basic Writing at Yale and Harvard, 1920–1960
Kelly Ritter

Writer's Block: The Cognitive Dimension
Mike Rose

Teaching/Writing in Thirdspaces: The Studio Approach
Rhonda C. Grego and Nancy S. Thompson

Rural Literacies
Kim Donehower, Charlotte Hogg, and Eileen E. Schell

Writing with Authority: Students' Roles as Writers in Cross-National Perspective
David Foster

Whistlin' and Crowin' Women of Appalachia: Literacy Practices since College
Katherine Kelleher Sohn

Sexuality and the Politics of Ethos in the Writing Classroom
Zan Meyer Gonçalves

African American Literacies Unleashed: Vernacular English and the Composition Classroom
Arnetha F. Ball and Ted Lardner

Revisionary Rhetoric, Feminist Pedagogy, and Multigenre Texts
Julie Jung

Archives of Instruction: Nineteenth-Century Rhetorics, Readers, and Composition Books in the United States
Jean Ferguson Carr, Stephen L. Carr, and Lucille M. Schultz

Response to Reform: Composition and the Professionalization of Teaching
Margaret J. Marshall

Multiliteracies for a Digital Age
Stuart A. Selber

Personally Speaking: Experience as Evidence in Academic Discourse
Candace Spigelman

Self-Development and College Writing
Nick Tingle

Minor Re/Visions: Asian American Literacy Narratives as a Rhetoric of Citizenship
Morris Young

A Communion of Friendship: Literacy, Spiritual Practice, and Women in Recovery
Beth Daniell

Embodied Literacies: Imageword and a Poetics of Teaching
Kristie S. Fleckenstein

Language Diversity in the Classroom: From Intention to Practice
Edited by Geneva Smitherman and Victor Villanueva

Rehearsing New Roles: How College Students Develop as Writers
Lee Ann Carroll

Across Property Lines: Textual Ownership in Writing Groups
Candace Spigelman

Mutuality in the Rhetoric and Composition Classroom
David L. Wallace and Helen Rothschild Ewald

The Young Composers: Composition's Beginnings in Nineteenth-Century Schools
Lucille M. Schultz

Technology and Literacy in the Twenty-First Century: The Importance of Paying Attention
Cynthia L. Selfe

Women Writing the Academy: Audience, Authority, and Transformation
Gesa E. Kirsch

Gender Influences: Reading Student Texts
Donnalee Rubin

Something Old, Something New: College Writing Teachers and Classroom Change
Wendy Bishop

Dialogue, Dialectic, and Conversation: A Social Perspective on the Function of Writing
Gregory Clark

Audience Expectations and Teacher Demands
Robert Brooke and John Hendricks

Toward a Grammar of Passages
Richard M. Coe

Rhetoric and Reality: Writing Instruction in American Colleges, 1900–1985
James A. Berlin

Writing Groups: History, Theory, and Implications
Anne Ruggles Gere

Teaching Writing as a Second Language
Alice S. Horning

Invention as a Social Act
Karen Burke LeFevre

The Variables of Composition: Process and Product in a Business Setting
Glenn J. Broadhead and Richard C. Freed

Writing Instruction in Nineteenth-Century American Colleges
James A. Berlin

Computers & Composing: How the New Technologies Are Changing Writing
Jeanne W. Halpern and Sarah Liggett

A New Perspective on Cohesion in Expository Paragraphs
Robin Bell Markels

Evaluating College Writing Programs
Stephen P. Witte and Lester Faigley

This book was typeset in Garamond and Frutiger by Barbara Frazier.
Typefaces used on the cover include Garamond and News Gothic.
The book was printed on 50-lb., white offset paper by Seaway Printing.